Sho tex anc strc gen nov rep in t pol bey the stu grip hov soc orig que furt var in comparable series, yet at the same time in a concise and compact handbook form. *Short Histories* aim to be "introductions with an edge." In combining questioning and searching analysis with informed historical writing, they bring history up-to-date for an increasingly complex and globalized digital age.

For more information about titles and authors in the series, please visit: www.bloomsbury.com/series/short-histories/

A Short History of ...

the American Civil War	Paul Christopher Anderson (Clemson University)
the American Revolutionary War	Stephen Conway (University College London)
Ancient China	Edward L. Shaughnessy (University of Chicago)
Ancient Greece	P. J. Rhodes, FBA (Durham University)
the Anglo-Saxons	Henrietta Leyser (University of Oxford)
Babylon	Karen Radner (University of Munich)
the Byzantine Empire	Dionysios Stathakopoulos (King's College London)
Christian Spirituality	Edward Howells (Heythrop College, University of London)
Communism	Kevin Morgan (University of Manchester)
the Crimean War	Trudi Tate (University of Cambridge)
English Renaissance Drama	Helen Hackett (University College London)
the English Revolution and the Civil Wars	David J. Appleby (University of Nottingham)
the Etruscans	Corinna Riva (University College London)
Florence and the Florentine Republic	Brian Jeffrey Maxson (East Tennessee State University)
the Hundred Years War	Michael Prestwich (Durham University)
Irish Independence	J. J. Lee (New York University)
the Italian Renaissance	Virginia Cox (New York University)
the Korean War	Allan R. Millett (University of New Orleans)
Medieval Christianity	G. R. Evans (University of Cambridge)
Medieval English Mysticism	Vincent Gillespie (University of Oxford)
the Minoans	John Bennet (University of Sheffield)
the Mongols	George Lane (SOAS, University of London)
the Mughal Empire	Michael H. Fisher (Oberlin College)
Muslim Spain	Amira K. Bennison (University of Cambridge)
New Kingdom Egypt	Robert Morkot (University of Exeter)
the New Testament	Halvor Moxnes (University of Oslo)

Nineteenth-Century Philosophy	Joel Rasmussen (University of Oxford)
the Normans	Leonie V. Hicks (Canterbury Christ Church University)
the Ottoman Empire	Baki Tezcan (University of California, Davis)
the Phoenicians	Mark Woolmer (Durham University)
the Reformation	Helen L. Parish (University of Reading)
the Renaissance in Northern Europe	Malcolm Vale (University of Oxford)
Revolutionary Cuba	Antoni Kapcia (University of Nottingham)
the Risorgimento	Nick Carter (Australian Catholic University, Sydney)
the Russian Revolution	Geoffrey Swain (University of Glasgow)
the Spanish Civil War	Julián Casanova (University of Zaragoza)
the Spanish Empire	Felipe Fernández-Armesto (University of Notre Dame) and José Juan López-Portillo (University of Oxford)
Transatlantic Slavery	Kenneth Morgan (Brunel University London)
the Tudors	Richard Rex (University of Cambridge)
Venice and the Venetian Empire	Maria Fusaro (University of Exeter)
the Vikings	Clare Downham (University of Liverpool)
the Wars of the Roses	David Grummitt (University of Kent)
the Weimar Republic	Colin Storer (University of Nottingham)

A SHORT HISTORY OF THE AMERICAN CIVIL WAR

Paul Christopher Anderson

BLOOMSBURY ACADEMIC
LONDON • NEW YORK • OXFORD • NEW DELHI • SYDNEY

BLOOMSBURY ACADEMIC
Bloomsbury Publishing Plc
50 Bedford Square, London, WC1B 3DP, UK
1385 Broadway, New York, NY 10018, USA

BLOOMSBURY, BLOOMSBURY ACADEMIC and the Diana
logo are trademarks of Bloomsbury Publishing Plc

First published in Great Britain 2020

Cover design: Terry Woodley
Cover image © stillfx/123rf

A catalogue record for this book is available from the British Library.

A catalog record for this book is available from the Library of Congress

ISBN: HB: 978-1-7807-6597-6
PB: 978-1-7807-6598-3
ePDF: 978-1-7867-3673-4
eBook: 978-1-7867-2667-4

Series: Short Histories

Typeset by Integra Software Services Pvt. Ltd.
Printed and bound in Great Britain

For Will Swinney

It don't matter where he turns up, he is on the side of victory . . .
Things move wherever he is.

Abraham Lincoln, 1863

Contents

Illustrations

FIGURES

MAPS

Preface

What follows is an attempt to explain the American Civil War to those interested in America but perhaps unfamiliar with its defining historical event. I have taught it for twenty years as a university professor in the United States, a Southerner teaching in South Carolina. The book is by commission and construction a short history: not nearly everything to know and not everything I know about the War (a substantial gap remains between the latter and the former) but what I perceive as crucial to know about it and its stakes. Moreover the imprint bears my own vital interests, which are in the history of the American South more specially. Certainly, the American Civil War was a central moment in the creation of a modern national state. Here, however, my emphasis is on what that moment promised to do – and in a real sense mortgaged itself by death to do – but did not. There is no real purpose to hiding behind the point. Many years ago the great American historian Allan Nevins finished an eight-volume opus called *The Ordeal of the Union* in which he postulated that slavery and "its complementary problem of race adjustment" were, at bottom, the reasons for the conflict. I see no complementary issue in race at all, but a fundamental one – so fundamental that it still roils the national state created by the War.

The central dynamic working toward dissolution in antebellum America was its growth and expansion in every way conceivable: demographic and geographic; economic and political and social. A country confined – quite literally – to the Atlantic seaboard in 1789 touched the Pacific Ocean within the lifetimes of some of those alive at its constitutional founding. How to direct that expansion and how and who controlled it were of course the power questions involved in secession and war. But the national questions were ultimately the same as the founding ones: what was America and who was an American? The founding generation answered in the Declaration of Independence with the clarion ideas of liberty and equality – ideas surely understood more conservatively than their own explosive expansion in democracy belied within a mere generation. We are still fighting the founding questions in America, only now we are far less certain than we once were that the American Civil War gave us the answers it formerly did.

A word is in order about the literature of the American Civil War. It is the vast hulking corpus of the most studied event in all of US history, embracing a multitudinous legion of other literatures (such as slavery) all voluminous in their own right. I will make no attempt to cite even a comparable fraction of it. It seems to me that readers of this small volume would rather I cite relevant general works where appropriate, the most topically or thematically relevant works where most needful, and, in cases requiring quotation or necessary fact, attribution where professionally proper. Particularly in cases where a citation or a quotation might be chosen from a myriad of secondary sources, I have tried to sample, by way of suggested reading, from some reputable works that are as I think most accessible to an interested audience. The most recent, most comprehensive professional review of the literature, and the state of the field, is to be found in Aaron Sheehan-Dean, ed., *A Companion to the U.S. Civil War* (Chichester: John Wiley & Sons, 2014).

I owe many thanks to many warm friends and colleagues, whom I hope will pardon me for conserving in words what I gratefully offer in a sincere generosity of spirit. I do wish to thank Emily Drewe, Olivia Dellow, and Kevin Hughes, and Samantha Town, all of Bloomsbury, and especially Joanna Godfrey and Alex Wright, who are now practicing elsewhere in the publishing world but without whom this book would not be. Macy Allison (MA, Clemson University, 2019) selected the illustrations. Special thanks are also owing to four colleagues for their kindnesses – Steven G. Marks, Michael Meng, and James M. Burns of Clemson, South Carolina, and Kevin M. Levin of Boston, Massachusetts – and one person without whom nothing is possible or desired, Keri Bradford Anderson.

Prologue: Battleground

The shortest way to introduce the American Civil War is to say that a nation created in words shattered itself on them. Americans would find ever-more murderous ways of killing one another, of visiting pain, and dealing out vengeance and suffering on one another, between the War's opening in 1861 and its close in 1865, but no weapons contrived in those years were as crimson-edged as the words they wielded. At least 750,000 soldiers, Union and Confederate combined, died in the American Civil War – and probably many thousands more; at least 50,000 civilians also perished – and certainly many thousands more. We will know better when and if we ever finish counting. Over 1.2 million Americans – probably many more – were wounded and maimed. They fell at the muzzle-end of the musket and the butt-end; at the hilt of the knife and the blade of the bayonet; at the mouth of the cannon and often at the breech; underneath the surgeon's saw; and at the noose end of the rope. They were scorched and blackened in fire and strangled and drowned in water. Vast swaths of them, the majority, were taken silently, quietly, by germs: by the sullen poxes of camp life or the ravenous infections and rotting gangrene of the hospital ward.

The harrowing pitilessness of such a catastrophic bloodletting was felt and understood as the greatest of the Civil War's sorrows at the time and has been perversely magnetic to Americans ever since. Such intimate devastation would be conceived of very differently now – after two twentieth-century World Wars, after the advent of biological and atomic and satellite warfare and industrial holocaust, after the chemical slough of Vietnam in the 1960s or the desert labyrinth of Iraq and crawling lurch of Afghanistan almost half a century later: all destruction wrought elsewhere, far from home. The physical and mental worlds of the present are capable of collapsing space and time in an instant, but paradoxically this can have the effect of throwing up impenetrable barriers to empathy and humanity by the sheer instantaneousness of violence in a world calloused or perhaps indifferent or maybe even expecting mass slaughter. But the Civil War still draws us. Its sacrificial ritual calls to us now as it has since it opened in Charleston Harbor in 1861, by the siren of its words. It is America's epic poem.

Union. Democracy. Liberty. Freedom. Equality. We continue to ask what caused the War, as well as to question its course, because such things are the imperative of history. Very little in those debates is basically controversial any longer, and very little of it sings the national epic. What draws us is a quest of identity: what these words, the protean cords by which Americans attempted to rebind themselves as a people when the Declaration of Independence dissolved the political bands connecting them to England, meant for the generation that fought the War; and what they mean for us, now, sinewed to the War. If the American Civil War was about anything, it was about what those words mean. Not *meant*: but mean. Because if we can say anything else about the War, it is that the meaning of them was in tumult and strife as it was fought, just as their meanings have been in violent quarrel in the fifteen decades of afterlife since.

It would be agreed upon in the immediate, romance-tinged afteryears, by many of those aged veterans who fought in it as well as the historians who wrote about it, that the Civil War settled some things. That may be so, if one considers the issues of the War narrowly. The nation-building question of permanent political union, which was the broadest consideration embracing all other economic and social considerations, including the fate of slavery, was settled. And if one considers the essence of what America means generally, as an idea, that may be so. What had been a tentative and uncertain experiment in self-government and republicanism became fixed, so that the protean cords that bound the Union became, as Abraham Lincoln put it, the mystic chords that sung the nation's everlasting promise. For many Americans who understand their cataclysm as both the trial and triumph of the nation's distinct place in the world, the War remade a perpetual Union, which saved democracy and, at unthinkable but unforgettable cost, secured liberty, freedom, and equality.

Yet not all Americans think the War did those things, and the triumphant national history underwriting such general attitudes has been stunningly revised in the last fifty years. In a few words, the perspective developing in the last half-century has discomposed us. The Civil War that preserved the Union and saved democracy was a limited victory, in part because it was a victory that betrayed itself. The War might have birthed freedom anew and secured equality but did so for the few, not the many; it was the deliverance of freedom and liberty, but liberty for the first, not the least, and freedom for the strong but not the weak – an all-the-more cynical result given its brutality and unimaginable cost. The War may have settled some things, but in the last generation we have begun to understand it, also, as distressingly unsettling. Afterlife generally is.

To say all that is to suggest somehow that alternative consequences were possible, and to suggest what might have been is to suggest a different mode of thinking about our relationship to the War. The objective outcome was and remains indisputable. The Union – "the North" in the often-used but inexact conflation describing the alignment of belligerents into (mostly) free states and slave states – won the War. But more subtly, even if less objectively, it is closer to the mark to say the Union won *war-making*. The South – the white South: the same imprecise conflations do not allow us to see black Southerners – won *peace-making*. This the defeated did by ensuring that the Union's triumph in war-making remained incomplete, by measures political and even paramilitary, by measures civil and social, and by measures enduringly cultural. The War saved the Union but by 1900 its reactionary aftermath had broken the revolutionary promises cresting with emancipation: emancipation, it must needs be known, was every bit as materially necessary to ultimate Union victory in 1865 as its guns and butter. The Union's triumph preserved a relatively limited, decentralized federal government and a democracy ultimately and sometimes violently reserved for white men and white supremacy. It destroyed slavery but the limits of abolition ensnared black Southerners and their descendants in a miserable system of economic repression begetting woe and hopelessness, in some places even today, down to the latest generation.

The Southern mastery of peace-making was a gritty political victory of power and interest and violence. Yet it was also, in the creation of a social and cultural mode, a way of thinking about and living with the War's outcome that reveals itself, up through to today, in our national fascination with it. If the immediate and unchallenged verdict of fact had been issued in 1865, the search for meaning was the imperative of remembering – the ongoing collective need to make sense of the War's pain and suffering, the need to find some larger purpose in its unimaginable sacrifice, the yearning for a vindication that might be shrouded in the present but would work itself out, for the greater good, over time, so long as the War was never forgotten. While both North and South struggled with the calamity of death and destruction, the victors did not long search their victory for redemptive purpose. The War's tragedy was that they did not. The stronger, better cause was self-evidently manifest in the outcome. Having secured the future, they also proceeded soon thereafter to live in it, eventually without much regard for what had gone before.

For Southern whites as well as Southern blacks, memory was a peculiar imperative and the War a passion-time that far outlasted surrender. For, on the one hand, black Southerners *did not* consider the thing settled, partly because they counted themselves among the victors but were soon abandoned by the victory. Because the promise of emancipation had been left unfulfilled, their memory of the War invoked its legacy for what it could have accomplished and was bound to accomplish in the future. The constant and ever-present memory of the War – or more narrowly and precisely, the emancipation begotten of it – would call the nation constantly to uphold its democratic ideals and the mandates of liberty, freedom, and equality.

White Southerners sought meaning in the past until finally they refounded their lost nation there. For them, ironically, the searching rendered essential by defeat sustained the South as a unique region and won for them what they could not obtain in their bid for a separate existence on the battlefields of the War. Defeat itself consecrated them as a people, became the larger purpose, became the vindication of suffering, became the redemption of pain. The War was not over and never could be so long as its memory worked to set white Southerners apart. The haunting but needful ever-presence of the past, history's verdict incontestably settled but its outcome constantly ongoing, dominated what came to be called "the Southern way of life" for more than a century after the Confederacy's collapse, and this, indeed, was comprehensive. Memory was indistinct from the political and social system of white supremacy – of it, whole and inseparable – which was "the way." Mode and system were one: the everyday civics of apartheid relied on living with memory, because it was, after all, a system designed to control all the unsettling possibilities unleashed by war and defeat in the past.

The War still comes. Its *ongoingness* is still with Americans, still *is* us. Just as white Southerners needed memory to set themselves apart and black Southerners conceived of emancipation as a biblical act marking them as touched by God, Americans in general – for better or for worse – have come to see themselves as a special people, and their nation's mission as an exceptional ordination. And so, union. So democracy. So liberty and freedom. So equality. If Americans would have it be that their distinctiveness exists as actuality, it is somehow dependent on those words and the eventual outcome of the American Civil War. The hollowness or the truth of what they proclaim is constantly and necessarily at issue. We are connected to the War generation not by the consensus of nostalgia in which they healed themselves in its immediate aftermath but by the discord of meaning that brought on disunion and then sacrificial violence. We still live with the War because we argue about what America is, and about who Americans are and ought to be. We want to understand in its violence not the vulgar possessions of the world: not power, not interest or advantage, not material benefit. Surely the Civil War was fought over those things and did confer those things, but so did other American wars that did not cost as much and did not vitally threaten the existence of the nation itself, and not coincidentally have become paragraphs in school textbooks. For Americans, as long as those words are the American ligature, tested supremely but fundamentally incompletely in the Civil War, we will continue to struggle over the War's meaning. Their battlegrounds became epic struggles over fiendishly bloody fields. Ours are the fierce struggles to control – to compose – the national epic.

****

Americans in 1850 would have been loath to predict the savage confrontation that would come upon them a decade later. They would have been even less sanguine to consider the idea that they would choose it. Certainly there had been contention and occasionally fierce debate among them, and at some periods, over some issues their struggles had been especially volatile. But Americans in 1850 did not live in any awareness of impending doom or slaughter. The fixed idea treaded quite the opposite way. To Americans who thought of themselves as advancing with the age, who thought of themselves as the vital new-world energy advancing the age, *progress* seemed to be inevitable. Twice in the past half-century had the country doubled in size, and twice had its population doubled as well. A fragile union of seaboard states in 1800, boasting five million inhabitants, was now a young colossus of twenty-three million people, with shorelines touching both the Atlantic and Pacific oceans. Prosperity followed commerce, and commerce followed an expanding network of roads,

Figure 1: Steam Boats docked in Saint Paul, Minnesota, 1858. *Grey Eagle*, *Frank Steele*, *Jeanette Roberts* and *Time and Tide* at dock in Saint Paul, foot of Jackson Street, Public Domain.

canals, steamboats, and, increasingly, iron-gleamed railroads. A vibrant American nationalism hailed these so-called internal improvements and proclaimed that they would bind the country together.

Most specially, many Americans believed that prosperity was their exceptional blessing, brought about in part by the virtues of citizen and institution, and in part by providential ordination. In 1776, a self-governing republic was an idea, a volatile proposition, an experiment that history suggested would end, futilely, in tyranny. By 1850, the republic had transitioned to a braggadocio democracy – a fuller form of self-government, to hear full-throated Americans acclaim it, sustained and declaimed by those who saw in the Union's promise the fullness of human freedom, liberty, and equality. Having reached in commerce the highest stage of social development, at least as such theories were promulgated by the enlightened philosophers of the previous age, what remained was the perfection of civilization, its refinement, the betterment of democracy through the ongoing reform of its institutions and the people who governed it. It was the nation's destiny, superintended by God and to be worked out according to His manifest purpose, that in its growth and betterment, and as a shining example to the world, America would rid itself of the last vestige of barbarism.[1]

By default, this short book is about the American Civil War, the years of disunion and conflict between 1860 and 1865, and not about the events and forces that led to it. Those antebellum questions have their own vast literature, and anyone who wades into it will not tarry long before discovering that it has always been fashionable to claim that civil war was inevitable. That notion seems to be in general circulation among Americans today, much like, say, a sense of inexorable fate often beguiles our understanding of the World Wars. Postures of inevitability usually have an easier time explaining oncoming disaster in hindsight than in fixing the points, at either beginning or end, of inescapable confrontation. Such perspectives do remind us of the profound importance of social or economic or political forces in history. They remind us that power and interest are prime movers. But perspectives of inevitability, if left to stand alone, are also profoundly ahistorical. The historical question is not merely *why* the American Civil War happened. It is – as the question is with any seismic historical event – *why* it happened *when* it happened.

Slavery, as we shall see, was the fundamental catalyst of the American Civil War. It was the lodestone issue that drew all other issues of political, social, and economic conflict to it, inexorably. But Americans had quarreled and compromised over slavery since the nation's founding – the makers of the Constitution even embedded the institution into the framework of government in an attempt to *avoid* future conflict over it – just as they had quarreled and compromised over many of the issues that ultimately would shape the Union's breakup in 1860. If inevitability has any bearing whatsoever, it was in a powerful direction moving exactly opposite to the direction typically associated with the War. The history of American political disagreement over slavery before 1860 was a history of inevitable compromise.

The perspectives of inevitability owe something to the stories the actors eventually told of themselves – which, especially in the War's aftermath, began to take on stage-drama elements of tragedy, of an appointment with fate, destiny, or providential commandment. It took form historically in perspectives emphasizing the fundamental incompatibility and inescapable collision of economic systems. Still others used it to stress what Southern extremists of the antebellum era insisted themselves as the heart of their cause: that Northerners and Southerners were different and distinct peoples, sharing little more with each other than disputed space on the North American continent. There is a truth in these perspectives. But it says something ineluctably important that when the War finally came, even Southerners understood it reflexively as a civil war.[2] The sense of profound, unbridgeable difference, of peoples separated from one another by the chasm between different ways of life, grew with the War itself – in the North, manifesting in the blood-welling desire to achieve retribution and punishment through victory, and, in the South, in the passionate intensity of a developing Confederate nationalism that grew more ardent as the sacrifices to achieve independence grew more devastating.

Still, and fundamentally, perspectives of inevitability impose a falseness of both experience and awareness on the consciousness of the people of any era. Americans shared more than might be obvious from the armchair perches and study rooms of hindsight, so often occupied by those keen to make decisions for the dead. Their common assumptions, their shared assumptions, help explain how quickly the Union was reconciled in the aftermath, and why, indeed, after four years of the bloodiest destruction known or imagined when it began in 1861, white Southerners bereft of almost everything they went to war to defend chose to surrender and to trust in their conquerors rather than fight to obliteration. The War itself would brutally illustrate one of its most common American features. They each – separately, entwined – chose to overcome what was not imaginable in 1861 with surprisingly swift fury, to unleash on one another the most terrifying elements of destruction and mayhem. The devastation would divide them but ultimately unite them again in nostalgia and remembrance of what they had done so horribly, commonly, to one another.

A fuller explanation of the War's fundamental dynamics would emphasize this: it was brought on by a relentless conflict over the future of slavery in a new and ever-expanding democracy arguing over the fruits of its prosperity. Americans, essentially, were arguing over a future that they were coming to believe was assured to them – the Founding generation and its successor brood in the early republic had not felt the same certainty – and confident they could control. That volatile democracy was not simply an institutional form of government but an ethic that emphasized a pugnacious egalitarian liberty among white men who denied the power of other white men to impose on that liberty. We can only begin to understand the far-reaching, interpenetrating power of the slavery issue to organize events when we comprehend slavery in the very foundation of this rising ethic of democracy. In a land of egalitarian liberty, aspiring to a future where the defining virtue was freedom and the signal promise was opportunity, to be *enslaved* was to endure the darkest, most abysmal form of tyranny.

It should not surprise us that enslavement was both a widespread metaphor, charged with a lightning-storm of emotional intensity, as well as a wretched condition to be vigilantly resisted. It is a word we find constantly deployed in the antebellum era but in ways that may be foreign if we do not learn their language. Slave society was not new in America. What was new and stupefying after the American Revolution was free society, and it was free society, not slave society, that was in constant need of definition. So when Americans of 1850 talked about slavery, they often meant their refusal to be enslaved to other white men – not literally to become the property of other white men, but not quite figuratively either, since a slave lacked a basic capacity in the very areas that were just beginning to be defined and celebrated in the practice of democracy: to vote, to choose and to judge for themselves, to seek even the meagerest fortune. Democracy meant above all things the ability and the right to control oneself.

With sensitive ears we can understand why Northerners responded in outrage when Southern extremists remarked that some Yankees, especially abolitionists, had been "suffered to run too long without collars," as one newspaper editor famously opined in 1856, or when we hear more and more of those Northerners insisting that a conspiracy of the "Slave Power" was afoot in the 1850s, yoked to Southern greed and bent on silencing opposition by stripping Northerners of political and civil rights. Just the same, we should listen for more than power and interest, although both were surely present, when we hear Southerners defiantly tell one another and their opponents that resisting Northern oppression and subjugation was a moral duty, as they constantly did in the 1850s. A sensitive ear also hears something of the vital reality at stake when white Southerners insisted on their equal rights to the nation's newly acquired territory, especially after the Mexican War of 1846–1848, or the pulse of their convictions when they insisted that the legitimacy of the Union required the equal protection of the Constitution. They did not fear becoming one another's chattel so much as they feared, and eventually refused to countenance, the reality or the appearance of being first beholden, and then controlled, by the political will and power of their opponents. A future in which independence was corrupted – politically, economically, socially – was enslavement.[3]

In that complex of values we also understand slavery's profound limitations as a moral issue. This is sometimes hard to grasp in the modern world, in which (ostensibly) the institution of slavery is abhorrent by consensus. Very few Americans of 1850 had much sympathy for the actual slaves, including people who lived in the North. Such indifference was primarily because those slaves were black. Almost perversely, from the modern point of view, bedrock color difference helped sustain what white Americans thought of when they thought about their own liberty. For liberty was not just a quality of one's life but a condition one possessed. Not everyone was entitled to it because not everyone was gifted naturally to exercise it. The virtuous were those capable of exercising independence, and independence was almost wholly set aside for whites and for white men in particular. Although Southerners had a distinct interest in portraying African Americans as dependent, childlike, lazy, irresponsible, ignorant, and much worse – among other uses, it justified the extreme physical torment and coercion to labor that one historian has recently isolated as the factor essential to increased cotton production in the antebellum period – that portrayal was largely accepted North and South. Slavery was sectional: but racism was national. The attitudes at the foundations of American racism had been in development for almost three centuries, and by the antebellum era many of them were fixed. If white meant virtuous independence and social progress, black meant abject dependence and licentious social devolution.[4]

Without racial slavery, liberty, already a bit ill-defined, would have been a completely abstract idea. It would have been more or less a universal quality ascribed to American life rather than what it was, a specific condition prescribed by and in American life. Slavery gave vision, reality, to the most distorted fears of metaphoric enslavement: one need not conjure what enslavement would look like or even theoretically feel like when it existed, already, in the wretched form of African Americans. But the presence of slaves also exalted the preciousness of freedom. Slavery made it starkly apparent to Americans – who, after all, thought they were a special people – that not everyone was entitled to it. *Denying* liberty to the unworthy and to the dependent was just as much a hallmark of American liberty as possessing it. In a sense they were one and the same. Liberty could be precious only if it was not universal, and slavery's presence heightened the sense of special possession that white Americans claimed as theirs, exceptionally.

As we will see, antislavery opinions ran along a spectrum in the antebellum North, from conservative to radical. Difficult as it can be to comprehend, those attitudes show us that it was possible – actually the general reality – to hold racist and antislavery sentiments at the very same time. That amalgam of attitudes is evident in an often overlooked but dire necessity within antislavery sentiment: one could not contemplate ending slavery without also, as an integral, inseparable act of contemplation, wondering what would become of the enslaved once they were freed. Most Northerners were antislavery, but most were also deeply conservative in their beliefs. So it was that when most Northerners said they were antislavery, or that they opposed slavery's expansion into the nation's newly acquired territories, what they really meant was that they opposed an institution that aggrandized the power of Southern whites at their expense. Expansion of slavery, for instance, meant to them the engrossment of the best lands and economic opportunities by slave owners. It meant to them the undemocratic engrossment of political power for slave owners, too, because one of the great compromises in the U.S. Constitution artificially inflated slave-owning power in Congress by counting slaves as interests to be represented. They did not tend to hate slavery for what it was, or for what it did to the enslaved. They did not tend to mean that they opposed the expansion of misery, unrequited toil, and degradation for African Americans. Slavery could not *do* to blacks what they were naturally given to *be* anyway, according to the general attitudes of the antebellum era.

Their emotional connection to antislavery, such as it was, tended to despise the institution more for what it symbolized, for there, only in the abstract, it was a contradiction to the ideals of liberty and freedom. In the abstract they were under no obligation to confront how slavery worked to preserve white liberty in the concrete. And precisely because their opposition to slavery was both self-interested and abstract, they also meant that they did not want African Americans around. They tended to shrug shoulders and click tongues when offering opinions on a post-emancipation future, or wag fingers and talk in vague generalities about colonization, or, as many did, throw up their hands and smirk in half-jests about quarantining freedmen right where they were, in the South. "Antislavery" they might be, but whatever might happen when slavery ended, African Americans would not be welcome among them. In 1860, one northern state, Indiana, entirely prohibited the settlement of free blacks – a national population of some 500,000, a slight majority of whom actually lived in the South. (For complicated reasons this fact does not count for irony). Four other states required such restrictive conditions that free black migration may as well have been prohibited.

A much smaller middle ground, typified in the antebellum decades by men such as Abraham Lincoln, did hold a humanitarian regard for the enslaved. Given the general feeling this was in itself a marked, noticeable departure. But as yet these could not imagine blacks living in America after slavery, either – for *their* welfare or for the welfare of whites. Like most Northerners, the humanitarians envisioned the gradual end of slavery over time, a slow change that would begin with halting its expansion into new territories and end, as some saw it, in another century or two. What to do with those who were freed was a question they might have thought about with feeling but could not quite comprehend. Their regard for African Americans did not trump their belief that white supremacy was a fixed fact, and that collision tormented them with both practical and sentimental difficulties. Not even Lincoln could come up with any plans better formulated than utopian schemes for colonization.[5]

The radical element was also the smallest. Perhaps fewer than 1 in 250 Northerners would have called themselves abolitionists. They were radical not because they called for the *immediate* end of slavery everywhere in the United States – most Northerners simply wanted to keep it confined where it was – but because many of them also simultaneously agitated for the abolition of the civil and social stigmas against blacks. The movement itself, while not integrated in the modern sense, was driven by leaders both black and white (among the African American leadership were Frederick Douglass and James McCune Smith). To a degree scandalous in the nineteenth century, it also included women and men. In the abolitionist vision, slavery would end and black freedmen would come to enjoy American liberty. And their position was uncompromising: that liberty was God-given. Slavery was wrong because slavery was a sin, not merely a political or social or economic wrong, nor a moral lapse, nor an ethical error. It speaks to just how radical the abolitionist proposition was in the North that one of the first martyrs to the cause was a newspaper editor murdered by a mob in Illinois – the land of Lincoln – and that William Lloyd Garrison, the most famous of them, was once dragged through the streets of Boston by a scrum of townsmen intent on humiliating him, or worse, into silence. In Philadelphia (!) riots were quite nearly *de rigueur*. In 1838 a mob not keen to pummel abolitionists – these were women, after all – instead torched their new meeting hall to cinders, a temple literally thrown down three days after its opening.[6]

One of the American Civil War's revolutionary dynamics, as will become apparent, worked to push Northern opinion along the scale. It liberalized attitudes the longer it went on, the more it cost, and the more urgently and immediately it forced on them the fundamental question of what the sacrifice would bring into being rather than simply preserve. It *became* an abolition war – at least, instrumentally so. The War was the instrument that ended slavery immediately, everywhere, and it was the instrument that ensured the future of now-freed African Americans was not elsewhere but in America. Whether it would become the instrument by which former slaves would live in liberty, freed of racism, was not yet ensured by 1865.

Abolitionists did not tend to live in the South or agitate if they did. White Southerners made no fine distinctions in antislavery opinion. Nor did they bother counting Northern abolitionists. In the decade between 1850 and 1860 more and more of them were convinced that any antislavery was abolition – in its fullest, most realized form. Of all the dynamics driving secession, none was more vital than the apocalyptic conviction that a future within the Union was a future in which their slave property was seized, then transformed, into men and women who were their equals. The hideous contortion of political and civil rights for blacks, as the South Carolinians suggested in a secession manifesto, was a "great political error invested with the sanction of a more erroneous religious belief."[7] Such opinions were widespread and proclaimed openly: first against abolitionists, then by an escalating series of conflations into all Northerners. There were in the South other opinions, not the less widely spread for being utterly, quietly, silent. Yet the attitudes of black Southerners, the slaves among them, require no conjuring. As we will see, as became apparent both on the battlegrounds of the War and in the aftermath of memory, slaves were the most radical abolitionists of all – in what they did and would have done, in thought and in deed, and in the imagination of their hearts for what would be left undone, in words.

1

UNION: 1860

On November 26, 1859, readers of the English weekly magazine *All the Year Round* were at last brought to the astonishing climax of what would become Charles Dickens's most popular novel. In those pages the hopelessly dissipated Sydney Carton gives up his life at the guillotine to satiate the Vengeance – a mob of revolutionary Parisians that has mistaken him for Charles Darnay, the selfless aristocrat whom Carton resembles only in appearance and the man wedded to Carton's ideal wife. So it was, in *A Tale of Two Cities*, unrequited but purposed, at the end, to make something lastingly meaningful of himself, the meekest of humanity laid down his life for love and redeemed the worst of times for the betterment of time.

Not quite a week later, in the languid noonhour of December 2, John Brown stepped upon a makeshift gibbet in Charles Town, Virginia, offered his head to an executioner who adjusted hood and noose, and with a grim resolution that impressed even those who feared him, fell through the platform to hang in the stillness, as it seemed to one observer, "between heaven and earth." We have come to understand the meaning of the American Civil War's violence in what we say to redeem a vengeful carnage. Yet it began with a prophecy. On the way from his jail cell to the execution field Brown had handed one of his captors a note. "I John Brown am now quite *certain*," it read, "that the crimes of this *guilty land will* never be purged *away*, but with Blood. I had, *as I now think vainly*, flattered myself that without *very much* bloodshed, it might be done."[1]

The prophecy was as remarkable for what it did not pronounce. Brown had hoped to shed some of that blood and perhaps even flattered himself as the avenger who would shed it in just the right tincture. Both hopes were vanities. On the night of October 16, he had led a small band of abolitionist revolutionaries into Harpers Ferry, Virginia, intent on capturing arms from the town's long-established federal arsenal and rifle works. Their number was twenty-two and would have been serendipitously Dickensian had not the great black leader Frederick Douglass, who told Brown his band "would never get out alive," positively refused to join them.[2] As Brown envisioned the dream marching on, word of his deed would spread to slaves near and slaves far off. They would rush to his banner, Brown's insurrectional band growing into a liberation legion as it moved southward down the spine of the Appalachian mountains, into North Carolina, into South Carolina, into Georgia, the legion multiplying again and again as it strode into the phalanx of a general slave rebellion that would destabilize the institution in America and destroy it once and for all. Far-fetched it might have been, but such operations always had a far-out quality to them. The swashbuckling American filibusters with Narciso Lopez invaded Cuba in 1851 with a provisional army of a few hundred. William Walker invaded Honduras in 1855 with a similar crowd. Filibustering – and Brown'sattempt was a kind of attempt to annex native country for free soil – always had in it the element of the fantastic.

Brown captured the arsenal fairly easily (it was guarded by one watchman) and even took among his hostages the great-grandnephew of George Washington, who lived nearby, and was wanted, Brown said, "for the moral effect it would give our cause."[3] Then, for reasons no one has ever come to know fully, Brown simply sat there, in Harpers Ferry, and waited. He even allowed free passage of the night-train to Baltimore, whose conductor soon spread the alarm via telegraph. Maybe such chivalry seems less inexplicably antic in light of Brown's first decision the next morning, which was to order breakfast for his hostages from the local hotel. By that time Harpers Ferry was alive with armed residents and oncoming local militia, its cobblestoned streets sparking with the spent bullets of a nasty affray in which the town's mayor was picked off and several of Brown's raiders killed and their corpses humiliated. Among these was the "very fair mulatto" Dangerfield Newby, whose hope to liberate his wife from slavery died with him. He lay "stretched along the pavement" with a "most hideous wound" in his throat "gaping open quite large enough to admit the fore part of an ordinary-sized foot." Presumably, other details were too grotesque to admit to either a public telling or a public confession of atrocity, for Newby's corpse was dragged into a gutter where a trophy-hunting townsman sliced off his ears. The rest of him was left there to be rooted by village hogs.[4]

Meanwhile, Brown had been driven into a small building housing the arsenal's fire engine. There did he, four of his men, and eleven hostages hole up during the night of the seventeenth. By the next morning a detachment of US Marines under the command of Colonel Robert E. Lee had arrived from Washington, DC. With Lee observing from a nearby hillside and at least two thousand local spectators on hand for the denouement, the Marines summarily stormed the engine house and ended the insurrection thirty-six hours after it began. Brown's "provisional army," as he styled it, included three of his sons. Five others were black, the now-mutilated Newby being one, the fugitive slave Shields Green another. The raid was less a plan than a vision, less an insurgency than a sacrifice. Ten raiders were killed, including Brown's sons Oliver and Watson, while seven were captured – two in Pennsylvania after they had managed to flee the immediate scene – and later executed. The last of Brown's raider-sons, Owen, and the others managed to escape entirely.

Brown probably would have been run-through and killed had the marine who attacked him been wielding a weapon other than his dress-sword. The old man was severely wounded as it was. Sometime in the long hours before the final attack, if not much, much sooner – again, no one has been able to embrace his mind – he had known failure the likely outcome but had also resolved that martyrdom, if acted heroically, was the best of all outcomes. This clarity he had achieved in the engine house during the frantic night before the final assault, where he stoically awaited the morning and urged his men "to sell their lives as dearly as they could," even as his son Oliver died of his wounds in the darkness; this determination he had made during his incarceration, in which he corresponded with friends and dignitaries and manfully impressed the governor of Virginia in a personal interview; this duty he had taken up during his trial, speedily convened a few weeks after the raid, in which the outcome was not to be doubted but in which he managed to make himself both an Old Testament Maccabee and a New Testament baptizer exhorting among a brood of vipers. It was almost as if he had been brought before Pilate. He remarked during his trial,

> I see a book kissed, which I suppose to be the Bible, which teaches me that all things whatsoever I would do that men should do to me, I should do to them. I say I am yet too young to understand that God is any respecter of persons. I believe [that] to have interfered as I have done in behalf of His despised poor, is no wrong, but right. Now, if it is deemed necessary that I should forfeit my life for the furtherance of the ends of justice, and mingle my blood with the blood of millions in the slave country whose rights are disregarded by wicked, cruel, and unjust enactments, I say let it be done.[5]

And this resolve he had taken to the gallows. "I am worth inconceivably more to *hang*," he wrote one of his correspondents, "than for any other purpose."[6] For all of the religious overtones of his manner and speech, critically vital as they were to perceptions of him in a pious age, there was also something of a narrative awareness in Brown's words, as in his actions, a way of patterning himself on the heroic and romantic literary conventions of the Victorian era. That sensibility should not be dismissed as a conceit. More than one historian has surmised that Brown could see the story after him – he understood what his death might do, how the tale *was supposed* to be written after his doom, if he could but write himself into it as the tale demanded. He acted a martyr's part, and acted symbolically, in essence, so as to make the story come true.

As it was no conceit, neither was the sensibility restricted to Brown. For much longer than many might imagine possible in a war that scraped romanticism off to its nubs, a considerable array of the era's most distinguished figures acted as dramatists in what they had already conceived as the fateful American epic. For many of them, it was as if destiny unfolded in vibrant possibility before them – only the substance and the tone of their part in it remained to be found, beginning with the peerless hostage Colonel

Lewis Washington, whose self-authored tale soon appeared in the newspapers in marvelous Thackerayian visuality. He was waylaid at home in his nightshirt by men carrying "lighted flambeaux, made of pine whittlings," and after inquiring about the weather ("rather chilly," he was advised; wear an overcoat) was allowed to dress for the occasion, then driven to his imprisonment in his own carriage and by his own servant.[7] The heroic ideal was a motive force indeed in a sentimental age.

Brown's fortitude in death, his utter acceptance, was all the more compelling because it redounded to his mystique then and later in stoic contrast to the reactions of his white countrymen. An atmosphere of spine-tingling fear and scramble gripped both North and South in the weeks and months after the raid. A search of the nearby farmhouse where Brown and his men lived as they prepared for their mission had turned up the old man's correspondence – which implicated six abolitionists as his major financial supporters, called then and afterward the Secret Six. Three panicked and fled to Canada to avoid arrest, another was conveniently ill and convalescing in Europe, and a fifth, Gerrit Smith, the wealthiest of them, checked himself into a lunatic asylum. Only Thomas Wentworth Higginson, previously renowned in Boston and elsewhere for his militant dissidence and famous during the War as an officer of an all-black Union regiment, publicly and stridently defended the raid and his own role in it.[8] None claimed to know exactly what Brown planned when they contributed to the cause, although it is hard to imagine they did not conjecture a stunning errand into the wilderness. Whether they fully comprehended its violence is also – odd as it sounds given Brown's reputation – a matter of some conjecture. Brown's presence, like his oratory, was mesmerizing, captivating, was charismatically persuasive beyond rationality. He would die insisting that he intended to incite no insurrectionary violence at all. If blood were shed, it would be on the hands of slaveholders who attacked Brown's innocent fugitives as they fled, equally innocently because freedom was God-given but man-taken. The lowly could not be blamed for killing in the self-defense that followed from self-emancipation. Something of the same logical magic had captured the imaginations of the Secret Six.

A far more nimble scramble was required of Northerners whose antislavery opinions and rhetoric had, according to white

Southerners unwilling to make fine distinctions in it, nurtured abolitionists and incendiaries and conspirators. Distancing themselves from that charge became yet more difficult after December 2. Church bells peeled in some Northern towns at the hour of Brown's death; memorial services were conducted; silence was kept. Those who sympathized with Brown's beliefs but condemned his act struggled to express their continuing support for antislavery tenets on the one hand and their rejection of insurrectionary violence on the other. This tack was particularly treacherous for leaders of the Republican Party, which had formed in the middle of the decade on an antislavery platform. Already, long before the raid, white Southerners and many Northern political opponents had perverted it into a coalition of radical levelers and Jacobins. Under circumstances that threatened to legitimate this caricature, the best many Republicans could do was to call Brown insane and attempt to prove it by the bewildering, botched monomania of his plan. They could also point up a family history of mental illness, long the gossip of old neighbors and acquaintances at home, an effective tactic perhaps as a mitigating defense in the court of public opinion, yet less so in the court of execution, where Brown himself utterly and eloquently rejected it. It would not have mattered: He was a dead man.

Frenzy in other forms shook Southerners, in Virginia and elsewhere. Insurrection was the blackest fear of any slaveholder. Although it is an exaggeration to say that white Southerners lived in daily hysteria, they were all too aware, and aware all too often, of the potential horror of slave rebellion. Memories were long, and nightmares leapt from one dream to the next. No one need remind any white Southerner of the Haitian revolution of the 1790s, in which masters had been overthrown, cut in half, and buried alive, especially not in South Carolina or Mississippi where the slave population outnumbered the white one. No jarring recall was necessary of the most recently sensational American example, Nat Turner's rebellion in Virginia in 1831, which was put down brutally and its leader executed but not before several of Turner's white victims had been thrown into fireplaces.

These were known, rote, but the slave system did not generally publicize its disturbances. Only those insurrections whose scale of terror made them impossible to ignore – Haiti, Turner, now

Brown – tended to become matters of discussion. Best to be silent. White awareness could not, after all, be hidden from black slaves, who very well might choose to accept slave rebels as role models and their rebellions as templates. Local outbreaks might take the form of loose collusions, such as an uprising thwarted in Camden, South Carolina, in 1816, or cabalist acts of violence, such as the poisoning of a master here or there. These were far more numerous than organized rebellion and tended to be hushed up. The actuality of any plot did not really matter. A suspected conspiracy was enough to set a considerable machinery of repression into service, as at Natchez, Mississippi, in 1861, where at least twenty-seven slaves were tortured and executed when whites began to fear vague talk among their slaves about something possibly happening sometime. What *might* happen was far more unpredictable – Independence Day in July or Christmastime could be edgy – and the anguish of not knowing more pervasive. Fear was glutted with a dread generated by the justification slave owners had created for their own domination. Very few rumors of rebellion did not contain a fantasy: the reputed uprising must include, not just as an inseparable act of insurrection but as the *objective* of insurrection, the rape of white women. Mastery contained within itself the loathing of its apocalypse.[9]

The military spectacle that accompanied Brown's captivity, trial, and execution was in many ways both a compensation for fear and a projection of it. The governor of Virginia, who had accused Harpers Ferry residents of acting like sheep in the face of Brown's attack and boasted that he could have captured Brown with a penknife, nevertheless summoned the state militia into service and spent $250,000 (a lot of penknives, then or now) to underwrite an arresting martial display of horses, guns, and chivalry. Vigilance justified such spectacular stage-drama, it was said, to prevent Brown's escape or his deliverance at the hands of spies or rescue parties rumored to be on the move from Pennsylvania and Ohio. Nor was drama or hysteria confined to Virginia. It radiated southward. Slaveholding communities everywhere redoubled vigilance, shined their boots and bolstered patrols, perked their ears to the murmurings of their human chattel in just the way their slaves had always perked their ears around them, and cast beady eyes on strangers white and black, road travelers, and Yankees known and unknown.[10]

Figure 2: John Brown, by John Bowles, *c.* 1856, Public Domain.

Such reactions might seem grotesquely out of proportion when measured against the broken plan of one man, whom many thought insane, and an army of twenty-two that its captain had rather optimistically called "provisional." More than one contemporary was overheard wondering whether it was the pathological reaction, rather than the act, which befitted lunacy. Yet Brown's raid was a critical matter: it proved powerfully destabilizing as well as transitionally unifying. Its incendiary cataclysm not only closed a pivotal, rancorous decade in which arguments over slavery constantly, continuously usurped all attempts to settle or suppress them. It gave Americans north and south a narrative of themselves, and of each other, they could live into, and that more dramatically and less messily than their politics had allowed. By fate or connivance it came on the eve of a presidential election in which the political system, formerly friendly to slavery and built to contain such shocks, was instead already fraying and reorganizing under them. When that election itself came to be understood as a hostile act – an act of conspiracy and civil insurrection, if not a terror itself in which legions of Northern voters were transformed into the ballot-box proxies of Brown's raiders – the Union was not to endure it. Some thought it was already doomed. Brown was guilty of a fiendish plot "to murder our wives, our children, and ourselves," one Virginian wrote to his son on the day of the old abolitionist's execution. "Methinks I can see you ... engaged on a Sunday evening molding balls and preparing for the conflict."[11]

****

By 1840, the American political party system was the most tangible manifestation of the nation's virtuous democracy. Modern elements of the national state were generally nonexistent or weak by design, and even the most concrete levers of tangible federal power, such as the army, hardly registered as institutions of majesty. For most Americans, the reach of the post office was the reach and influence of their government. There were, as well, precious few symbolic representations of nationhood. Power existed locally and identity took root provincially, especially in the South. In Washington, DC, a traveler or statesman still had to contend with dirt, mud, and bog half a century after the capital's founding, and no one would have occasion to appreciate the Washington monument because it was still a decade from having a cornerstone. The Union existed in felt ideals – a vague but instinctive liberty chief among them – and in filial piety, in the mystical reverence Americans paid to the Founders, who in speeches and songs and stories and Fourth of July parades were constant apparitions among them. It existed rhetorically in a kind of democratic eloquence, in orations, at lyceum addresses, in Noah Webster's dictionary and schoolhouse speller, but also in the courthouse stump speech, the tavern, in newspapers and debating societies, or in the hagiography-as-history of Parson Weems's *Life of Washington* or William Wirt's *Sketches of the Life and Character of Patrick Henry* (which another founder, Thomas Jefferson, who lived until 1826, sneeringly shelved in his personal library under "fiction").[12]

This otherwise maturing civic culture transcended its generally smallish outlook through political participation, and it is possible, even to a cynic of today, to marvel at this vibrancy, at the mad American intensity of political association. The parties of the antebellum era commanded loyalties as devoted and committed as the passionate followings of modern sports franchises, and the pageantry of political experience was often as exuberant. (The distinctly American word *booze* entered the lexicon courtesy of a Philadelphia distiller, one John Booze, who bottled whiskey during the rambunctious 1840 presidential election.) In no election between 1840 and 1860 did voter turnout fall below 70 percent, a remarkable figure even allowing for the restriction of the franchise to white men. More importantly, the parties were considered essential – they were *good* things – by those who led and supported them. They promoted democratic participation, they channeled opposition into legitimacy. As national institutions they softened the cutting abrasions of sectionalism. As broad-based coalitions they subdued forces of ambition and interest. As cultural entities they connected Mississippians and New Yorkers and Carolinians and Iowans and made the political United States not only a practicality but a reality.

It is impossible to grasp the pivotal turmoil and the eventual destabilization of American politics during the 1850s without comprehending that the party system had not always been this way nor would remain this way. The mode of politics in the founding decades of the American experiment was republican. So too was political language. Both mode and language were the legacy of a commonwealth tradition radicalized by early British Whigs in the 1720s and shaped by American experience into a temper of zealotry for all-precious liberty. Even into the 1820s in America, political parties were suspected as corrupt factions, as conspiratorial combinations of ambitious interest, indeed as usurping forces. Extreme virtue, extreme vigilance, were necessary to defend the common good against them. A generation later, with the system still in the throes of transition toward a more expansive democracy, the antique attitude about parties had become glossed in the reverent, old-fashioned sepia tones of the old school – in no small measure because the good of new school was tantalizingly tactile in the spoils of patronage. Political parties were now understood as guardians against subversion rather than agents of it. Once deemed local or interested factions, they were now, vitally in the vibrant 1840s, the organizing and facilitating institutions of national bonding.

And yet if the American system had begun a metamorphosis, its idiom did not, and that it did not was one of the critical elements of systemic disturbance. The language of the republican mode remained democracy's most accessible vocabulary and posture. Its stark contrasts and demands – virtue against corruption, extreme vigilance against conspiracy, precious liberty against engrossing power – were used to persuade and wheedle a consuming, voracious public opinion, and to organize opposition to whatever party had achieved power. The ideology giving it voice filtered and explained expansive events that otherwise might seem disjointed or unconnected. The Slave Power Conspiracy was an instance. While surely conspiracy was effective as propaganda, as spin, as a talking point, more and more Northerners were in fact becoming increasingly persuaded that at the bottom of Southern aggression in the disturbing 1850s was an insidious, caballing plot to engross their power (and snatch away Northern liberty) by extending slavery from sea to shining sea, and maybe even to the next sea over if the caballists could but get themselves a navy.[13]

In short, by the middle of the 1850s, the relentless reach and bitterness of the slavery issue had placed the young American party system in a constant turmoil it did not survive, and its disintegration was both cause and effect of accelerating political dysfunction. A fundamental realignment after 1854 produced not a new national unity but a sectional party, organized around antislavery impulses and strong enough to succeed without the necessity of intersectional ties – appealing to its adherents because it was formed, as many of them thought, to combat a conspiracy; debilitating and threatening to its opponents, as many of them believed, because it *was* one. At the risk of leaping too far ahead, the immediate cause of Southern secession, the breaking up of the Union, was neither military invasion nor legislative assault, not groaning taxation and not a military coup, but the free, fair, and constitutional election of a new party, the Republican Party, to power. To white Southerners, to the most ardent secessionists, *this* was the act of irredeemable hostility. If a sectional party hostile to the one institution foundational to their interests and their way of life could come to control the government by outwardly Constitutional means, no recourse to the Constitution could protect slavery. Their only protection was secession, because as far as radical Southerners and slaveholders were concerned, the face of that party's president, Abraham Lincoln, was painted black.

The Republicans were many things. They were a party of economic growth and government activism, a party of social and educational reformers, a party, especially in its earliest manifestations, of nativist shades and sober Protestant predilections. Foremost it was a party of antislavery, pledged by its central pillar to halt the future expansion of slavery in the United States, with the goal, sometimes stated but always implied, of putting it on the path to ultimate extinction everywhere in the country. The end would come, but it would come gradually not apocalyptically, and by stages so subtly advancing, under such a modernizing prosperity, that perhaps a century or maybe two would pass and the institution would seem vanished. This was a position owing somewhat less to the violence slavery had done to the enslaved, and mandated more by the harm slavery had done to the country, to its white citizens, to the very idea of progress and civilization. Many Republicans were no different than most white Americans who, when they saw victims, tended to see ciphers or to see themselves. Yet there were some, a few, who privileged the moral conviction that slavery was primarily wrong for its unmitigated trespasses on African Americans, and they would grow in stature and influence as time, and war, came to pass.[14]

Understanding the origins of the Republican Party requires peering into a teleological dimension that accompanied its birth pangs in more than fifty years of American westward expansion. The party had begun to coalesce only in 1854, in the aftermath of the so-called Kansas–Nebraska Act, perhaps the decade's original destabilizing political event. By that act Congress formally organized the territories of Kansas and Nebraska in preparation for eventual statehood – but not before its champion, the Illinois Senator Stephen A. Douglas, was cajoled, prodded, and eventually forced to do something he knew, as he remarked during a carriage ride with two Southern congressmen who were doing the coaxing and buttonholing, would raise "a hell of a storm": it repealed a compromise that had governed in those territories for more than a generation, the Compromise of 1820.[15] The famous Compromise had resolved the fate of slavery in the entirety of the Louisiana Purchase – the huge swath of middle America between the

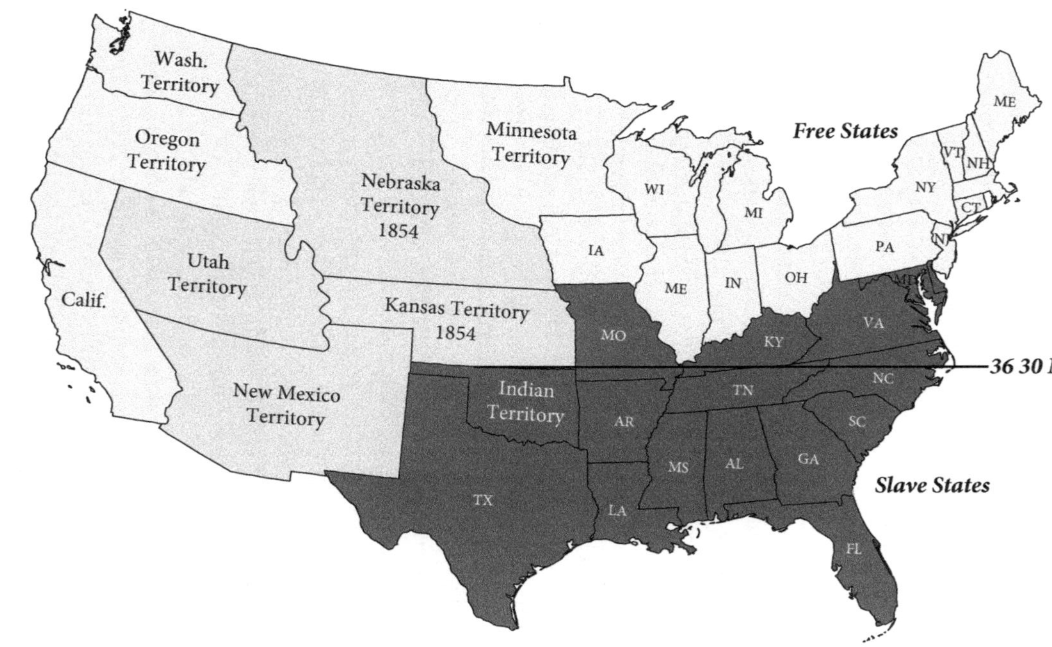

Map 1: America in the Age of Expansion and the Kansas–Nebraska Act.

Mississippi River and the Rocky Mountains – by allowing slavery in Missouri and south of it, but prohibiting slavery more or less north of it. And that was Douglas's hell and storm. Kansas and Nebraska were both north of Missouri. Slavery had been forbidden there.

The intrigues are less important than the storm, as Douglas had proven a worthy political meteorologist. On the surface of things, the debates about the territorial expansion of slavery leading into the 1850s were about slavery's future, about where it might go. By 1854, its present status, where it was, was already settled. But the debates were never solely and separately about the future. To talk about where slavery might go – to attack it as an evil to be stopped or to extol it as a good worthy of extension – was necessarily to define or redefine slavery *where it already was*, even the plantation South, where it had existed for almost 200 years. The future moved toward a definite end, be what it will, and the tendencies of the present shaped and reshaped both what would be, as policy, and what already was, as history. Lincoln voiced this teleological element when he proclaimed in 1858 that the Union could not permanently endure half slave and half free. His was not an assertion of power or a threat or even a platform, although it is often read to be (and was read by white Southerners to be). One way or another the thing would be settled totally, and permanently. What made the atmosphere suffusing the debates especially volatile was the collision of the teleology with the powerful language of the political idiom. It was one thing for events to tend more or less naturally in one direction or another. It was another – quite another – when those events were somehow manipulated by mysterious cabals of men who conspired to bend them to their own interests.

This, as far as many soon-to-be Republicans were concerned, including eventually Lincoln himself, was what happened in the Kansas–Nebraska Act and its aftermath. Slavery had been on the road to extinction: that was the purpose of the 1820 Compromise, to limit it, to cut it off, to kill it. Perhaps it was true that events since 1820, particularly the acquisition of the far western territory between the Rockies and the Pacific Ocean in the Mexican–American War, would delay the final end. After all, some portions of that new territory had been opened to slavery. But even the Mexican cession, ultimately, would not prevent extinction. And now the Kansas–Nebraska Act had fundamentally reshaped things. Slavery was now allowed into places it had been explicitly proscribed. It was not only moving forward, into the far West, but seemingly backwards too, across territory it had passed over, to reshape the final end. Worse still, its menace was corrupting free institutions – the institutions of American liberty ostensibly apart from slavery – as it did so. Slavery's tentacles violated the sacrosanct agreement of 1820, would do worse damage in Kansas, would choke liberty in the very halls of Congress. Slavery would most ominously corrupt justice itself, when in 1857 the Supreme Court ruled, in the infamous case of Dred Scott v. Sandford, that no power could prevent its expansion. For good measure, sayeth the Court through its cadaverous chief justice, Roger B. Taney, black men were not, were never, and could never be American citizens. The final end was not merely the expansion and utter completeness of slavery in America. It was the extinction of free institutions and of free government.

The ostensible point that there were no Republicans in the South is true only if four million potential Republicans – African American slaves – are banished from thought in the same way the Dred Scott decision attempted to banish them forever from any path, even as freed persons, to citizenship. Such may seem a historically invasive comment, the briskly superior remark of a modern, morally smuggish world. In fact the awareness of them is a necessity to see just how visible they were to those in the South who appreciated the potential, manifest in its very denial, suggested by the Supreme Court. *Only* with that sight can the bleak threat represented by the Republicans be understood. Tellingly, white Southerners rarely referred blankly to the Republican Party, but, instead, called it the "Black Republican Party" and their adherents "Black Republicans." The intended insult had its particular political and social uses, each complementing the others. *Black* conjured darkness and degradation and evil, corruption and conspiracy; *black* insidiously created a leveling association with the "red republicans" of Europe, whose social radicalism convulsed the continent in the 1848 revolutions; most penetratingly, *black* suggested an affinity of "true inwardness" between Republicans – whose skin was white but whose hearts were black – and the slaves they would surely free. Their liberation would be not just from bound labor but the freedom to become the equals of their former masters, at liberty to vote, to hold office, to acquire property, to live daily in social ease and familiarity with whites.[16]

Of course most Republicans wanted no such thing. Most *Northerners* wanted no such thing. It was Douglas, Lincoln's rival in Illinois, who suborned the distortion of Black Republicanism and the politically powerful affect of his own assertion when he accused Lincoln's minions of craving black wives. (He put it that way, and not the other – the corollary that free black men thus craved white wives – since the other was too crassly indelicate to mention. He merely need wink and nod to imply that Republicans would free slaves and then free black men would be free to marry white women.) Yet these national attitudes on race and the divisions and cleavages over them in the North were of no matter to white Southerners. Many of them were already too far gone in their association of any antislavery attitude with abolition. The formation of the trope "Black" Republican first conflated all Republicans, a useful tool for Democrats and Southerners alike after 1854. But it was the beginning of more volatile extremism that would soon conflate all Republicans into all Northerners. And this was a deadly development. What white Republicans there were in the South were few indeed, and brave, and the rough examples of their harassment and intimidation cowed all but the bravest. Yet if the Black Republicans came to national power, the proof of the party's essential ability to maintain its power, and govern without the necessity of white Southern votes or a coalition with Southern interests, or even the barest Southern influence, was manifest.

The exclusion of the South was obviously potentially devastating on many levels, yet one is often unremarked, and was what might loosely and for lack of a better be called psychological. Since the founding, the peculiar workings of the American system had not merely counted Southern power but fundamentally privileged it: slave populations were used to apportion power in Congress and in presidential elections. (Jefferson was mocked by his enemies as "the Negro president," for instance, not because he kept the slave mistress Sally Hemings, but because he was elected on the strength of artificial votes created in the South through its slave population.)[17] Southerners had been used to being masters of the Union. To insist upon equality in the Union, as they would do in harsher tones in the 1850s, was to redirect in inverse their declining influence even as it was to assert conspiracy. Black Republicans would govern without the South, and if that happened Republicans could halt the extension of slavery and even abolish it where it already was, and if that happened white Southerners would become a permanent, and utterly powerless, minority in the Union – all the more galling because Black Republicans would guarantee their permanency (and become a national party) by aligning with newly freed and empowered former slaves.

Those who were once masters – not merely of their chattel – would become slavish dogsbodies.

****

Republican ascendancy had almost come to pass in the first national election the party contested, in 1856. Its nominee for president, a famed US Army soldier and explorer named John C. Frémont, would have been President had he been able to carry just two more key Northern states. The victor, instead, was James Buchanan, a Democrat, a Pennsylvanian by birth but a political careerist by profession, by turns congressman, senator, cabinet secretary, and twice-appointed diplomat who possessed not merely offices but enough self-awareness to call himself the Old Public Functionary. Perhaps it is getting ahead of things to note that almost thirty years would pass before another Democrat was elected to the presidency, but in that fact is the convulsion of the age. The Democratic party had been dominant in American politics since its organization under Andrew Jackson in the 1820s, or, if one prefers, even longer if the party is considered the heir of Thomas Jefferson's coalition of the 1790s. Like the Republicans, the Democrats were a composite of many interests, held together generally by an emphasis on local rather than national power, the individual's freedom from government taking some precedence over the collective good imposed through government. If its strength was traditional, its reach into both sections had enabled the party to hold onto power in 1856. Maintaining its national appeal was necessary if the threat of Black Republicanism was to be contained.

Difficult, even touch-and-go, it was accomplished in 1856 by selecting Buchanan as candidate. Aside from his unfortunate association with the Ostend Manifesto, a saber-rattling, proslavery state paper demanding the seizure of Cuba, Old Buck (as he was called by others) was safe in the North. He had been out of the country functioning as minister to England during much of the recent trouble and could not be battered with its political rocks nor bruised with its clubs. He was even safer in the South – the slaveholding states there voted in phalanx for him. By the end of Buchanan's term, the Democrats were a national party in name only, its organization riven into sectional wings unwilling and unable to hold together because, as it turned out, Buchanan's one remarkable quality was his bumbling incompetence. Or at least that was how the story used to be portrayed in the hindsight of Buchanan's weak-kneed, frozen indifference to secession in 1860–1861. The reality is somewhat more complicated than a narrative making of a milquetoast presidency. If a portfolio of credentials and qualifications for public office mattered, no American in 1856 had more of either than Buchanan. Far from being weak-kneed or indifferent, it was Buchanan's stubbornness, and even perhaps his scorn and insolence for opposition, that triggered the eventual fissuring of the Democratic Party. The very things that seemed appealing about him, careerist and political loyalist that he was, those things that on the surface of matters seemed to make him eminently qualified, also contributed to the failure of his administration. The Old Public Functionary could see no opposition that was not essentially, and to him cynically, political and opportunist in turn.[18]

The issue that would come to define his presidency had been nearly three years joined by the November elections of 1856. Kansas was, in both the literal and figurative senses, a battleground, and not just between northern opponents and southern supporters of slavery, but between the northern and southern wings of the Democratic Party. When the Kansas–Nebraska Act repealed the Missouri Compromise, which had forbidden slavery in Kansas, the Act substituted the principle of popular sovereignty. Under it, the settlers of Kansas would decide themselves, for themselves, whether to allow slavery to enter the land. The southern wing of the Democratic party, whose most militant members were stung by the longstanding frustration and humiliation of being unable to obtain *absolute* protection of slavery's extension into the territories, fought to achieve on the ground what it could not ensure in Congress. The northern wing, led by Stephen A. Douglas but grievously weakened by the very passage of the Kansas–Nebraska Act, was publically tolerant of slavery's extension into Kansas, *provided* slavery was established according to the popular sovereignty doctrine – its integrity was, and rapidly became more so, the proxy for every issue in slavery's expansion.

Popular sovereignty's doctrinal history preceded Douglas's adoption of it, but the position has come to be associated with him almost exclusively. Among its virtues was nebulousness – it might even be called an oddly resonant Buchanan-like quality – of appearing to have perfect credentials as a solution only to be utterly ill-suited and unbecomingly cynical in practice. For it was cloudy by design: the doctrine's valence was in Douglas's refusal to stipulate precisely *when* settlers were empowered to apply it. The American system of territorial organization unfolded in phases. A provisional authority, called the territorial government, initially set the machinery of governance in motion; at a later stage, when the territory was established on a more permanent footing, settlers formally petitioned for admission as a state by submitting a proposed constitution to Congress. Only Congress was given to determine whether a new state was organized in accordance with republican forms of government, and if it was so, as deemed by the US Senate, the territory could be admitted to the Union. And there was the rub, for in the timing was the dilemma of Kansas and the failure of popular sovereignty as a solution. At which stage was popular sovereignty binding? If it was at the earliest stage, proslavery forces could arrive early and seize the upper hand. But over time, as most observers understood, the dynamics of emigration favored so-called free-soilers, as antislavery settlers were known. The answer was somewhere drifting in the abstract because Douglas avoided the question entirely. Possession on the ground was a simple matter of getting there first with the most men.

And so as early as 1854 the forces of slavery and their free soil opponents began streaming into Kansas to decide by force what popular sovereignty had hoped to organize by consent. The hothouse, guerrilla-style violence of Kansas – to say nothing of its befogging, labyrinthine corruptions – unfolded over several years, in several convolutions, and was challenging even for

Figure 3: *Bleeding Kansas.* Woodcut of Peace Convention-Fort Scott, Kansas.

contemporaries to follow with any sense of clarity or control. Often local issues were as compelling as the national stakes, but the complexity of forces and events there were quickly reduced in the public eye to symbolic epitome: intimidation (common), propaganda (effusive), rigged and bought and stolen elections (also common), financial and material subvention by the proxy underwriters of both proslavery and antislavery living elsewhere in the United States (extensive), usurpation of territorial governors (conspicuous), mayhem and murder (disturbingly all-too-common). John Brown began his career as an antislavery guerrilla in Kansas, most notoriously at a small settlement near Pottawattamie Creek in the spring of 1856, where he and a midnight band of followers murdered five proslavery settlers, execution-style. Brown had a kind of ideological double in David R. Atchison, whose proslavery was just as red-tinctured, and who had proclaimed that he would rather see Kansas sink in hell (with it, one supposes, free-soil Kansans) than see it a free territory. Atchison organized a fluid posse of armed Missourians who crossed the Kansas border on necessary occasions to intimidate free-soil voters, to vote illegally themselves in Kansas elections, to stuff or steal ballot boxes, and, when occasions seemed most needful, to shoot people. In view of Brown's ideological commitments and later notoriety, Atchison certainly possessed no monopoly on distressing human behavior. But he was US senator from Missouri at the time.

The fate of popular sovereignty in the Kansas territory must, like the origins of the Republican Party, be set against the larger political pattern of expansion that gave it urgency. And understanding the pattern also recalls the urgency of an earlier point: to debate the possible extension of slavery, to talk about where it might go in the future, was always and necessarily to talk about its fate where it already was. Particularly after the War of 1812, the addition of new states to the Union had been accomplished in a kind of political mirror. Free states and slaves states were admitted in pairs, a serendipitous twinning that preserved the balance of power between the sections in the US Senate, where each state was awarded two senators regardless of size or population, and where the relative advantage enjoyed by the free states in the composition of the lower chamber of Congress, the House of Representatives, was mitigated. The American system gave the Senate power to check potentially demagogic legislation emerging from that lower, less prestigious body.

But disturbances were on the horizon. The demographics seemed indisputably tilted northward. Its population was already larger and growing more so, and with that grew the likelihood, if not the certainty, that free states would in the future be admitted without slave-state pairs. If the free states eventually dominated both houses of Congress, and if antislavery forces also captured the presidency, those interests might act entirely within the constitutional framework to ban slavery's expansion and eventually abolish it entirely, everywhere. From this perspective the question of sustaining the economics of slavery in Kansas or in any other western territory was moot. There were never more than 1,000 slaves in the Kansas territory – many argued, in fact, that it could not profitably move west, that nature would control what Congress could not. Those arguments failed to grasp human nature or the connection to the goings-on in other phases of American expansionism. Slavery might or might not make a go in Kansas, but it would certainly – would richly, imperially, dreamily – make a go in South America, in Cuba, in places where quasi-American filibuster armies were even now, concurrently with the events in Kansas and elsewhere in the 1850s, already seeking the extension of slavery. For those places to be annexed by the United States, slavery must needs be defended and expanded where it was. So it did not matter that slavery might not turn profitably in Kansas. It mattered that *proslavery interests* controlled the Kansas government.

The goings-on in "Bleeding Kansas" provisioned opinion in press, rostrum, and pulpit, and ultimately generated pressures that boiled at a common point: the utter failure of popular sovereignty. Douglas's hope had been to tack between the extremes of proslavery, whose adherents demanded the absolute right to take slaves into territories, and those of antislavery, who wished to impose an absolute ban on extension altogether. Popular sovereignty's appeal had been in its seeming grassroots moderation and indifference to ideological posturing from afar. Actual settlers on the ground, local people with local interests, would decide for themselves. In the doctrine's emphasis not on slavery but on democratic choice, Douglas hoped to keep the Democratic Party from obliteration. Its political appeal was mainly to northern Democrats who could hold to it without threatening antislavery opinion at home or proslavery opinion in the party's southern wing.

In practice, and as more and more contemporary opinion was given to understand, popular sovereignty corrupted every freedom it was designed to reflect, and instead of becoming the virtuous expression of American democracy's most sacred civil freedoms, it became a carnival perversion. Consent was murder. Choice was manipulation. Opportunity was fear. Free expression was, ultimately, a plea or murmur at the muzzle of a gun. As if in hideous corroboration that the debate over slavery's future was inextricably twinned to slavery's present, corruption reached beyond the local. When in 1856, infamously, a cane-wielding South Carolinian named Preston Brooks beat the Massachusetts abolitionist Charles Sumner into a bloody heap of unconsciousness on the floor of the US Senate for Sumner's gratuitous insults and "libels" in a speech entitled "The Crime Against Kansas," and when some proslavery editorialists huzzahed their approval because saucy abolitionists such as Sumner had "dared to be impudent to gentlemen" while other admiring Southerners gifted Brooks with new canes for the one so gloriously shattered on Sumner's skull, it was perhaps as clear as it ever had been: where slavery might go was fastened, on a chain, not just to slavery where it was but to liberty at its root establishments.[19]

By the time Buchanan was inaugurated as President, in March of 1857, matters had seemingly come to froth – on the ground in Kansas, as well as in Washington DC, where Buchanan stood in the winter's cold and pronounced his faith that the issues long disturbing the country's peace were near a final, agreeable settlement. His confidence on the inauguration rostrum was an insider's knowledge – the Old Public Functionary not only knew it was immanent but tampered with the judicial process to ensure its immanence. The comprehensive decision in the Dred Scott case was issued two days later. Under the aged, palsied hand of its author, Chief Justice Taney, the decision guaranteed the absolute right of slaveowners to take their slaves into any national territories, anywhere. If Taney's dictum made the Republican Party's central pillar extra-constitutional, it less obviously or noticeably did the same to Douglas's popular sovereignty doctrine, since, as it turned out, settlers did not have the right to decide for themselves what to do with the property of other settlers. The right to slaves was inviolable. Finality, indeed.

From that day, Buchanan was inaugurated into his beleaguerment, and never lifted from or above it. Only partially was he encircled by the Republicans, who, rather than being silenced by the Dred Scott decision or the upraised gutta-percha canes of Southern zealots determined to lash them into submission, actually grew in strength thanks to the opprobrium of their opponents. Douglas and his supporters were also yet determined, perhaps to tilt quixotically for popular sovereignty despite its bankruptcy in Kansas, its evisceration under Taney, and Buchanan's indifference to its propriety or its merits. Ultimately, Buchanan's own allies parked their siege trains around him as well. For the Old Public Functionary owed his presidency to the southern wing of the Democratic Party, which had delivered the slaveholding states of the South for him *en masse*, and which he rewarded by reserving for their counselors the plum portfolios, and so the closest voices, in his cabinet. He would not risk governing by deserting his political interests, and perhaps he could not risk a functionary's sense of either practicality or honor by abandoning his political friends.

Desert them he would not, not even over Kansas, even though it threatened to blow up the party of which he was the nominal head, to say nothing of the Union, of which he was the elected head.

Figure 4: James Buchanan, by Mathew Brady, *c.* 1850–1868, Public Domain.

Time had indeed brought demographic victory in Kansas to free soilers, as many had predicted, but the early race had been won, also predictably, by proslavery forces nimble with the devices of corruption and fleet afoot in capturing the machinery of territorial government. They were readying to submit to Congress the issue of those designs, a document called the Lecompton Constitution, so named for the territorial capital in which it was drafted. The constitution was itself emblematic of their dexterity. It had been ratified by settlers, ostensibly in keeping with popular sovereignty – that process had been completed before the Dred Scott opinion was issued. (In any event, the full force of Taney's absolutism had fallen on Republicans and was yet to be realized by Democrats.) But of course that "election" was bastardy. Settlers were given, it was true, a choice to ratify their proposed constitution "with slavery" or "without slavery." The version "without slavery" was no such thing, merely a bowdlerized rendering of the proslavery document that would still protect the limited slavery already in existence under the territorial government. In effect ratification was a choice between some slavery and even more of it, and either way under Lecompton, Kansas would be admitted functionally as a slave state.

In Lecompton, then, was the measure of Buchanan's urgent desire for settlement, to be rid of the slavery question as a political and constitutional matter once and for all. When the document was submitted to Congress for approval in the winter of 1858 – "with slavery": the majority of free-soilers had recognized themselves as tools and boycotted its ratification – the Old Public Functionary declared it an "administration measure." By that he meant he would punish any Democratic senator who opposed it and would reward supporters using every available party emolument. The man most in need of Buchanan's presidential bullying was none other than Douglas, who determined to thwart Lecompton to salvage popular sovereignty – a doctrine he still considered lawful, sensible, and politically needful, despite its fraudulent application in Kansas, and despite the edict of the Supreme Court. In Buchanan's bare-knuckled push for approval and Douglas's brawler's opposition, was a battle for control of the Democratic Party and with it the imprimatur to lead it. Going back to the birthing days of the party under President Andrew Jackson, Buchanan told Douglas, no senator had opposed an administration measure and managed his political survival. "Mr. President," Douglas told him acidly, "I wish you to remember that General Jackson is dead." When Douglas, the father of popular sovereignty and the leader of the northern wing of the party, won the fight and Lecompton was defeated, Buchanan was dead, too. It remained to be determined whether the Democratic Party was among the casualties.[20]

****

Beginning as it did in turmoil, and closing as it did with the election of 1860 and, in its immediate aftermath, the breaking of the Union, Buchanan's presidency was an extended crisis in legitimacy. From a supreme judicial perspective, the only legitimate position on slavery's future was its unbounded extension into western lands, with federal protection of slave property in the territories an implied but no less important corollary. And yet in a democracy, legitimacy is also and more fundamentally a matter of public sanction – a point perhaps comprehended in the reach and depth of the concept of constitution. The constitutional idea is not solely limited to a frame of government but unmistakably associated with vitality, with vigor and strength, even with living and breathing, of *constituent* parts working in health and harmony together. So it is no real error, but directly to the point, that many modern Americans are in the habit of mistaking the living words of the Declaration of Independence – self-evidently: all men are created equal – with having been written into the US Constitution, where in fact they nowhere appear. Nowhere do they appear, but the words are indelibly, inseparably constitutional, in that they constitute America and are fundamental to its common health and welfare.

In that spirit, the US Supreme Court might have deemed proslavery doctrine the only constitutional position on the question of slavery's extension. But legal sanction did not and could not command public countenance. Many if not most Northerners, Democrats or Republicans, could not bring themselves to sustain it. Where to go when the middle position of popular sovereignty was disgraced and exploded? The only remaining positions on slavery – both "constitutional" in different ways – were at the extremes, either taken up by the Republicans, a sectional coalition, or by the southern wing of the Democratic party, which, on the slavery issue at least, was becoming increasingly and unmistakably sectional as well. If Lecompton, in other words, was the measure of Buchanan's administration, the measure of the slavery question by 1860 was legitimacy itself. Slavery was utterly and powerfully a foundational issue, for it drove right to the heart of the validity of the Union as both a form of government and the ideals of which that government was constituted.

By 1860, the fissuring of the Democratic Party was nearly complete, and the storm-driven chaos of the party's convention that spring, held in Charleston, South Carolina, made it total. A harried and exhausted Buchanan, no longer the unmarked man of 1856 but scarred with the stubborn defiance of a proslavery administration, decided against a campaign for re-election, and like so many American presidents eagerly awaited liberation at the advent of a successor. Siting the nominating convention at Charleston was fortune or misfortune, depending on point of view. It was then a

Figure 5: Stephen Arnold Douglas, by Mathew Brady, Public Domain.

city famed for politesse and cavalier gentility but also the citadel of Southern radicalism, the ideological seat of flame-tongued secessionists called fire-eaters, whose fire was a scourge for being kindled in various sectional crises going back thirty years, and now all the more scouring for having been stoked by John Brown's insurrectionary attempt on Harpers Ferry. The most incendiary of them, led by William Lowndes Yancey, a dissolute Carolinian who had scampered off to Alabama more than a decade previously to make name and fortune, arrived in Charleston determined to break up the Convention, at the very least, and perhaps break up the Union with it. Their condition for party harmony was nonnegotiable. They would support no nominee, and no party platform, uncommitted to enforcement of the Dred Scott decision by means of a federal code protecting slavery in the territories.

Not that negotiation was really theirs to offer. Douglas, as the leader of the numerically superior Northern wing of the party, was the presumptive favorite for the nomination. Douglas controlled the most convention delegates. Douglas was still committed to popular sovereignty. Even after Lecompton he had sought to rescue it by posturing that it could still function in a territory, since, practically speaking, settlers could choose not to enact local police laws specifically protecting slavery or refuse to enforce those that were passed. This was the very position the federal slave code demanded by Yancey was designed to nullify. With the Convention standing ready to nominate Douglas, Yancey and followers from six states of the Deep South stormed out. They considered breaking up the proceedings not due to a failure of the system but for the glorious achievement of its ruin. "Perhaps even now," Yancey crowed to a reveling, moonlit throng of admirers, "the pen of the historian is nibbed to write the story of a new revolution." Nibbed, yes, but also blotted by the blearing uncertainty of convolution. In the intraparty confusion that followed the unfinished business of Charleston, two successor conventions of Democrats gathered, where two different nominees were selected as candidates to run on two separate Democratic tickets for the presidency. John Breckinridge, currently Buchanan's vice-president, was a Kentuckian of statesmanlike bearing and ancestry. He would be the nominee of the Southern wing convened at Richmond. Douglas handily secured the Northern wing's nomination when it met in Baltimore.[21]

No one knows, or can know, what might have happened had either Democratic nominee secured the election. The division of the party made that outcome unlikely, especially considering that its disarray had contributed to the last-minute formation of yet another party, an ersatz coalition of cautious moderates who preferred to call themselves the Constitutional Unionists but who were jested by many others as the Old Fogeys. Perhaps, however, had the unlikely if not impossible occurred, the Democratic Party, having secured power, might have eventually mended itself and gotten enough support from the Constitutional Unionists to govern in the face of a common Republican opponent. It does seem highly improbable, at the very least, that Southern states would have responded to the hypothetical election of Stephen Douglas by seceding from the Union. The Democracy had splintered, with disastrous results in the short term, but it was not clear that the splintering in itself implied a crisis beyond the pale.

The crisis of legitimacy, instead, was gathering in the strength of the Republicans. Following the narrow loss of 1856, the party's quest was to find a candidate capable of holding the winnings from that election but who was sufficiently unmarked by controversy or radicalism to win in a couple of key states that had then tipped the other way. Democrats had pursued something of the same politics when they elected Buchanan, and the candidate the Republicans selected was considered by many party leaders to be just such a milquetoast man as the current incumbent: selected for availability, but, if elected, a functionary to be governed under the influence of strong-willed party voices. What Abraham Lincoln of Illinois lacked was Buchanan's cachet. A long-time state legislator, Lincoln had been elected to Congress – once – but had twice been defeated for the US Senate, most recently and bitterly in 1858 by his Democratic rival Douglas, who derided Lincoln in public, even hectored and belittled him on the stump, but in less partisan settings grasped much more about his adversary's abilities than many in Lincoln's own party. In point of fact, Lincoln's probing assault on popular sovereignty during a famous series of campaign debates helped force Douglas into his awkward position on local police laws that eventually shattered the Democratic convention at Charleston.

Whether Americans are more prone to the sentimental underdog than other Westerners, whether they are particularly taken with the underappreciated, underestimated hero who succeeds to riches from rags or rises to fame from oblivion, may be a debatable thing, yet for that Lincoln *was* poor as a youth, *was* ambitious, *was* a meritorious riser made good against earth-leaning odds – was, in a profound sense, self-made – and was also, in 1860, still relatively obscure and unknown. He did not impress by appearance. His giant gaunt ungainly limbs poled out of his trouser legs and prolongated out of sleeves and coat cuffs; his voice was a nasal-pitched whistle that cloyed as it carried; his penchant, déclassé to the sophisticate, was for proverbial backwoods aphorisms, homespun parables, and ribald jokes: a bony, broad-shouldered, big-handed town lawyer, by circumstance David Copperfield, by appearance Uriah Heep, by his bootstraps an attorney whose hard won middle-class respectability as yet ill-fitted his rough, rural-hewn edges. A famous photograph of

Figure 6: Abraham Lincoln, Republican Candidate for Presidency, by Thomas Hicks, 1860, Public Domain.

him by Mathew Brady, taken in New York City in February, 1860, was the first of what would become many Lincoln-as-classical-statesman portraits done up by America's most illustrious photographer. Yet in 1860 Brady designed to conceal by his art as much as he revealed. Lincoln's neck was too long, as were his legs. His ears were too big and his chest too narrow. "I had great trouble," Brady said later of his efforts, "in making a natural picture."[22]

Melancholy and endurance would give Lincoln's face its transcendent wisdom, and to his bearing a kind of weary, patient paternalism, that we now associate with the affect of Brady's later images. That transfiguration would be the War's doing. He was in New York City purposefully at that moment for an important speech arranged by supporters who sought to capitalize on the notoriety of Lincoln's debates with Douglas, and to parade him before eastern voters. The setting was an assembly hall called Cooper Union. There, as he would so often during the cataclysm to come, Lincoln attempted to engage by argument, reason, and persuasion: with words, and with ideas, to which he paid more scrutiny, and with which he was far more agile and penetrating, than most American presidents before or since. The country's framers, he argued, had acted and were committed to limit slavery's expansion – the Union when it was constituted in 1787 embraced the eventual end of slavery. Republicans were not radicals, then, but fundamentally conservative. As heirs of the fathers they attempted to fulfill the founding vision. And, as he did in his debates with Douglas in 1858 and would do more famously in the blood-seared

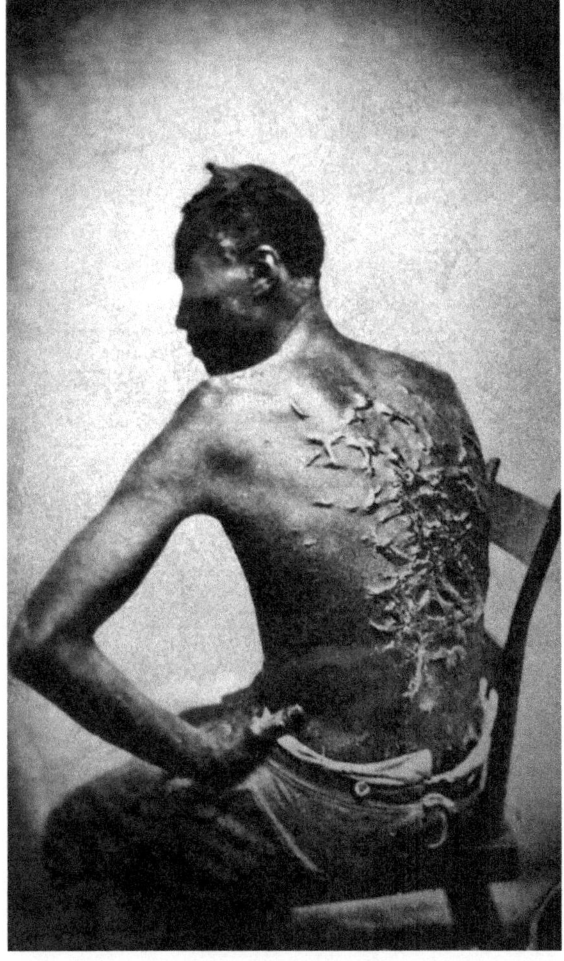

Figure 7: Scars of a whipped Mississippi slave, McPherson and Oliver, 1863, Public Domain.

future at Gettysburg, Lincoln set America's constitutional ideals in the Declaration of Independence. The nation sought to perfect in its mission what was promised in its vision: democracy and equality, endowment to life, liberty, the pursuit of happiness. Those words and not solely the prosaic ligature of the Constitution were the protean constituent words of Union.

In that belief, oddly, Lincoln shared something with John Brown, who had been moldering in his grave for only two months, and with the abolitionist movement, to which he took pains at Cooper Union to distance himself and his party. "You charge that we stir up insurrections among your slaves," Lincoln said, addressing Southerners who would certainly read the speech in their newspapers. "We deny it; and what is your proof? Harpers Ferry! John Brown!! John Brown was no Republican; and you have failed to implicate a single Republican in his Harpers Ferry enterprise."[23] And Lincoln was not Brown. But beginning in 1860, first on the rostrum at Cooper Union, and then in November, when he was elected to the presidency, and, then, when the exhaustion of war settled in the sorrowing battle lines of his face as the grim resolve to carry through a blood purge, he began to resemble something like the Old Testament warrior, come to appear again.

2

REVOLUTION: 1861

In long afteryears, the Southerners who had been defeated in war, and to this day many of their descendants and cultural heirs as well, crafted a number of euphemisms to name the meaning of their experience. To them the crucible became the War of Northern Aggression, the War for Southern Independence, Mr. Lincoln's War, or even the Late Unpleasantness (a term of forgetfulness also used by Germans after the Second World War). A more popular variant, the War between the States, eventually became vernacular. That awkward articulation owed something to the origins of the United States, for "a war between the states" had been conjured up as an apocalyptic counterpoint to the benefits of a peaceful Union, appearing first under the pen of the ultranationalist Alexander Hamilton during the ratification debates accompanying the Constitution. Increasingly it became the frequent rhetorical device of those among the Confederates who by the earliest months of 1865 had begun to see the writing on the wall. They redeployed it beginning then and ever after to deny the winners the lexicon and the ideological fruit of victory.

Anything to avoid calling it a civil war, which denoted a struggle among a common people rather than a war between separate peoples. Anything to deny the smug victors their term for it, the War of the Rebellion, which stripped from the Southern cause its legitimacy and any principle in its underpinnings. Anything to avoid confronting dissonance: that the psychological need for such a term was itself powerful evidence of reintegration with the United States, or a recognition that the sheer viciousness of the American Civil War owed much of its ferocity to a common people slaughtering one another violently over the meaning of a common heritage – a kind of brothers' war that the shift toward a sentimental modality of reconciliation, a generation later in the 1880s, cast in a different light entirely.

The War between the States remains the best-known euphemism, yet each was a name loaded up with freight. Each evoked a kind of denial. And each retains a unique complexity that is immaterial to many white Southerners, who today tend to use the terms indifferently – and without recognizing that they also double back to betray the experience and the ultimate intentions of their forebears. The Confederates who strove to create their own nation never would have called it the War between the States had they won. Such are the difficulties of revolutions when they fail. Whatever might be the verdict of history on their endeavor, secessionists eagerly awaited the trial in 1861, awaited what they would call the War for Southern Independence in the full bloom of their optimism. They awaited it as avowed revolutionaries, some as avowed radicals. Although many were romanticists of the archaic persuasion, they did not expect to fail.[1]

Much ink has been spilled, especially recently, on the period between secession, which occurred in two waves over four months in late 1860 and early 1861, and the War which began in April. The implication in some of it is that secession did not necessarily lead to or predetermine a war. Those perspectives capture the tense interval of contingency between Lincoln's election and his inaugural. But the grim threat that secession and war were combined, that they were of the same motive force, was the far more prevalent feeling, the far more anticipatory feeling, the feeling more firmly set in American history – colonial secession from the British Empire had not been achieved peacefully, a fact every American considered essential – and the far more general understanding of the decline and fall of classical republics. From the formation of the American republic in 1787 to 1789, as Hamilton well knew when he contributed his efforts to what became *The Federalist Papers*, the word disunion was virtually a synonym for a dystopian war between states.[2]

Lincoln was indeed elected in November of 1860, taking not just the electoral votes of key states but sweeping the free states of the North, while the three other candidates, led by Breckinridge, divided up the slaveholding states. That result is arresting and important in at least two respects, for on the one hand it obscured significant and potentially devastating divisions in the North. A surprisingly strong Democratic opposition on the home-front bedeviled Lincoln throughout the War. The result also foreshadowed the halting and uncertain response in the South to Lincoln's election, and underscores the prevalent unfolding fear that secession meant war. Few were left in the white South who did not believe in the abstract right of secession. The major question was not over right but over timing and mechanism. For some, mainly fire-eaters of the Deep South such as Yancey, time and circumstance demanded an immediate, triggering response: even if secession were undertaken by a single state, others would surely follow, as they must, like falling dominoes. For so-called cooperationists, the circumstances might demand secession but timing required several aggrieved states to act in concert. Relying on the dynamics of immediate secession was too risky if a single state found itself outside the Union in isolation. For still others, mainly along the border of the upper South, neither timing nor circumstances were fitting or proper. Lincoln's election was not enough to drive them to secession and certainly not, as it was for many immediatists and cooperationists, an irredeemably hostile act. They were called "conditional unionists," but that way of identifying them was not nearly the same as "loyalist." Their unionism was cased in a fragile carapace. To no one was their quivering loyalism more an insult, in fact, than to hardcore secessionists of the fire-eating variety, who rather than curry or flatter sought to shame them, and taunted them as submissionists.

No single form of secession was primal; all forms were technically employed. What should not be forgotten often is, in convenience, by those who see abstract political principle and not the all-embracing slavery crisis as the dynamic of secession. Far from being undertaken in righteousness to protect state sovereignty, as those who see a political principle at stake claim for it, secession was accomplished in the understanding of a central

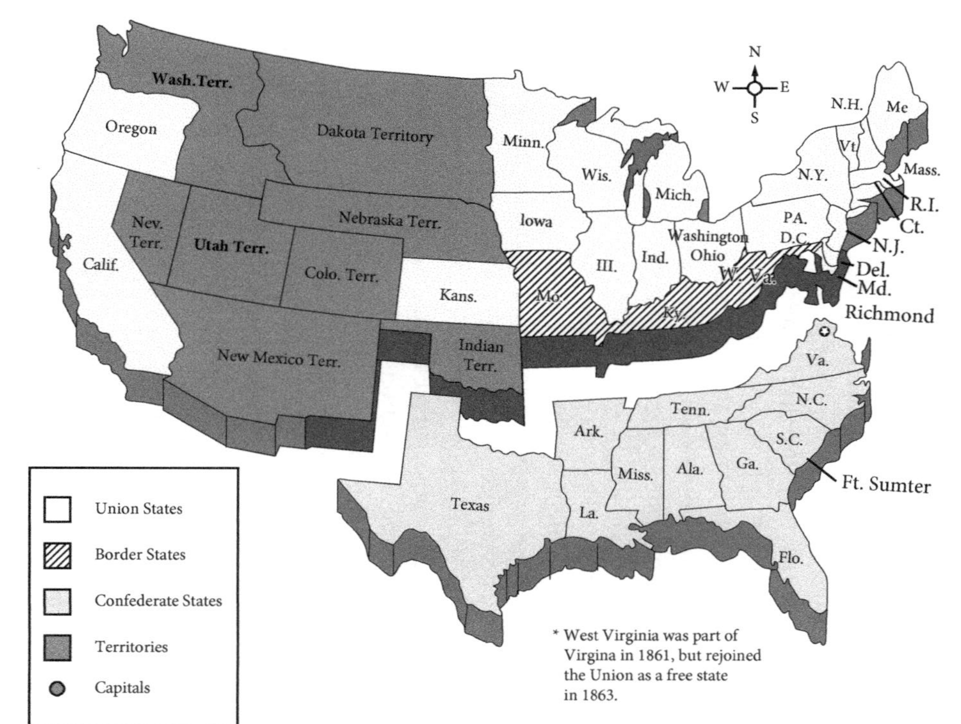

Map 2: Secession and the Confederate States of America, 1861.

alliance of slaveholding states waiting in its aftermath. The first thing undertaken after secession, ostensibly once the slaveholding states freed themselves from a corrupt and centralizing power, was the immediate formation of a new one: precisely because a war for preservation seemed the impending consequence of their act. In warfare, the Confederate States of America became a powerful authority perhaps even more centralized than the Union they had left.

No state seceded absolutely alone. It is more accurate to say South Carolina, long the most radical Southern state, left first, on December 20, 1860, hardly a month after Lincoln's election, but with a tacit assurance that Georgia would follow. Soon enough, in the six weeks to come, Alabama, Mississippi, Texas, Louisiana, and Florida also left the Union, and together they framed the Confederacy in Montgomery, Alabama – the new nation's first capital – in February 1861. It bears repeating, because in the emphasis is the urgency of secession, that Lincoln had been elected, yet not inaugurated; he had been promised power but did not have it, did not wield it, and would not succeed to it until March. Indeed Jefferson Davis, whom the Confederacy soon chose as its leader, was a president before Lincoln was. The election of a Republican, the fair triumph of sectional antislavery at the ballot box was, *in itself*, the corruption of the Union – the accession to power, by the peaceful, legal process of democratic government, which foreboded and even promised the destruction of slavery by the same ostensibly constitutional means. Therein was the pith of the secessionist moment. "For twenty-five years," the South Carolinians had pronounced on secession, antislavery "agitation has been steadily increasing, until it has now secured to its aid the power of the Common Government. Observing the *forms* of the Constitution, a sectional party [now] has the means of subverting the Constitution itself."

Because race remains an explosive modern dilemma, many contemporary Americans are sometimes quick to deflect it or are hesitantly embarrassed to acknowledge its force in the past. This was not so for those who undertook disunion. They declaimed their sentiments openly in documents modeled on the Declaration of Independence. The Carolinians "deem[ed] it due to [themselves], to the remaining United States of America, and to the nations of the world, that she should declare the immediate causes which have led to this act." They were not self-conscious or embarrassed, nor were Georgia, Texas, or Mississippi, whose secession conventions adopted their own declarations in deference to a decent respect for the opinions of mankind. Later generations of white Southerners, many claiming abstract right but some tortured by defeat and some by fear of moral ostracism, would deny that their fathers had entwined secession and slavery. Their fathers were not squeamish. "Our position," the Mississippians proclaimed in their declaration's preamble, "is thoroughly identified with slavery – the greatest material interest of the world. Its labor supplies the largest and most important portions of commerce of the earth. These products are peculiar to the climate verging on the tropical regions, and by an imperious law of nature, none but the black race can bear exposure to the tropical sun."[3]

Just how thoroughly they also identified their position with the American Revolution ought not to be esteemed lightly. Although the delicacy of race in modern America owes something to an inability or unwillingness to see the nation as anything other than the linear, unfolding realization, over the generations, of the founding virtues of liberty and equality, the secessionists identified slavery as the irreducible foundation of the American political and social compact. They understood it more elementally as the fundamental understructure of economic life and vibrancy – not only in the South, not only in America, but in the world. Its vastness as an engine of commerce, and especially its essential complicity in the development of American capitalism, has only recently been well articulated and established by writers engaged in the enterprise.[4] Those expert explanations confirm what many secessionists understood about the wealth of their institution more generally. The Mississippians calculated slavery's worth at "four billions of money" and reduced the matter to its pointed equivalency: a "blow at slavery is a blow at civilization." Just as the Revolutionary founders saw security of property as the security of liberty, the secessionists feared that the Republican conspiracy to take their property would reduce *them* to a kind of slavery. From that inevitably followed racial devolution and decay. Removing the bonds on African Americans would lead to licentiousness and the destruction of civilization. The Mississippians declared this also: "Utter subjugation awaits us in the Union, if we should consent longer to remain within it. For less cause than this, our fathers separated from the Crown of England. Our decision is made. We follow their footsteps."

Only their postwar declamations would take on the tone of self-conscious justification. At secession, during their war for independence, even after defeat, they mantled themselves as the legitimate heirs of the revolutionary forefathers. Like them, they thought of themselves as revolutionaries – and like them also, as conservative revolutionaries. They would *return* to founding principles rather than overturn or revolt against them. Their national symbols said as much (the first national flag of the Confederacy was easily mistaken for the Stars and Stripes) and even their national Constitution, adopted at Montgomery as part of the February convention, said as much. Aside from several important modifications regarding states' rights doctrine and slavery, among them the significant emendations that slavery was named and explicitly protected in the document, where it had been hidden away in silences and euphemisms in the Constitution of the United States, the Confederate republic was framed as a replica of what was already being called the "Union as it was."

As president, the Confederates selected Davis, a Mississippian who had been named after the most idealistic of the old revolutionaries. Time, and war, revealed Davis's limitations, among them a prickly, ramrod bearing, a stiff resolve to protect his own honor – neither of which, incidentally, necessarily stood in contrast to the touchiness in many of his honor-obsessed countrymen – and a sharp temper turned dyspeptic by chronic ill health. (The worst of these maladies was a facial affliction known as neuralgia, its torment suggested in the word-roots *nerve* and *pain*.) However otherwise the choice of Davis proved to be, at the time it was greeted with gladness and a measure of relief. Davis, at 52 years old, was both a planter and a political stalwart, having been secretary of war during the 1850s and more recently senator from Mississippi. He was also, as far as Southern opinion went, a moderate: he had called his Senate resignation in January the "saddest day of my life." The selection was further evidence of the conservative nature of the Confederate enterprise. William Lowndes Yancey and his fire-eaters might be prancing along the dirt thoroughfares of Montgomery, parading their joy in kicked-up dust and kicked-back whiskey, hope and hard liquor perhaps inspiriting a desire for recognition as fathers of a new country. But by the lights of those same men empowered by the actions of the radicals, the Yanceys of the world were destroyers. Most of those who seized control at the Montgomery convention understood the task of Confederacy as state-building. Davis was a governor. Among the radicals, only a few served the Confederacy in any meaningful leadership capacity.

Davis accepted his duty with reluctance. This was not because he was a moderate but because he hoped to lead the Confederate army. In a technical sense, he would – among those facsimile elements of the new Confederate Constitution was its provision that the civilian president was also its commander-in-chief. Yet Davis yearned for field duty, for combat, for the consummation of his youth, part of which had been spent as a cadet at the US

Figure 8: Jefferson Davis (1808–1889). He governed, as it were, from the heights downward.

Military Academy at West Point, and for the consummation of his young man's ambition, which he had tasted first as smoke-and-primer friction while a colonel of Mississippi volunteers during the Mexican War. The most successful Confederate generals would find themselves managing him and his martial ambition. That is a story to come. Like so many in the new nation, Davis understood that the immediate issue of secession, its birth-child, was war. And like so many of them, he welcomed it, even treasured it, in part because he saw in it the traditional fulfillment of national destiny. War was not a radical force of demolition but a historical force of creation through preservation – of nations, and of life's blood and ambition.[5]

****

In the North, disunion generated a reverberating, volatile wave of passion and a range of opinion, the most hostile of which was the white-hot patriotism of *la rage militaire*, and smugness the most bemused. Indifference was perhaps the most flummoxing. Indifference was a genuine reaction, but among those who subscribed to it also erratic and occasionally calculating. It could turn wildly under the unpredictable to and fro of events. Among those buffeted was the President – still, at the time of secession and the formation of the Confederate nation, James Buchanan. Despite the tossing and churning uncertainty surrounding him, Buchanan maintained an oddly defiant clarity of perspective that seems almost genetic in the least capable of the country's leaders: the Republicans were to blame for having gotten themselves elected and thereby instigating this crisis. He was not bound to address it. He did not want any moral responsibility for starting a war for the Union and did not fear any moral culpability in letting the Union tumble to ruin. In his annual December message to Congress he declared that secession was illegal. He then promptly declared that armed coercion to prevent secession was, alas, also illegal. Thus did the Old Public Functionary functionally abdicate his office months in advance of its term.

Indifference in the North took many shapes other than these and could even be reconfigured in the contingency of daily developments. In Buchanan's case it should not be conflated with indecision. He was *decisively, actively* indifferent – a kind of benign neglect superimposed on the opinions of scores of other Northerners, including many abolitionists all too beneficently content to be cut off from the sin of slavery and from ties with slaveholders, no matter how partial the severance was and remained in the winter of 1861. But abolitionists were not presidents. Buchanan, committed by oath to uphold the Constitution, pursued an active policy of noninterference, and for that he has received the scathing *cum laudibus* of one (perhaps too presumptuous) writer who distinguished him for having come "closer to committing treason than any other president in American history," and another who graced such distinguished imbecility by embellishing it with one of the rare exclamation points ever to bedeck the ponderous pages of the era's scholarship (!).[6] Among that policy's fruits were the uncontested handing-over of Federal forts, courts, customs-houses, and post-offices in the South – to call these surrenders would be inaccurately to insinuate even a dice-throwing contest over them. Buchanan continued to heed the even more brazen and self-serving influence of Southerners in his cabinet and among his advisers. Some of that influence was not so much self-serving as it was double-dealing.

Belatedly, and on one rock, Buchanan chose to make something resembling a stand over the Federal fort in Charleston Harbor, Fort Sumter, which had been occupied on Christmas eve by a small garrison of US soldiers who had abandoned the untenable Fort Moultrie nearby. Even then, and after that continuously, did Buchanan wobble toward resolve. His newfound Unionism was partly a result of Southern advisers leaving his side for the work of secession and nation-building at home, and partly the acute dismay of discovering, like a tidy householder who suddenly discovers a forgotten bill, that without *something*, even some minimum deposit, the ground in Washington and in the North, of the presidency itself, would collapse beneath him. In January he ordered the commercial steamship *Star of the West* (donated to the expedition by shipping magnate Cornelius Vanderbilt, soon to be floating on even more stupendous wealth as a railroad tycoon) to reinforce Sumter with men and supplies. No one bothered to inform the garrison at Sumter that it was being reinforced and provisioned. When enemy batteries along the Charleston waterfront opened fire on the *Star of the West*, the guns of Sumter offered no reply. The ship turned around without entering the harbor or reinforcing the fort, and although there were voices screaming about the insult to the flag, the stillness of uncertainty drifted northward with a forlorn supply ship. Nothing, seemingly, happened.

The drift also listed westward, to Springfield, Illinois, where Lincoln had maintained an indomitable silence – for some an inexplicable and frustrating aloofness – since his election. At home, Lincoln was busy with the demands of building an incoming administration and with drafting his inaugural address, doubtless to be momentous. Harrying him also were suitors for patronage, who descended on town and Lincoln's shabby, one-shingled law office by the score and even the four-score. To those who unctuously demanded action of him, it could have been said, although it was not, that he did not yet hold power. To those who demanded a statement of policy, it was said, although reluctantly and abruptly, by way of a third-party letter whose contents Lincoln expected to circulate, that his views were already well and widely known. To those who demanded compromise – some appeasement to mollify the seceded states and, as the word then meant, to reconstruct the Union by compromise – Lincoln was direct but still discreet, preferring confidential letters addressed to influential Republican leaders. "Entertain no proposition for a compromise in regard to the *extension* of slavery," he wrote in December. "The tug has to come, and better now than any time hereafter."[7]

There was more naïveté in such sentiments than military steel, at least initially. Although its smugness can be exaggerated, Lincoln's instinct on secession was political. He thought of it as a cynical, tactical maneuver and even a bluff by those whose power had been curbed, and who then resorted to brinksmanship to have their own way. The tug was civic, not martial. If secessionist politicians were met with self-assured political resistance, if the bluff were called, they would back down and their states would return to the fold. In this Lincoln assumed that the Slave Power acted at home in the South much as it acted elsewhere in the country. It had cowed or silenced or drowned out the opinions of white Southerners who might never support Republicans but who would never support disunion either. The Power had simply hoodwinked the typical Southerner, a sturdy farmer who surely would be tugged to his senses. Lincoln's faith in a persistent, pragmatic conservatism in the South, his belief in the existence of loyal Unionist sentiment needing only the resolve of the North to fatigue the holding power of an indigenous conspiracy, was shared by many Northerners, both Democrats and Republicans. Many of them never completely shook off this dream – for that is what it was – even after they were wide awake. Because it carried over into the belief that war would be a three-month affair and then, after that mistaken apprehension was exploded, into the belief that it could be won by conservative means, the misapprehension was fateful.

Congress did discuss several proposals to redress the secession crisis but these can be dismissed frankly. The most comprehensive, crafted by the Kentucky senator John J. Crittenden, would have amended the Constitution permanently so that it protected slavery explicitly where it already existed and allowed its future extension into territories below the old Missouri Compromise line. In actuality, this, though it gained traction, was no compromise measure. It would have forced Republicans to disown the results of their own election. The simple truth is that nothing short of the Republicans handing back their victory would have reconciled the secessionists of the Deep South. The legitimacy of secession might make debatable philosophy in the abstract, divorced from motive and interest and considered as a right. Yet settlement under these terms would have been a corruption of democracy, a failure of it more damning than secession. That such a measure was even considered (many of those pondering it were Republicans who needed Lincoln's bucking-up) says a great deal about the whipsaw instability of Northern opinion. The saber-shaking coercionists rattled those Northerners who feared war's disruptions. The self-assured, those all-too-willing to call the secessionist bluff, spooked those who doubted the strength of their hand. Even the apathy of the indifferent threatened to expose those who wore their disregard tactically, as a mask of diplomacy – behind it they designed to lure the seceded states back to the Union while simultaneously keeping the remaining slave states from joining the Confederacy. Eight of them yet remained as United States: Virginia, North Carolina, Tennessee, Arkansas, Missouri, Kentucky, Maryland, and Delaware. It all seemed interminable.

In February, Lincoln began a twelve-day, roundabout trek eastward that started as a post-election tour and ended in an atmosphere so riven by plot and intrigue that he finally entered

Washington secretly, as one newspaper scoffed, "like a thief in the night." On March 4, while Federal sharpshooters overlooked the steps of the US Capitol, he delivered an inaugural address renowned today for its beatific imagery of majestic fellowship, of the better angels of our nature, yet greeted then by those who heard whatever they wanted to hear. He had called for peace and forbearance but also promised to hold and maintain Federal property in the South, including forts nominally within the new Confederate nation. What, precisely, did that augur? What chorus, after all, had swelled higher in the mystic chords of memory than the last decade of strife? "We are not enemies, but friends," Lincoln said upon closing. "We must not be enemies." Such was either argument or assurance – but of what, of peace or a sword, depended on the ears of the listener. "If you are as happy on entering the White House as I shall feel on returning [home]," Buchanan told him in their carriage afterwards, "you are a happy man."[8]

Buchanan knew the immediacy whereof he spoke, for no sooner had Lincoln opened his office door than he discovered word from the Union commander at Fort Sumter, Major Robert Anderson, that the Federal garrison was running out of supplies. The tug had come. If Lincoln abandoned Sumter, he might as well have pushed for something like the Crittenden "compromise" as a next step. Only something like the surrender of national power to Southerners could offset the recognition of secession and the independence of the Confederacy, which the peaceful surrender of Fort Sumter implied. Yet if he determined to hold the fort, and particularly if he did so under the auspices of an armed flotilla that would have to blow its way into Charleston Harbor, he risked a divided Northern opinion and, beyond that, the secession of the slaveholding states in the Upper South. Acquiescence was *de facto* recognition of Southern power within a reconstructed Union, if not a practical recognition of a Southern nation outside of it. Coercion was *de facto* recognition that the American ideal of self-government had failed, even as it portended, by means of a second wave of secession, the tangible strengthening of the Confederacy and perhaps the irreparable fragmentation of Northern opinion. And that was no point from which to begin a war for the Union. Happy man, indeed.

The chroniclers of the chaotic first days of Lincoln's administration and the circumstances that begot the opening guns of the American

Civil War have been studious, but there were also subtle complexities underlying the position of the new Confederate nation. For all the qualifications that can be enumerated to avoid simplifying Lincoln's response, and for all the superficially pacific tones of Jefferson Davis's public pronouncements before the confrontation, the drift of the secession crisis had carried the new Confederate president into narrower straits than it had his counterpart. "All we ask is to be let alone," Davis would say famously, after the immediate fact of Sumter and war.[9] The realism in that sentiment owed more to pre- and post-Sumter diplomacy than desire. It was a tactful wedge deployed to strengthen divided opinion in the North and, as well, to appease the slaveholding states still remaining in the Union. The border states might yet be enticed to join the new Confederacy by sentiments designed to offset the Upper South's lingering mistrust of fire-eating hotheads. In point of fact, the Confederacy, ostensibly desiring merely to be left alone, actively ministered to those same slaveholding states long before Sumter – by means of the artful propaganda of the secession declarations and state emissaries appointed as special commissioners of Southern fraternity. In February, one of these emissaries addressed an undecided convention of Virginians on the irreversibility of secession and its benefits.[10]

Much more remains to be said about the new Confederate nation's institutions, structure, and social makeup, yet, fundamentally, the Confederacy was the assertion of a value-laden culture, a way of life, framed and formed on the foundations of a slave society. It could ill afford to be let alone: it would have collapsed in on itself under various internal pressures all the more intense for having been shaped in the age of martial, romantic nationalism. The South had for years been defined against the North in traditional terms, and the content and tone of the definition emphasized a tangible, here-and-now presence, not an idea, in which a white Southerner lived and moved and had his being. For it was a culture of honor and of assertion, of the exertion of authority and of dominance, of expressive, primal physicality at all levels yet polished at its uppermost in superimposed chivalry and the habits of gentility. Such a society professed but not called on to prove would have crumbled under cultural pressures to assert itself. Otherwise the Confederacy would exist intolerably under the absurdity that an irrepressibly hostile, supposedly insulting, and permanently threatening antislavery power along the length and breadth of its borders had, instead, in profound, utter indifference, been allowed breezily to ignore its provocations – in the language of today, to get away with it; in the cultural language of honor, to give the lie. The fullest realization yet of another absurdity would have been existential crisis: being let alone also assured the Upper South of its place in the Union, and thereby proved the greater security for slavery to lie *within*, not without, the more powerful United States. The Confederacy's very legitimacy rested upon the imposition of itself and then the test of that assertion as a test of strength. For *Southerners* the tug must come, better now than later.[11]

On April 12, the Confederate guns in Charleston Harbor opened on Fort Sumter. Lincoln provoked the first shot – and as far as these things go, avoided the moral responsibility of starting a war – by authorizing a resupply effort much like what had been aborted in January. A prior message informed the South Carolina authorities that Fort Sumter would be supplied "with provisions only." "If such an attempt be not resisted," it read, "no effort to throw in men, arms, or ammunition, will be made." This Jefferson Davis could not allow without admitting that the Confederate nation was utterly hollow, a spirit without form. To be real, it needed to bleed. For thirty-three hours the bombardment continued, until on April 14, and although no casualties were inflicted on or by either side, the shaken and exhausted Federal garrison inside Fort Sumter surrendered. As the ladies of Charleston stood on the housetops of the city, watching the epic unfold like the Trojan women of ancient times, the American Civil War had begun.[12]

****

One of the Civil War's keenest chroniclers thought that the Americans who waged it "surprised themselves, but the surprise consisted, in part, of getting what they had asked for."[13] For many years, history's standard emphasis has been that neither side expected a long struggle, certainly not one that would consume four years, and neither side expected to levy or to bear the fullness of its destruction. The emphasis remains important, but therein also lay the surprise: they did not anticipate in 1861 beholding in themselves the brutality they knew they were capable of unleashing. It might be that the War's relative restraint in its first year – which nevertheless collapsed furiously under a relentless revolutionary escalation – was as much about restraining what they feared to realize as it was an element of grand strategy. More and more and more of them, on both sides, eventually began to understand violence as regeneration. But what they feared in 1861 was barbarism.

Lincoln responded to the surrender at Fort Sumter by issuing a proclamation the next day, calling for 75,000 military volunteers. The volunteers would be in service for ninety days, a telling chronology for what he understood and even characterized as a conspiratorial rebellion too large to be put down by existing forces but small enough to stamp out in three months. They were to be drawn in quota from the state militias. His call provoked two feverish responses: a blast of enlistments from the North (several governors shrieked that they must be allowed to exceed their quotas or risk the back-drafting firestorm of their constituents) and a volley of outrage from several leaders in the slaveholding states of the border, whose harsh rhetorical attacks on "coercion" prefigured a second secession crisis. "The people of this commonwealth are freemen, not slaves," the governor of Arkansas telegrammed, tellingly, "and will defend to the last extremity their honor, their lives, and their property, against Northern mendacity and usurpation." Within days, Arkansas joined the Confederacy, as did Tennessee, North Carolina, and, most importantly, Virginia, whose governor accused Lincoln of inaugurating a civil war. Still, four other slaveholding states of the border remained in the Union – Missouri, Kentucky, Maryland, and Delaware. All but the last were home to large populations sympathetic to secession. Those states were to be erstwhile allies in the quest to restore the Union, but their allegiance would prove troublesomely tenuous.[14]

Meanwhile Jefferson Davis and his government wasted little time packing things up and heading northward, to Virginia. The capital of the Confederacy would now be seated in Richmond, merely 160 kilometers from Washington, DC. As with so much in the Confederate experience, the transfer of government was a strategic decision gilded in political and cultural circumstance. Montgomery wasn't much, after all, except a state capital in the Deep South happening to be more or less centrally located within the boundaries of the original seven states of the Confederacy. Lacking amenities, lacking infrastructure – lacking anything approaching grandeur: the tales told of a team of oxen that had once drowned in its mud-batter streets – Montgomery attracted not much beyond mosquitoes. Far more than comfort was at stake. Virginia was the most populous state of the Confederacy. It was also the wealthiest and the most industrialized. More immediately, and more agonizingly, the state's secession was contingent on voter ratification. The voting was scheduled in mid-May, by which time anything might happen, including a Federal invasion, to change her new course. Virginia must not only be secured but constantly secured thereafter. What was true of her was true also about the accession of the other three slave states of the upper South, which now nominally fell under, rather than outside, the protective umbrella of the central government now planting its shaft among them.

Over time there would develop consequences, for with transfer of capital came also transfer from the relative safety of the Deep South as well as a transfer of attention and resources from the lower and western Confederacy. Too much can be made of those consequences. Despite its proximity to Washington, the Virginia theater flummoxed Union efforts for the War's entirety, in large part because its military geography proved advantageous to skilled Confederate commanders. Nor were any of the other considerations superficial or cosmetic. Virginia, a seeding ground of the American heritage that mattered so much to the new national experiment in the 1790s and 1800s, lent to the Confederacy that same tradition as well as a direct connection to the Revolutionary legacy and the legitimacy important to statecraft. Legitimacy also powered the development of the intense Confederate nationalism that eventually stoked the war effort, which itself was one of the more dynamic and surprising developments of the entire era. Like the rest of the border South, Virginia was critical to the Confederacy's military fortunes. But that was so because Virginia was also imprimatur.

Moving also was General Pierre Gustave Toutant Beauregard, the hero of Fort Sumter, and the bearer of a name that would have been invented to embody Southern effervescence in 1861 if

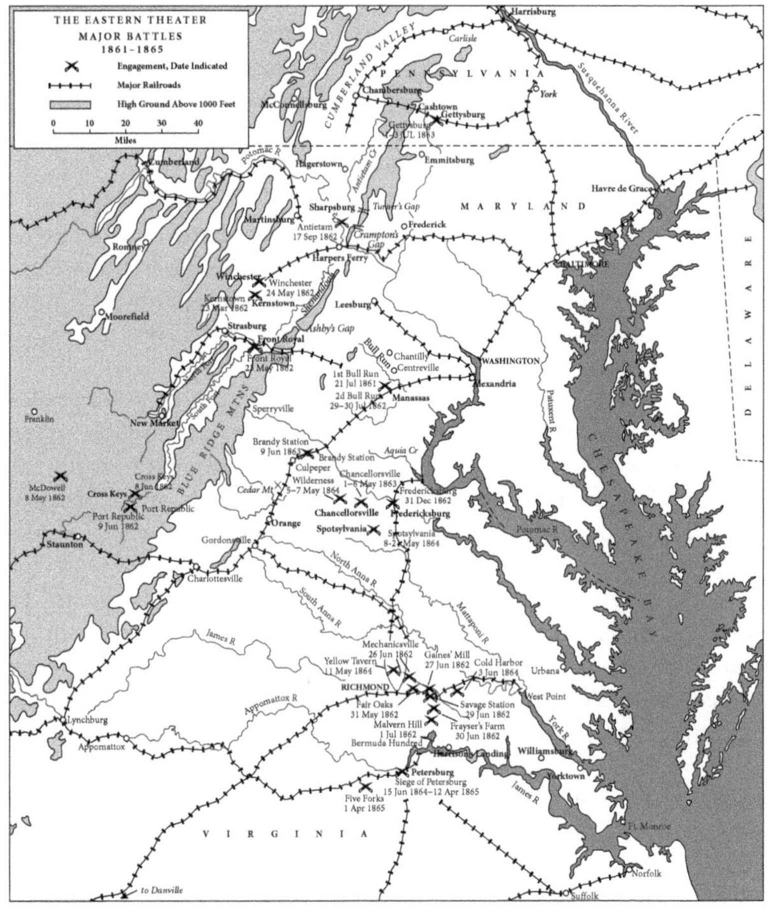

Map 3: Major Battles in the Eastern Theater, 1861–1865.

both personage and flamboyance were not already very real and living elements of a nascent cause. Pete to his friends, a Louisiana creole by birth and rearing, Beauregard's flair for *le beau geste* was almost theater-made for the War's opening drama at Sumter, which he supervised as the Confederate commander in Charleston – man and city were one in chivalry – and where, in obeisance, he had received the fort's capitulation from Major Anderson, who had instructed him in artillery when Beauregard was a young cadet at the US Military Academy. Just as complaisantly, that is to say, naturally, Beauregard expected to be given command of Confederate forces in what most understood to be the seminal, if not the only, major campaign of the War. Sumter's harbor had been the symbolic test of Confederate legitimacy, but the ground north of Richmond became its symbolic test of vitality. It was one thing to toss bombs at one another from ships and shore batteries and encasements, and quite another mettle to raise, equip, and deploy armies. Sumter was a measure of exuberance, battle a measure of strength. And in the spring of 1861, very few were considering *duration* as a matter of endurance but rather of stamina in the moment. A Union victory would be like decollating cork from a bottle, the pretensions of the Confederacy whisking into air and oblivion as the Union army marched in high superiority past the shattered cause on the way to Richmond. A Confederate victory would not merely collapse the facetiousness of would-be conquerors. It would forge the consciousness of a nation: it would create unconquerable form from the spirit of a people.

Beauregard gathered some 23,000 volunteers above a strategic railroad junction called Manassas, some 50 kilometers distant from Washington, DC. He was supported on his left, to the west, by a contingent of Confederates in the Shenandoah Valley under the command of a Virginian, Joseph E. Johnston, whose smaller force of 11,000 could move to Manassas Junction quickly, by rail and foot, if need arose. Both Johnston and the Valley he defended were to prove critical to Confederate fortunes over the course of the War – the former because he seemed indifferent to holding territory; the latter because it was territory imperative to hold – but those were issues virtually no one expected to matter much in 1861. Least of these was Beauregard himself. His charge was defense of northern Virginia, but his desire was not unlike the spirit animating many of the men in his army, who for their part were enrolled mainly not to miss the moment and secondarily not to defer to it. Beauregard surely would accept and even count on Johnston's aid should he be attacked – but rather than be suffocated in passivity, he had hoped to wheel the flower of Southern manhood around by the east, into the very dens of the enemy, and strike garishly for national independence in the Napoleonic fashion.

Lincoln, also, was restless for confrontation, even apprehensive, like a man summoned to a dueling ground on which the paces had been counted off but the code of rules half-remembered. Having called 75,000 volunteers for three months' service and then left to excruciate over hours and minutes when, in the heady, time-warped days immediately after Sumter, those who had been destined for service in the capital were delayed, he grew agitated to use them. As spring became summer, as April became July, his nerves curdled. The force near Washington consisted of 35,000 men under the command of Irvin McDowell, a career officer who had been chosen only after another career officer of greater reputation, the Virginian Robert E. Lee, had been offered the Union army but refused it. That loss was palpable. By reputation Lee was the nation's second-greatest warrior. Its first was Winfield Scott, whose glory was won in the War of 1812 and then marbled during his heroic march on Mexico City more than three decades later. Scott had since that triumph campaigned unsuccessfully for president, gathered up laurels, and now served as general of the army. Yet he had also accumulated age and hoarded flesh, and his joints were now wreathed in gout. He could no longer mount a horse. Thus Scott had recommended that Lee be offered field command, and when Lee refused – he resigned rather than condone the usage of the army against his native state and, not surprisingly, was now in Confederate service – Scott had settled on McDowell.

McDowell's own gluttony and girth were perhaps the only things by which his reputation paced ahead of him, or for that matter were anything near the equal of Scott's. For that he was gifted with the relatively rare quality of self-awareness in a war in which brag was trite. He attempted to decline the command on the pardonable grounds that he had never before directed men in combat: he was a general, sure, but a *commissary* general. His expertise was supply. Scott persisted, McDowell acquiesced, Lincoln approved.

Having attempted to talk the Union high command out of hiring him, McDowell now attempted to talk Lincoln out of rashness. His men possessed exuberance but lacked experience and, worse, any awareness that discipline and training might, perhaps, come in handy. Sending that mob to Virginia, on to Richmond, was foolish.

McDowell's argument against a too-bold attack was the first of many experiences Lincoln would have with generals who did not quite appreciate the politics of war – that a democracy could not ignore the tremors of public opinion. Not only were the ninety-day enlistments ending: the entire period was set to expire without the battle that would settle the thing. Summoning volunteers only to send them home might achieve by bureaucratic proxy what the Confederacy had hoped to earn in battle, namely, collapse the Union in fatuous hot air. We are not ready, McDowell told Lincoln, as the president pressed him to move out of Washington. "You are green, it is true," Lincoln replied, perhaps realizing but perhaps not that for a career supply officer uncertain of his own capacity, the second-person was piercingly singular as well as plural. "But they are green also; you are all green alike."

On July 16, they moved out, McDowell's infantry packed down as if the short-haul distance to Manassas was the winter road to Moscow. The army needed three labored days to cover the ground. (Picnickers following in carriages, including members of Congress, were also well-larded – their vistas over the landscape would surely be painted when the sublime battle was commemorated in art, as surely, yes, surely as it all would be.) Whatever reservations of self and army, McDowell's plan was executed with surprising cunning. A portion of his command moved on the center of the Confederate front, which was located along a sluggish piedmont stream called Bull Run. There McDowell designed to hold Beauregard's line in place while the larger element of his attacking army forded Bull Run upstream and fell upon the Confederate left flank. Fortunately for Beauregard and his Confederates, an alcoholic brigadier was one of several subordinates who recognized the gambit and began moving their forces piecemeal to the actual point of attack. On the afternoon of July 21, a hot Sunday and breezeless, the greens and green-alikes fought for five oppressive, sweat-baked hours, taking and giving, back and forth, the undulations of momentum palpitating over the ground in vicious mimicry of rippling summer heat.

Beauregard was doubly fortunate. His colleague in the Shenandoah Valley, Joe Johnston, recognized that need had indeed arisen, and had given the slip to the small Union force watching him. The job, bumbled by an old army veteran, was simply to keep him where he was, but Johnston had begun getting his men to Manassas a few days earlier. Now, in the late afternoon of the battle, the rest of Johnston's reinforcements also began arriving. These men were fresh. By happenstance their movement to the field brought them naturally on the exposed right flank of McDowell's attacking column. The afternoon's hard-fought, indecisive momentum turned straightaway. McDowell's first-timers had acquitted themselves ably, but there is no callow quivering quite the same as the hyperventilation of a novice army crumpled up by an unexpected blow. In ones and twos, and then in spasms of

Figure 9: General P. G. T. Beauregard, Confederate States Army, *c.* 1860, Public Domain.

tens and hundreds, McDowell's army simply dissipated on the run, dropping guns and packs and shame behind them. The worst of the spooked commandeered ambulance wagons to ensure they made it back to Washington in far less time than it had taken them to come. When night fell over a hard-fought field, as Jefferson Davis, who had come up by train from Richmond, was soon to report, it fell on a stunning Confederate victory.

Whether Beauregard could have ended the War with a counterstroke against a collapsing enemy was a controversy that began almost immediately and fully emerged somewhat later, on the Confederate side, once it became clear that bitter attrition would decide the War's outcome. The issue has remained provocative ever since, though mainly for reasons that split the question into two. One seems answerable just as the Confederate high command answered it at headquarters on battle day: if anywhere sheer rawness was self-evident on July 21, it was in the confused, exhausted aftermath. The mayhem of victory disorganized the Confederate army nearly as much as defeat harassed and disordered their foes. A crushing follow-up strike was a phantasm.

The other half of the question lingers because it is really a question of historical imagination. Assuming one hypothetical condition – that the War in 1861 was considered a political affray, an 1850s squabble writ large – and then overlaying that with another one – that a merciless blitz against a panic-stricken Union army that had been shooed forward because a good fight seemed like the right way to go about teaching these bullies a lesson – would a blow have been enough to end things? There is no knowing. But considering it compels an answer different from the one asked for. "I don't believe there is any North," Lincoln had fretted back in April, awaiting in agitated, anticipatory distress the delayed arrival of his volunteer forces. After Bull Run, there wasn't. The task had become one of summoning the *Union*, of making it so. In the mere unwillingness of their opponents to go belly up after a battlefield defeat, the Confederacy was confronted with the same manifest revolution. This was not to be a simple armed extension of the last decade's quarrels, a pitting of mere northern interests against southern interests. *Quarrels* were becoming *causes*. While Bull Run may have been strategically and militarily indecisive, that does not quite do justice to the grand picture. The astonishing realization of victory on the one side and the equal astonishment of defeat on the other surprised both – in summoning from them not what they had been but what they were willing to become.[15]

****

One measure of Bull Run's romantic folly was in those picnickers – several of whom, incidentally, were swept up and captured during the retreat. (The congressman presumably survived imprisonment on more meager fare but was eventually exchanged and released.) Another was in casualties. Some 1,600 Union volunteers were killed and wounded, while Confederate losses approached 2,000 men. In one afternoon, casualties nearly approximated the nation's entire battlefield losses during the Mexican War. Soon enough these were unobnoxious. Killed also, while invalided in her house, was Judith Henry, an aged widow over whose hill and farm the battle's fiercest fighting took place. The bedridden old woman was blown up by a Union cannon ball intended for other white Southerners equally stubborn in their refusal to vacate the premises. Such picaresque details have often provided the gloss, just as foolish picnickers have provided the innocence, for storytelling historians touching up their own vistas and landscapes of war. They tell more of a brutal fact that until recently has been benignly neglected: the War's ravaging exactions on civilians began in the beginning and shot all the way through to the end.

Still, that military casualties seemed almost individuated and a civilian death poignant in 1861 is important to note. The Battle of Bull Run, or Manassas as it came to be called in the Confederacy, took on a quality reminiscent of the old Revolution's Bunker Hill. It was big enough to recognize something massively, qualitatively abstract about war and experience, for nothing would be the same hereafter, and no one knew quite how or why. Yet it was intimate enough, as well, to clutch at fate, as if virtue and honor were still in the deeds of each soldier, as if each held the outcome in his very hands.

Certainly, there were, now, abstractions to consider as well as other figures. What was there of each nation to be summoned and sacrificed for war, and at what odds of success? The balance sheet favored Lincoln's minions. More than 22 million people lived in the states of the Union, and slightly less than half as many lived in the Confederacy. The Northern advantage in population actually tripled in comparison, at least on surface consideration. The white population of the Confederacy, the only population from which its armies would be drawn, was closer to 6 million: all the rest were slaves. In theory, the Union could mobilize 3.5 white men of military age for every soldier the Confederacy could entice or impress into its armies. Measures of industrial capacity also overwhelmingly favored the Union, with potential to be decisive. Combatant forces – armies, navies – can do nothing unless they can move, and they cannot move unless they can be supplied: food, shoes, clothes, bullets, guns, tents, horses and mules, and wheels and widgets. A typical army of 100,000 men devoured 600 tons of supplies each day and needed 2,500 wagons to move and store it all. On balance, the Union could make more, move more, replace more, invent more, and pay for more than the Confederacy. More industrial goods were produced in the state of Massachusetts in 1860 than were produced in *all* the states of the Confederacy. The states of New York and Pennsylvania each produced twice as much. Lincoln would eventually call these advantages, simply, *the arithmetic*. For the Confederacy, at least on paper, it was a hard math.[16]

But while account sheets and census rolls mattered, there were also other kinds of paper. There were, for instance, maps – and overlaying one of those on the balance sheet of war suggests leveling facts. For all of its advantages, the Union still might not have enough of what it needed for victory, while the Confederacy might have just enough to forestall defeat. In the margin between victory and defeat was resistance, and the calculus to achieve or resist subjection was the arithmetic that really mattered. The Confederacy was not charged with winning the Civil War. It needed merely to avoid losing. Maintaining the military contest was the imperative always on the Union cause, because cessation was tantamount to acknowledging Confederate independence. On a map, the Confederacy claimed to consist of almost 1.3 million square kilometers of territory, a landmass greater than that of western Europe. Its coastline ran 5,000 kilometers from Virginia to the Florida keys, and then almost another 1,000 kilometers along the Gulf of Mexico to Texas. Whatever the legitimacy of its claims, Confederates would have to humbled by land and by water. By sea, especially, Union numbers didn't propitiously add up: the United States merchant fleet was strong – the *Star of the West* was a merchant vessel – but in comparison the navy was pipsqueakery. Only forty-two ships had remained of John Paul Jones's offspring. Most of these were sailing the oceans of the world in 1861 and not immediately available. None were worthy to navigate the country's multiple rivers and streams, and these interior water borders would have to be controlled, as well. The sea was the Confederacy's vital connection to the transatlantic world, and to overseas markets and potential allies, but rivers were the seams holding the Confederacy together.

The crosscutting dynamics of conquest made the Union task all the more difficult. The Union bled men even when it didn't fight with them. The farther its armies marched to control Confederate territory, the more manpower it lost in detachment as occupiers, pacifiers, and guardians of supply lines. Meanwhile, the presence of slavery freed the Confederacy to mobilize white manpower as a kind of *levee en masse* – more than 80 percent of its military-age men eventually found their way into service, while its slaves provided essential labor on the home front or even as teamsters, camp laborers, trench-diggers, or fort-builders at the seat of war. The immediate circumstance of slavery, Sparta-like in its effects, helped drive the effective Union manpower advantage drastically downward, from 3.5-to-1 on paper to 2.5-to-1 on the ground.

Before it was over, the slaves themselves would strip the Confederacy of the offsetting advantages of forced black labor. Yet that revolutionary circumstance also required a fundamental transformation in Union war aims that was two years in gestating, begotten ironically by stupendous Confederate successes, and which took place against a countervailing revolution in the South. For the Confederacy was far from static, though its culture and war aims were originally conservative. Its quest would generate an intense modernizing process that mushroomed its industrial capabilities, liberalized its society, and transformed it into a modern war-machine. By population ratio, it was to become one of the most organized, centralized nation-states of the West.

Still another form of paper can be overlaid on raw data. These were ballots. Nothing remains more crucial about understanding the American Civil War than its democratic dimension. Neither Union nor Confederacy was a democracy in the modern development of the term. Yet both enfranchised most adult white men, and both at least subscribed broadly to the egalitarian ethos of American citizenship that penetrated all layers of the conflict. Citizens who were volunteers fought it; citizens who shaped public opinion debated it; citizens on home-fronts supported it, often circumscribed it, and sometimes undermined it. The War would last as long as the citizen-antagonists on either side desired it and only for purposes the people would sustain. National will was not a banal question of endurance so much as it was a simple matter of essential character: because both nations were democracies, public morale was translatable directly to power. In the North, a major election of one kind or another – state or national – took place in twenty-four of the forty-eight months of the War, and the Democratic party remained a potent force, sometimes of fiery opposition but always of contestation. Each of these elections might be a referendum on the War's mission, its course, and its management, although, as we will see, none was more vital than the presidential election of 1864.[17]

Elections were less frequent in the Confederacy, and after the fall of 1861, when Jefferson Davis was elected to a full six-year term as president on the expiration of his provisional first year in office, the Confederate high command was somewhat more insulated than the Lincoln administration. That same insulation, because it obviated the occasional need for opponents to muzzle themselves and reinforced a predisposition against a formal party system, also subjected Davis to an electrically fractious public opinion as well as bitter, sometimes withering personal attacks. His war-making came under attack almost before McDowell's army had beat its embarrassing retreat after Bull Run and was a constant source of internal turmoil thereafter. The arithmetic, Lincoln's summation of the Union's enormous paper advantages in men and materiel, is often quoted and remembered for its pith. But as he well knew, as Jefferson Davis well knew, as modern interpreters sometimes forget, the arithmetic was also and vitally a calculation arrived at by democratic politics. The will to use those resources, the will to destroy blood and treasure, was a translation of the numbers either side could command at the polling precincts in thousands of cities, towns, and rural crossroads across thousands of kilometers of territory, disputed as that territory was.

The central element of the War was not raw data or paper advantage, not numbers abstracted from substance. As a general idea, the Numbers Thesis has found its way into any number of otherwise capable military studies. Our occasional overreliance on statistical measures gives too much to determinism and sometimes to pettifogging numeracy, and not enough to the critical, historical element that lies not in how we confront the odds but how *they* did. The Confederates did not think themselves an overmatch. Nor did Unionists think themselves so muscular as to be capable of victory even with one arm prostrate. We cannot understand the massive transformations overspreading each would-be nation, each driven by both hope and fear, without understanding their catalytic and common dynamic in uncertainty. Nor can we – historical actors ourselves, well aware that life is uncertainty, that our humanity is the experience of time and time is merely how we measure living in hope and fear – be so arrogant as to make their decisions for them. They did not know how it would go. They chose to find out.

Only after defeat did white Southerners claim to be overpowered by Northern resources, an interpretation of events that became creedal in their postwar mythology. In 1861 the reverse sentiment seemed prevalent in the Confederacy: they were the sons of the American Revolution, the *legitimate* sons of the Revolution, and their hero-fathers were now immortal precisely because they had vanquished similarly long odds. Confederates were, if anything, brash. Their confidence was born of their culture, which emphasized power and mastery and honor, and this their trine of indomitable self-assertion was set upon the glorification of the physical violence necessary to maintain it. Their surety was also within their profound sensibility of God in the world, a facet of nineteenth-century American life that is often misunderstood or ignored in a more secular modern day. Many Southerners did not doubt, in piety, that righteousness would make their cause mighty.

As many in the North felt that God was with them. These believed He would march with the strongest cause, not necessarily that He marched with the strongest battalions. The most surprising thing encountered in a Union so relentlessly and physically powerful, even while shorn of eleven seceded states, is the volatile swing of its morale, its deep malaise after setbacks, its sheer uncertainty of whether the nation was capable and worthy of its task. For many in the modern day, it can be a stunning thing – a heart and mind-stopping thing – to realize that had those in the North believed or known their victory was inevitable, as the odds-makers of history self-assuredly proclaim it was, Lincoln never would have issued the Emancipation Proclamation.

That, too, was an important piece of paper, and perhaps the most crucial one. For if citizens fought it and debated it, if citizens supported it and often circumscribed it, the War's most unpredictable element would come to involve the fate of four million slaves who were not citizens but subjects, and yet also fought it, supported it, or undermined it, and ultimately shaped its course. Although very few in the North and South doubted that slavery was the true inwardness of the War, very few hoped or wanted slavery to become the War's central dynamic. Both Union and Confederacy desired a quiet war – a conventional, tidy war to establish independence, on the one side, to restore the Union as it had been, on the other. Neither wanted what Lincoln feared and loathed as "a violent, remorseless, revolutionary struggle." In this Americans were not only blind to themselves and the kind of transformative violence they were capable of attaining, but wishfully and willfully blind to the expectation of their slaves. For if conspiracy-minded white Southerners seceded in part because they feared Lincoln and the Republicans meant to free their chattel, black Southerners interpreted events to mean that freedom was coming whether any white person willed it. They acted in anticipation of emancipation even as both sides counted on their passive, peaceable acquiescence to the tidiness of *as you were*. Slaves, too, believed: Yahweh was a living God, from everlasting to everlasting, and His deliverance of the Israelites from bondage was not merely an example of His strength, but the surety of His ever-presence. To Him, as to the slaves whose faith was in Him, the salvation of the Israelites was as near in time as His own promise to deliver them from evil.

"This is," Lincoln wrote in a special message to Congress on July 4, 1861, "essentially a people's contest." At that very moment, thousands if not tens of thousands of expectant slaves in the South had fixed on the American Independence Day as the day of their jubilee: the grapevine telegraph, that remarkably efficient line of communication by which slaves everywhere passed news and rumor to one another, brought word that Lincoln meant to free them. The new president did not, but that was because even Lincoln did not yet grasp the potent voltage of his own sentiment. Precisely was this the very question at stake. Who were the people? Over four years, Americans would come to realize that the magnitude of their conflict *actualized* "the people." The War's incomprehensible scope expanded what had been an abstraction of political theory into a tangible fact of real democratic dimensions. It not only relied on "the people" to sustain it, but engaged them and demanded of them, and demanded more of them, far beyond any event in American history, even the American Revolution. It mobilized millions for its armies, but millions also for its support – men as soldiers and clerks and bureaucrats; women as nurses and wage laborers and farmers and teachers (and in a few celebrated cases, soldiers); slaves and free blacks as teamsters, as runaways and agitators and reformers, and finally as soldiers. It collected out of their hands the goods made on farms and in homes and in business houses, in tens of thousands of places, and marshaled them into the material of war – foodstuffs, clothing, munitions and metals, livestock – in order that an idea substantiated in their blood and treasure, a nation, might be established.[18]

The central aspect of the American Civil War, its central arithmetic, then, was *time*. Rather than pass indeterminately, rather than pass inscrutably, time's integral connection to the practice of democracy made it real. Time was counted against events past and events present and calculated against events to come, the spending of time inseparable from the spending of men and material. All were *measured*, all were reckoned, so that expenditure was always contingent. The War would go on only for as long and for purposes that the people were willing to sustain. The longer it went on, the more it swallowed, and the more it demanded, the more it expanded – the more searching questions it provoked: questions about purpose, about sacrifice, about benefit, about what kind of victory was worthy recompense for destruction. The knife's edge of such questions was all the keener because victory, after all, was hardly inevitable, but uncertain even as the payments were being made. The longer it went on, the more colossal it became, and the more consequential were its premiums: they were worthy only if victory created something new. In its scale, in its picnic-basket innocence, in its *rage-militaire* enthusiasm, the Battle of Bull Run was a beginning worthy of the assumptions and expectations surrounding it. What began in 1861 as a war of conservation, on both sides, ended, on both sides, as a war of revolution.

3

LIBERTY: 1862

"The world has never had a good definition of the word liberty," Abraham Lincoln once remarked, "and the American people, just now, are much in want of one. We all declare for liberty; but in using the same *word* we do not all mean the same *thing*." In that, as in many other instances, Lincoln had put one of his rangy fingers on the matter, but it was because so many Americans had been willing to put their fingers to the trigger that the matter needed addressing. Liberty's mixed meanings and multiple valences had existed more or less peaceably in American political life for generations. Not least among these was the volatile but heretofore contented acceptance of a union of liberty with slavery. And while destruction wrought a blur of convulsion to many things, it was also bringing a stunning lucidity of vision: peaceable life might exist in the muddle of routine, and democracy in sloppy compromise, yet civil war on an engrossing scale, by increasingly destructive and anomalous dynamics, demanded clarity.

Liberty was the American Civil War's core contested idea. As Camille Desmoulins had been fatally mistaken in his reckoning with the Reign of Terror – "I shall die in the opinion," that Jacobin had written (and die in it he did), "that to make France republican, happy and flourishing, a little ink would have sufficed, and only one guillotine" – just so would we mistake the intractable confusion of the word to believe that by the middle of 1862 ink could have substituted for blood. A year's fighting, bridging the summers of 1861 and 1862, reified the idea of liberty. It became a palpable and even carnal objective rather than an abstraction of the American tradition or the hyperactive rallying cry of the *rage militaire*. Frustrated by incomplete successes but also desperate after wounding reverses, and more than occasionally frantic in inertia, Union and Confederacy abandoned the imperatives and even the assumptions of conservative war by the autumn time of 1862. They committed instead to a voracious, all-consuming trial. The very uncertainty of the War's outcome generated the powerful, spiraling forces of escalation. The in-gathering forces of centralization made nation-states of both of them, especially of the Confederacy, whatever the world might make of its claim to independence. The centrifugal forces of separation did the very same. By collecting unto itself, each side sundered ties that, in 1861, might still have tended toward convergence and reunification.

In separation was definition and purpose, was lucidity, was clarity. Thus Lincoln sought to break apart the ambiguous but tenacious American pairing of liberty and slavery. That he was speaking in 1864, and not in 1862, is not evidence of a lag in the force of the separating vision but a measure of its ongoing progression. "With some the word liberty may mean for each man to do as he pleases with himself, and the product of his labor; while with others the same word may mean for some men to do as they please with other men, and the product of other men's labor," he said. "Here are two, not only different, but incompatible things, called by the same name – liberty. And it follows that each of the things is, by the respective parties, called by two different and incompatible names – liberty and tyranny." He meant that emancipation – tangible, carnal, bodily freedom – had become the most conspicuous example of liberty's reification on the Union side: a restored, reintegrated Union, always the primary goal of the war effort, and in 1861 the only objective of the conservative war, would in victory become a Union liberated from slavery.

Confederates wondered which word was just then in need of definition. "The tyranny of an unbridled majority [is] the most odious and least responsible form of despotism," Jefferson Davis declaimed as the provisional Confederate government of 1861 shifted into its permanent form in 1862. "Therefore we are in arms to renew such sacrifices as our fathers made to the holy cause of constitutional liberty." Even so, and even then, the momentum of the War had begun to obscure the Confederacy's instrumental purpose. There cannot be and should never be misunderstanding that the Confederacy's primal imperative was the preservation of slavery: it was an aim equivalent, as a categorical, fixed, and constant necessity, to the North's fundamental objective of preserving the Union. But just as the twin forces of nationalism and separation drove Union war aims toward transformative regeneration, those forces accelerated a transitional, revitalizing shift from Confederacy as means to Confederacy as ends. Independence moved beyond a mechanism for conserving slavery and toward an encompassing, visionary force of creation, a catharsis in and of itself. Through it a new chosen people would be born to the earth. Liberty meant self-government; tyranny meant subjugation. And slavery defined not merely their economic and social interest in African Americans, but a state of abject, humiliating subservience they, themselves, as a new people, would suffer on the death of the Confederacy – a ghastly abortion, stillborn before christening. The reification of those abstractions was embedded in the incessant, abrasive grind of war. For many white Southerners, the War's absolute military requisite for the Union armies – invasion – sustained a tangible, even gritty fastening of liberty and the life of the Confederate nation to the material defense of their homes and their families.[1]

They thought, just as Lincoln thought, theirs was a definition of liberty they could justify before the world, if only they could sustain it on the field.

****

West of the Appalachian Mountains, a vast expanse almost beyond imagining in the eighteenth century, was called the backcountry when English colonists still looked across the water to Great Britain for identity. It became known as the frontier when the American gaze shifted with independence, but more than one hundred years of conquest, white resettlement and exploitation, and economic development had not dislodged some eastern conceptions about the region or the people who lived in it. Despite the growth of new cities such as Cincinnati, Chicago, or St. Louis, or the older cosmopolitanism of New Orleans, the bustling of railcars and the whistling of steamships, or the prosperity of enterprise, many urbane Americans of the seaboard states still ridiculed the West as an uncouth boondocks ill-adjusted to the refinement of civilization and the prim comfort of the Victorian family parlor. If the region – today's American Midwest – was not yet the Wild West of the dime-store novel, if it was not the dusty, sun-scorched frontier of low-belted gunslingers and cowboys-and-Indians and cardsharps in saloons who kept aces up each sleeve and dirks in each boot, it was still, in stereotype, the ranging ground of the raw and the vulgar, and a rough place for rough men. None were more legendary already than the gamblers and con artists who plied the Mississippi River on the great steamboats of the era, and who pricked the imagination of British travel writers such as Arthur Cunynghame or Frances Trollope, and populated Melville's *The Confidence-Man.* Lincoln had been regarded, initially even by some of the men who served in his cabinet, as a boorish, half-literate lawyer from the sticks: even his most important general (whose conceit would have been gratified at being thusly designated) snubbed him alternately as the "original gorilla" and "nothing more than a well-meaning baboon." The hubs of American culture, its vitality and its fidelity, its civic centers of political, religious, artistic, intellectual, and scientific life, were grounded in metropolitan Boston, in New York and Philadelphia and Baltimore, in Washington and Richmond, and in Charleston.[2]

But taken purely as a military consideration, the American Civil War was won, as it was lost, in the West.

Both high commands were directed by westerners, and neither thought in ignorance about the theater beyond the Appalachians. The first Union approach to grand strategy, a proposal developed by Winfield Scott in 1861, was continental in scope. Scott conceived of victory as a process of containment rather than conquest. His plan called for Union forces to encircle the Confederacy by land and sea, using armies to hold key points and naval forces to blockade Southern ports and control Southern rivers. Mutterers who preferred something dressed in the pageant of Napoleonic confrontation scorned this as meat-handed strangulation and belittled it as "the Anaconda Plan," but they were to be never-minded. Scott was especially keen on major western waterways, which, unlike their eastern cousins, generally flow vertically. They

Figure 10: Portrait of US President Ulysses S. Grant, *c.* 1870, Library of Congress. Public Domain.

were potentially avenues of movement and transport into and through the Southern heartland, and so to control them was to fasten the Confederacy in a logistical chokehold. Mastery of none was more vital than the mighty Mississippi River. To govern the Father of Waters (in Lincoln's arch-christening) was to split the Confederacy in two. If New Orleans were captured as an added advantage, western Unionists might also breathe easier. As before the War, their commerce could move freely downriver.

Sooner and not later it stands noting that the Anaconda Plan offered elements of eventual Union victory, especially its foresight on water. By late 1861 the Union had begun a blockade, despite two initial diplomatic blushes caused in first case by Lincoln's misunderstanding of how to impose a blockade under international law, and in the second by a swaggering Union sea captain who stopped a British packet and manhandled two Confederate diplomats on-board to Europe. Scott's plan even prefigured the way in which the Confederacy was eventually suffocated by attrition. But it was not the plan of Union victory, as is often breezily professed. Occupation meant containment, and containment meant not conquest but pacification that would promote reconciliation and reunification.

Scott's vision was sustained by all the assumptions and fortified with all the objectives of a conservative war. Its object was to restrain destruction, its intent to forestall Lincoln's much-feared "violent, remorseless revolutionary struggle." The hand of war was only as firm as necessary to quell, to secure, to quiet, to control, to govern – and even to protect and to make peace. It was not to loose havoc, retribution, confiscation, or radical upturning. Scott's enemies jeered his plan with winning metaphors and catchy nicknames, yet oddly they misunderstood that even their "constriction" was a much more violent grip than the so-called Anaconda Plan envisioned. The crueler the clenching of war, the more difficult the clasp of hands in peace.

It took time to secure victory and reunion, as Scott predicted. All the same, the transformative assumptions of 1865 were not the conservative assumptions of 1861. Sober aims did not survive a year's fighting. The revolutionary impulse was initially more forceful on the Confederate side, odd as that sometimes sounds to modern ears and especially to a still shrill (but mercifully small) element of contemporary white Southern opinion whose present is often refracted through a lacquered illusion of the past. For although the first Confederate assumptions of warfare were similarly traditional, and its initial objective was similarly preservative, expectations were soon overborne. Confederate nationalism quickened desperately under the pressure of military failure. These developments were felt first in the West, where Confederate ambitions were just as continental as those of their adversaries, and, as military, economic, political, and diplomatic necessities, just as acute. All rested on the integrity of their undertaking. Could it be held together to make a nation? The conservative ethos of its beginnings almost necessitated that question as a physical one of institutions. But it was specially a territorial one.

Welcome strength that it was, the secession of the slaveholding states of the border and their accession to the Confederacy accentuated practical defensive difficulties. Confederate grand

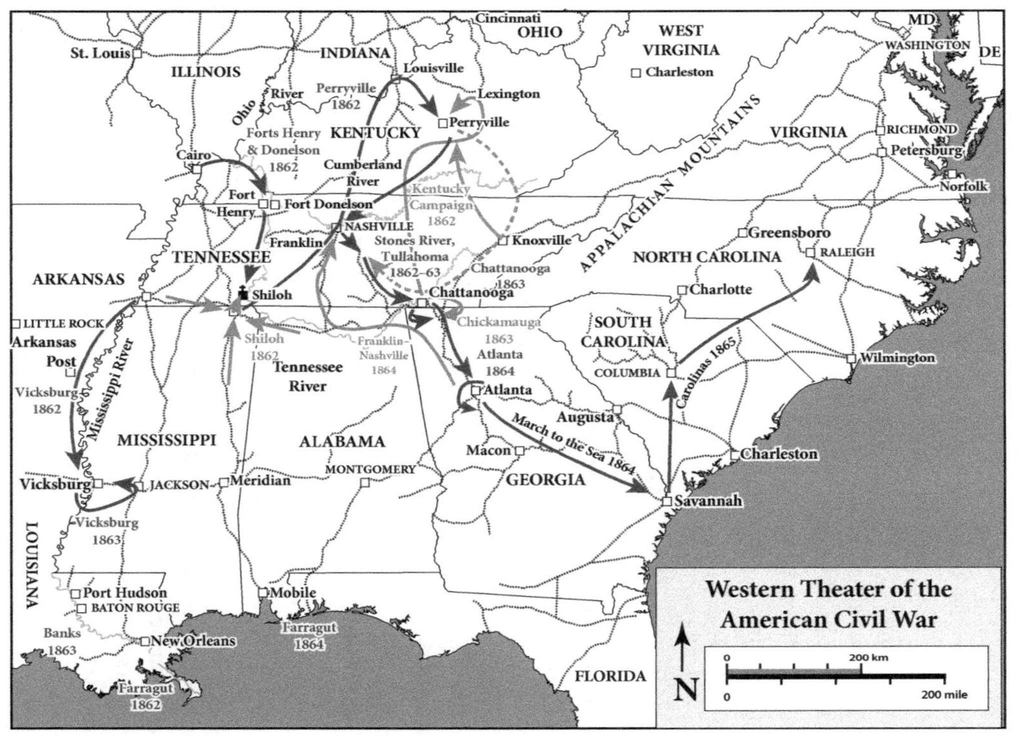

Map 4: The Western Theater, 1861–1865.

strategy in 1861 and early 1862 called for protection of a line stretching from northern Virginia through the rugged mountains of western Virginia, running the length of Tennessee, until it reached the Mississippi River. Across the great river, in what was called the trans-Mississippi, matters were strategically different. The relative isolation of Texas, Louisiana, and Arkansas allowed a certain independence of operations. The struggle in Missouri, in particular, where brawling had been instantaneous after the surrender of Fort Sumter in 1861, swiftly devolved into a guerrilla carnival, a kind of haunted reprisal of the outlawry in antebellum Kansas, and perhaps recompense, as well, for what Missouri's border ruffians contributed to the bleeding masquerade of popular sovereignty.

Coordination across the Mississippi River was a difficult war-long task for the Union and a nearly impossible one for Confederates, but then again the same impossibility was evident on the nearer side. The Confederacy had not nearly enough volunteer manpower to cordon 800 kilometers from the Appalachians to the Mississippi and beyond. Their border was, plainly, a fragile wall of sand, easily toppled – and to hold even this, the Confederates occupied Kentucky, which though a slaveholding border state and wobbly on secession, remained as yet in the Union. (The state had declared its "neutrality," a convenient fiction Lincoln honored to avoid losing it and its strategic importance for control of the Ohio and Mississippi rivers – but the Confederate violation in the fall of 1861 helped insure Kentucky remained in the Union for the duration of the War.) Beginning in the latter part of 1861 and into the winter of 1862, the line began eroding, first on the western flank – where the Confederate general in charge, an Episcopal bishop named Leonidas Polk, already was showing his preference to take orders only from God – then on its eastern one, and finally, with crashing speed, at its center. The Confederates had tossed up a pair of fortifications on the Cumberland and Tennessee rivers, Fort Henry along the former and Fort Donelson on the latter, but neither one Scylla nor Charybdis. They fell in February when, eight days apart, they were assaulted by combined land-and-water forces under Ulysses S. Grant. Grant had issues of his own – just now they were scruffy, beard-bedraggled anonymity and a weakness in him for whiskey that preyed elsewhere when distracted, as it was now by the scent of combat, but somehow never seemed to stray too far off. The War would work those issues out. But the harlequin absurdity in Confederate headquarters at Fort Donelson, where the generals decided to leave, then to stay and fight it out, and then to leave, and then finally bickered all over again over which of them lacked enough illustriousness to surrender his sword to Grant, foreboded churlish, debilitating quarrels to come.

All along the line, in gritty clumps, the Confederate army funneled south and slipped through Nashville, which straightaway fell to Union naval power along the Cumberland. The army collected again along a new base at Corinth, Mississippi, about fifteen kilometers from the Tennessee border. A thin line theirs was, but in losing a burgeoning industrial and supply center at Nashville (and all of the Tennessee heartland for that matter) the Confederacy lost a vital source of manpower, of meat and of harvest, and of beasts of burden. If it was a wall of sand before the collapse, it was sand whisking in an hourglass now, frittering to the bottom. Sudden disaster had flipped the triumphant national morale of last summer upside over. Howling critics launched vicious denunciations of their leaders in Congress and in the newspapers, but sniping was in soldiers' ink, too, in letters home, where it became whispering conversation in the parlor and clatter around the courthouse square. Jefferson Davis stood accused of imbecility generally, but of turning his back on the Confederate west especially.

Yet the complainers ignored what Davis considered the salient counterpoint: he had, verily, appointed his best general to command the western army. This was Albert Sidney Johnston. Davis met him while both were schoolboys in Kentucky, and reunited with him at West Point, where Johnston, two years the elder, became a fraternal mentor as well as a model of ideal martial manhood. Davis's image of Johnston, it seems, never grew old. The allure in Johnston's character blended boyish generosity and antique self-restraint, and his career, at least glazed by distance, was an ode to gallantry. At turns private citizen and failed planter, at turns a soldier and Texas revolutionary, Johnston was in California just prior to the War, soldiering again. Friends and connections had rescued him from the poverty and paralytic melancholy of private life, among them Davis, who during his stint as secretary of war appointed his idol to a colonelcy in the US Army. (Not a small favor in the antebellum army, where advancement accrued at geologic pacing: Robert E. Lee, who lived no such in-and-out existence, having never left the service after his appointment in 1831, and acquiring a better soldier's reputation besides, was Johnston's second-in-command.) When Texas seceded, and although he hesitated, Johnston couldn't help himself. "It seems like fate," he told his wife, "that Texas has made me a rebel twice." With that he journeyed cross-country on horseback, adding yet another lyrical tale of perilous adventure to his *oeuvre*, and in the fall of 1861 presented himself in Richmond. Davis appointed him immediately to lead the western army. "If Sidney Johnston is not a general," Davis would say when the carping at Johnston reached a crescendo in the spring of 1862, "we had better give up the war for we have no general." To him, Johnston was the gray-eyed man of Confederate destiny.[3]

Meanwhile Grant had taken up a new fix on an old habit – a raging and ultimately life-killing addiction to the cigars admirers had gifted him after the victories at Henry and Donelson – while revealing a quintessential one. With some 45,000 men he moved southward to consolidate the heartland, tethered by the Tennessee River on one flank and by his orders on the other. The giver of those, Grant's superior, was Henry Wager Halleck, already known as "Old Brains" for his two published volumes before the War, the later book an acclaimed translation of the life of Napoleon by the French military thinker Antoine-Henri de Jomini, which acquired for him a vicarious reputation as a grand theorist and strategist. In truth he was neither, though administratively competent, and, as Lincoln later remarked with stinging insight, "worth but little except as a critic and director of operations." A Democrat in his politics, Halleck's natural conservatism also told in his presence. "Old Brains" rubbed at his elbows absent-mindedly, obsessively, in conversation or in thought, surely a quirky human mannerism but also irksome to more than a few annoyed auditors and guests. His hooking self-possession was as essential to his personality as Grant's relentless determination was to his. Holding tightly to his reputation, Halleck would risk nothing to lose it, either to Confederates, or to Grant, whom he correctly if suspiciously regarded as a striving man.[4]

In early 1862, safekeeping did not reveal what it would in time, for Halleck's caution was consistent with the larger Union strategy of possess and pacify. Even Grant thought the War would be over in six more months. He marched along the Tennessee river to a small riverboat docking called Pittsburg Landing, where he could be supplied by water, and in time reinforced by a second Union army moving from Nashville under the command of another conservative general (and, like Halleck, a Democrat) named Don Carlos Buell. The landing, some twenty kilometers inside the Tennessee border from Mississippi, was no town, it was not even a hamlet but a rustic way station where local planters and farmers could put aboard cotton and produce. It was nothing more, unless it was the epitome of urbane eastern stereotypes. Above towering river bluffs were woods and bramble for miles on miles, a wilderness broken now and again by cabins and small farms and dirt roads and trails, teeming with living things of all kinds – deer, boar, turkey – and even the promise of eternal life, for nearby also was a Methodist log church that the local buckskins called Shiloh.

Grant fixed in at the landing to wait on Buell's army without doing much more than setting camp. His mistake was in underestimating Johnston's desperate ingenuity – somewhere out there, prowling, were thousands of fierce Confederates. Although dispirited and gloomy, Johnston had lost nothing of daring, and certainly nothing of his gray-eyed gallantry. If anything, the nagging doubters fed him with their rancor. Johnston boldly devised a concentration of his own, bringing together scattered western commands to the main army's rendezvous point at Corinth, and in early April began moving 44,000 men along muddied, rain-sopped wilderness roads to launch a surprise attack on Grant's exposed army. To subordinates who worried about Grant's numbers, Johnston professed chivalric indifference: "I would fight them if they were a million," he told a staff member; and to subordinates who wrung their hands after spattered entanglements in the mud, he accepted no counsel for delay and none for abandonment of the surprise, not even after some of the greenhorn innocents in his army began shooting at deer and rabbit in the woods. "Tomorrow," he said, "we will water our horses in the Tennessee River."

The battle of Shiloh was fought over two days, April 6 and 7, in messy, undressed collisions that owed something to the ground and something also to rattled inexperience on both sides. In a word, it was *stripped*. Its rawness, its skinned ferocity, shook young soldiers on both sides, and if their memoirs are any guide, they never experienced their instincts, or sensed their very flesh, in the same way afterwards. Day one, despite the confusion, was a hard-punching Confederate success – the gray minions broke through the woods at dawn, suddenly shrieking, and achieved absolute, fear-rising surprise – but rather than drive Grant away from the river and his link with Buell, as apparently was the plan, crushed him backward on the landing. Johnston's moment of glory was not in this world. Seeing a chance in the afternoon, he couldn't help it; on horseback he teed off to join a Confederate infantry charge. Thoroughgoing extrasensory ecstasy was in the moment. He knew his thew again only in the aftermath, when he felt blood pooling in his boot. A musket ball had severed an artery below the knee. Johnston reeled in the saddle before being smuggled off to die, hidden away so as not to demoralize his army, in a ravine just behind Confederate lines. Command passed to none other

Figure 11: Confederate General Albert Sidney Johnston, Public Domain.

than Beauregard, whose prickly falling out with Davis during the winter led to his sacking in Virginia and this, his exile to the western army. The touchy problems of leadership and relationship in the Confederate high command evinced, at the same time, how intimately Davis valued Johnston's high-toned loyalty. Now, he was gone.

Overnight came a lashing rain, lightning shattering the skies to illuminate the black pitch of the wilderness, thunder clapping the firmament shut again, as if God determined that throwing light on horror was beyond the senses of his creatures to endure. Wounded men, some unrecognizably maimed and immobilized on their backs, cried for water, and perversely drowned in its torrent. Hogs rooted on the dead and gnarred also after the mangled living. A pond near a peach orchard on one edge of the battlefield was said to be rose-soaked in blood. Underneath the river bluffs, back at the landing, thousands of terrorized Union soldiers looked to Buell's coming not to reinforce them but to deliver them away from this wilderness Gehenna. They huddled under the cliffs while Grant's roaring gunboats blasted away at the field. Grant, meanwhile, stood soaked under an oak tree at headquarters, puffing a waterlogged cigar. In time, William Tecumseh Sherman would become the officiant of such scenes as a transfigured archangel of war. He saw Grant there. "Well, Grant, we've had the devil's own day, haven't we?" Grant had been shaken, but he kept smoking. "Yes," he said. "Yes. Lick 'em tomorrow, though." Which, rallying his army, he did: Buell's timely arrival with 25,000 men allowed Grant to deliver a ferocious counterpunch on the battle's second day that drove Beauregard and his army back to Mississippi, beaten but also confused by Grant's sudden strength.[5]

Never had there been such concentration of firepower on an American battlefield, and never had there been such carnage. More than 1,700 were killed and 8,000 wounded in each army. The missing and anonymously mangled perhaps ran up the spoilage to 24,000 men, more than the combined losses of every major engagement of the War thus far, and quintuple the innocent costs of Bull Run. In those first days the newspapers wrote of valor. Today they told macabre tales of slaughter. It was last year a question of gallantry. This year was a matter of meat. Stunned, outraged Northern editors roared that Grant was no soldier but a butcher, yet the truth was pinking in themselves, though still too raw to be realized. If in death Sidney Johnston bestowed anything on the field, it was not his errantry, which he took to the grave, but instead in leaving to Grant, his brother in arms, the hue and cry.[6]

****

Lincoln's trenchant support of Grant in the aftermath of the Shiloh carnage – "I can't spare this man; he fights" – was perhaps more than a sanction of dogged steadiness. In Washington, in the east, Lincoln had by then a general who wouldn't fight, but yet he couldn't spare. George B. McClellan was a prodigy. He distinguished himself as a youth, entering West Point at the age of fifteen (the academy waived its minimum-age requirement) and graduating four years later with the class of 1846 as its second in standing. He distinguished himself on Scott's staff during the bold march to capture Mexico City in 1847 and later was handpicked as American military observer during the Crimean War, a working assignment but also a coveted ceremonial and diplomatic one. Lately, he had been distinguished as president of not one but two railroads, lucrative positions both, and soon to be the perch of the archetypal American captain of industry. But to McClellan, still only 34 years old, these captaincies were an iron-dulled rote. In 1861, he had commanded a small army in the mountains of western Virginia and of course led it to victory, after which the Union controlled part of the territory that in two years' time would be kerfed from Virginia to become the Unionist state of West Virginia. After the disaster at Bull Run, in the sucked-out welkin of humiliation exhausting the camps and leadening the streets and the offices of power in the capital, Lincoln turned to McClellan to transform his embarrassed eastern army into a supreme fighting force. As McClellan saw things, his admirers were right to call him the Young Napoleon. Lincoln was right to call on him when the chips were down. In a matter of months he ascended to command of *all* the Union armies. His – and nearly his alone: neither Lincoln nor anyone else was up to the mark – was the burden of saving the Union.[7]

The relationship was fractious from the start, most writers faulting McClellan. But its fragility rewards curiosity. Aside from

Lincoln, no other figure was more central to the Northern cause than McClellan, not even Grant, unspareable though he was.

For in Lincoln's relationship with McClellan was his fraught relationship with everything McClellan represented in the war effort, politically and militarily most of all. Their contentions originated in the *conduct* of the War, but festering, they eventually became about *the War* itself: its vision, its revolutionizing tendencies, its destruction and despoliation, and ultimately emancipation. It bears repeating that the tendency to talk in too-general terms of *a* Union, or *the* North – or even Democrats and Republicans on some matters – risks obscuring the fissures and divisions that troubled the struggle for the Union from the beginning. When, in 1864, two years after Lincoln shakily sacked him and exiled him to New Jersey, McClellan ran as the Democratic nominee for president, the stress of those divisions came within two months of bringing the War to a blunt, decisive halt.

Beginning with the War and continuing to our time, it has been the custom to attack or defend McClellan frontally. He is better revealed at the flanks and *en echelon* – pressing in one area of his character exposes supple pockets of strength and weakness in others. McClellan was thoroughly a professional man. He disdained ill-disciplined volunteers, horse-traded political generals, and at one level even the rabble and the wasteful messiness of a democracy at war. And yet having trained, equipped, and disciplined a people's army into what now was called the Army of the Potomac, he loved it, possessed it in a real sense, as polished of its egalitarian coarseness. His army had become a grand army of the republic, an extension of his own excellent technical prowess. War was a discipline; war was a science; war was, in the most competent sense, *organization and application.* He could and would not conceive of it, ever, as bureaucratic, because its diplomatic function was also, as practical statesmanship, a classical art conforming to rules of substance, style, and manner. And although its machinery and its logistics functioned in its details, war was essentially grand. Its accomplishments best be taken not on the ground, where it was wasteful and things broke, but at the birds-eye.

Yet it was messy, it was wasteful, and it was a force of its own that resisted order by men, if indeed it did not discipline them and seek to teach *its* ways. Its cruelties beggaring any refinement, as

Figure 12: General George B. McClellan, 1861, Public Domain.

William Tecumseh Sherman soon phrased his instruction in it. Its merest incidents, as Lincoln articulated his, might produce mighty consequences that no one, and especially no one in the democracy that fought it, could predict or control. Try as McClellan might to impose his own control on it, he could not, and never accepted the lesson that he could not. The possibility that its rules were less principles to be discovered and applied than perverse justifications organic to its nature was not merely anathema to him but hateful.

As with Halleck and Buell, a conservative pedigree in McClellan was no disqualification for command, or even necessarily dysfunctional to the prosecution of a restrained, conservative war. Neither were his Democratic politics. And neither, necessarily, was his ego. Instead it was a personal quality, a drum-major instinct, as it were. The pulsing, pounding need for distinction, to be in front, to be seen at the head of the corps, never left him. In itself ambition for recognition could have served the cause well enough – Lincoln quested, too – had McClellan not been undercut by a puny thing in him beating meticulously, relentlessly: a chronic need for assurance, a constant insecurity about his performance and his importance. Lincoln might have managed this, as well. He recognized it and tried to quiet it by attempting to relate to McClellan as a father-figure. The paternal way, as he grew into the War and the War grew in him, became Lincoln's mien. It would work with other generals, even with other politicians. In 1865 it spoke to the people in his Second Inaugural Address as an ancient patriarchal wisdom. Yet the mien and voice were both immature in Lincoln in 1862, and not likely to resonate against McClellan's insecurities and youthful arrogance anyway.

For McClellan, Lincoln's manner seemed to recognize him not as the prodigy but as a kind of prodigal son. By the War's first winter, when McClellan had been in command half a year, the general even descended to a series of public slights by which he seemed to delight in forcing Lincoln to wait on him for an audience. In private his disdain was vicious. Letters to his wife – reading them leaves the distinct impression that McClellan never quite lived beyond her and her father's initial rejections of his courtship – began referring to the commander-in-chief as the "O.G.," shorthand for "the original gorilla." More is telling in that insult than the mocking of Lincoln's homely appearance and folksy frontier wit. Baboons, monkeys, gorillas – these were all racist lampoons and pseudo-scientific stereotypes of inferior blacks and submissive slaves: never to be civilized, never to be educated, never to be uplifted from brutishness. Those caricatures were also deployed to attack the Republicans as the party of amalgamation and degradation. The "O.G." was no primal father McClellan would have accepted. "The good of the country," McClellan wrote home, in what might have been his most searing confession, "requires me to submit to all this from men whom I know to be greatly my inferior socially, intellectually and morally! There never was a truer epithet applied to a certain individual than that of the 'Gorilla.'"[8]

McClellan kept the commander-in-chief in the dark about his planning as long as he could, suspecting leaks, and fearing most of all the hidden agendas and stashed daggers of his political enemies. He planned to move the massive Army of the Potomac by water, down the Chesapeake Bay, and land it on the peninsula between the

York and the James rivers. Thereby he would flank the Confederate army in northern Virginia and move on Richmond from the east, avoiding, as he saw it, a costly, slug-it-out campaign for the rebel capital over land. Knowing what in hindsight we do about McClellan wobbles our judgment. It was a cautious plan, relying on the deployment of massive physical and human resources, but bold in carrying on after the fashion of Winfield Scott's grand landing at Vera Cruz in the Mexican War. Yet when McClellan eventually ferried his army down the Chesapeake he convoyed with it both his narcissism and his fear. Care in coordination became diffidence in execution. He built a sterling-proud army but could bring himself to move it only by ponderous, dangerous plods.

Lincoln came to understand McClellan's gluttonous consumption of time as fatal, dawdling timidity, a chronic case of the "slows," a diagnosis that must also take into account McClellan's paranoia about the motives and events around him. Ever vigilant to hidden agendas, dark political maneuvers, and stage-managed appearances, McClellan became convinced of a conspiracy to stab him from behind and poison his success. It was true that he had been gifted a hulking army of more than 100,000 men, with all provision and accouterment, not to mention the massive tonnage of naval transport to land it. But in some historical actors is just this, the histrionic flaw. McClellan interpreted the generous largesse at his command not as confidence in him but as a cynical set-up. His conceit was – as self-rationalization – also part of his essential planning, not perhaps in the conventional sense, but in the sense that he had prepared arrangements for the outcome. If he succeeded, he in fact did do it all – and all by himself, against all odds. And if he did not, the fault rested not with him but with connivers and rivals who resented him and made possible by their very largesse the spectacularity of his failure.[9]

He had been denied only one thing, and for McClellan this denial ultimately became the tell of "true inwardness." When finally, in February, Lincoln forced the matter by summarily ordering a simultaneous movement of all Union armies before McClellan was ready to move his, McClellan revealed his plan only to have Lincoln balk. A movement around the enemy would leave Washington exposed to a Confederate counter-thrust, the president argued. McClellan doubted that contingency but agreed

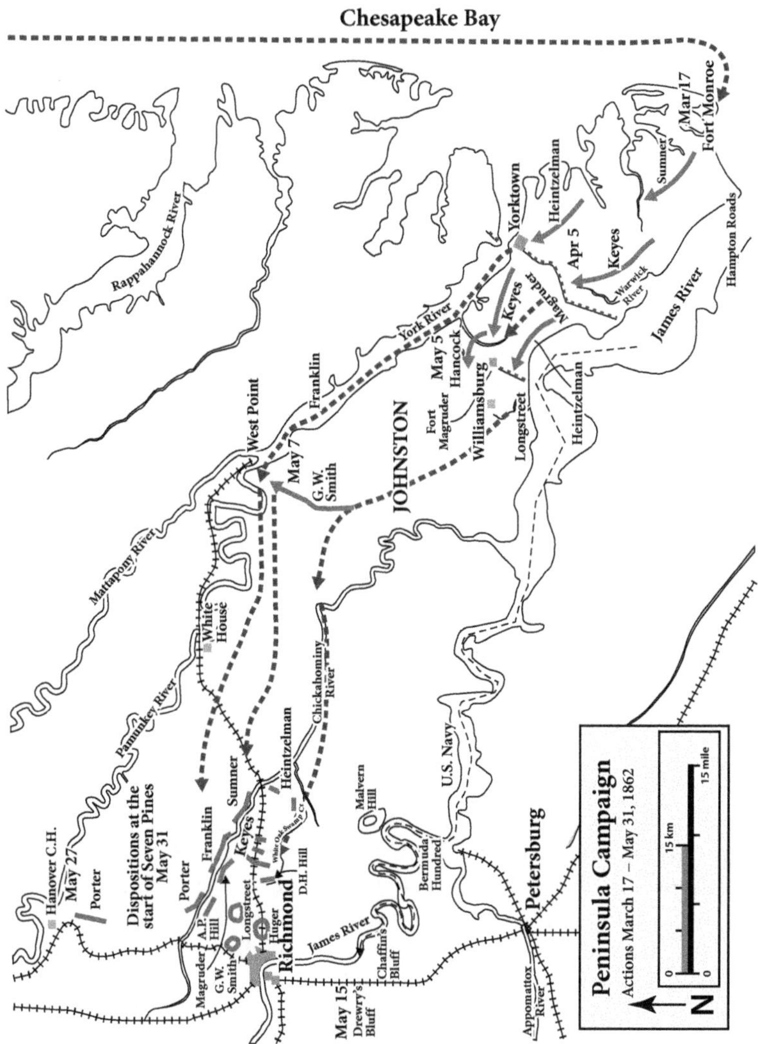

Map 5: The Peninsula Campaign, 1862.

to safeguard the nation's capital with 40,000 men. But when the Army of the Potomac landed on the Peninsula in March, Lincoln counted and found paper soldiers. Teamsters, engineers, state militia: they were not trained combat troops. Forthwith he detached 40,000 men from McClellan's army and positioned them between Richmond and Washington. If they were needed at Richmond they could move over land and cover Washington at the same time. McClellan howled and operated thereafter in the echo chamber of his protest.

He had been given just enough to make it appear that he had everything, including the responsibility of having everything, only to be denied that last little bit to ensure his success. Even as he moved – slowly, ponderously, mechanically – up the Peninsula, even as he drove methodically on to Richmond, here and there fighting for the ground, but mainly bulldozing the opponent in his front under the hulk of his army, even as he cumbered forward through swamp and bog and mud, closer and closer to the Confederate capital, even as it seemed, by late May, that he would defeat the menace ahead and behind – in front, where he was fantastically convinced that the enemy vastly outnumbered him; in rear, where he was just as fantastically convinced of the plot to snatch from him his victory and transform his war into a radical crusade – despite these and all odds, he and his army had inched close enough to Richmond to hear its church bells toll, the telltale thing beating inside McClellan all the while.

****

There was, between Lincoln and his general, one other point of profound difference. It touched politics, of course, because nothing in their relationship failed to touch politics. Yet where it rubbed up against the tactile present it also punched through to grasp at something beyond. "I claim not to have controlled events," Lincoln would write in 1864, "but confess plainly that events have controlled me." Or, more often, as a kind of nimble, overarching mantra of either wiliness or shrewdness, depending: "My policy is to have no policy." McClellan rejected the latter posture as noodling cant, an unconscionable disavowal of principle and duty, but he repudiated the former as an abdication of *history*. For if

McClellan's thorough professionalism made him something of a forerunner to the impersonal American Progressive of the 1890s, he was also romantically and temperamentally a Great Man. He had put that self-conception succinctly, when asked whether he could conceivably direct the entirety of Union operations everywhere on the continent while personally overseeing his Peninsula campaign in Virginia. "I can do it all," he replied. But Lincoln ultimately came to believe (as did Tolstoy, far away and consumed with writing *War and Peace*) that events moved beyond the control of man. Something – necessity; ultimately, God – moved them; war as a force of nature moved them; messy, fickle democracy moved them; and, as he came to realize by 1862, the idea of liberty moved them.[10]

All were possessed of a kind of superior authority, ineffable and impersonal though all of it ultimately was. Lincoln rightly is understood as a master of words. Rightly, too, on that genius has he been judged an incomparable war leader. Yet the truth, as any writer knows, is in a subtle irony. Lincoln pondered words ceaselessly and chose them with such care, with such power, and with gashing precision by way of the constant, futile search to define what it was moving beyond them. No sooner had it been captured than it moved again. The spirit of God, the spirit of war, the spirit of democracy, the spirit of liberty: all blew where they listed, the sound of them unmistakable, the source of them impenetrable, their destination unknowable. To it man must not give obedience – that would presume knowledge of the motive force itself – so much as be reconciled.

Hardly any actor in the American Civil War was immune to the Great Man theory of history, not even Lincoln. He was pushed to an alternative conception by increments. Some of these were biological and biographical. Lincoln's churning ambition was offset by a mixture of humility, fatalism, and melancholy. Others were chronological, to be found in the profound contingency of major events or as the cinder cast by "mere friction and abrasion – by the mere incidents of war." In his annual message to Congress in late 1861 he had written that "the struggle of today is not altogether for today – it is for a vast future also." Then he urged acceptance of "the great task which events have devolved upon us." A year later he had been carried to an altogether broader conception, past acceptance to reconciliation, past men as masters of destiny to men as instruments. "Fellow citizens, *we* cannot escape history," he wrote. "We of this Congress and this administration, will be remembered in spite of ourselves. No personal significance, or insignificance, can spare one or another of us. The fiery trial through which we pass, will light us down, in honor or dishonor, to the latest generation."

Between the two messages was an idea in motion. In 1861, the Union conserved liberty. The great task was to preserve it as its vessel. In 1862, liberty overflowed the Union: the great task was to preserve it in a new vessel worthy of its fluid potency. He continued:

> We *say* we are for the Union. The world will not forget that we say this. We know how to save the Union. The world knows we do know how to save it. We – even we here – hold the power, and bear this responsibility. In *giving* freedom to the *slave*, we *assure* freedom to the *free* – honorable alike in what we give, and what we preserve. We shall nobly save, or meanly lose, the last best, hope of earth.

Something like that message had been delivered long before, in the Bible that the president, a skeptic in his younger days and never a creedal church-goer but never quite a freethinker either, had begun ever more empathetically contemplating if not centering himself within. He looked there to find meaning in the War's vast, interminable destruction, and comfort after the traumatic death of his favorite child, the 11-year-old scapegrace Willie, in February 1862. Saving the Union was no longer possible by preserving the form of it. The new wine that was liberty would burn through old wineskins.[11]

The least of men were the proofs of the teaching, for the embodiment of liberty was no longer the Union but its slaves. They, too, were in motion. Almost with the first shots, they knew of the War, and knew it would involve them, many plainly that it was *about* them. Rumor and war news moved along a remarkably efficient slave network of mouths and feet – a so-called grapevine telegraph of intelligence gathered from multiple sources and completely impossible for Southern whites to control or contain. Among the revelations brutally extracted under the whip at the torture and execution of those twenty-seven slaves in Mississippi in 1861, for instance, was their anticipation of something akin to the capture of New Orleans and Winfield Scott's Anaconda Plan. An ideological bent in modern writing (in seeking to correct an opposite, longer-standing ideological bent in previous writing, but there more insidious for often being silent) has overcorrected matters in asserting that American slaves freed themselves. Less so that than as with Lincoln: the enslaved did not control events so much as recognize that events controlled them. Many if not most were awake for contingencies. They were anticipatory agents of deliberative activity where they could risk success and masterly, attendant inactivity where they could not. Over and again they proved to be shareholders of opportunity. But the primer of those opportunities was the presence of Union armies. Where they were, slaves went to find escape and protection, and because where the armies went was also where the slaves already were, the abrasion Lincoln spoke of was a constant rub.[12]

On two occasions prior to the summer of 1862 Lincoln's generals attempted to attack slavery by fiat and link emancipation to the Union cause. The more imperious of these was none other than John C. Frémont, the Republican Party's nominee for president back in 1856, who during the War's first summer commanded Union forces west of the Mississippi, including the dystopian state that already was Missouri. In August he attempted to quash guerrilla bushwhacking with an edict confiscating and emancipating the slaves of secessionists, frankly targeted at nonenlisted civilians in arms against the government (who presumably would have no further need of their slaves anyway, since by the same proclamation they could be court-martialed as freelancers and executed). Lincoln, who had not been consulted, initially asked Frémont to revise his order, and when the Pathfinder refused with less than Chesterfield manners, immediately revoked it. He told Frémont's protesting emissary (who happened to be Jessie, Frémont's plucky, well-connected wife) that she was "quite the female politician" and that the Pathfinder "should not have dragged the Negro" into the War. Nine months later, as Grant consolidated his victory at Shiloh, the Union navy captured New Orleans, and McClellan lumbered inexorably toward Richmond, events were looking up, or at any rate still had not devolved "the Negro" on him. When in May another

Union general, David Hunter, attempted another emancipation edict, this one covering slaves in South Carolina, Georgia, and Florida, and this one in concert with arming them (a fiendish chrysalis their terrified owners likened to inevitable summary execution), Lincoln revoked that, as well. The conservative war still prevailed.[13]

The trouble was, nevertheless, that "the Negroes" were dragging themselves into the War. All talked, of course, ceaselessly. All listened, actively and expectantly. Others plotted, and thousands escaped. Wherever and whenever Union armies made incursions, runaway slaves were sure to appear in their lines, eventually in great throngs that one Union chaplain could conceive of only as "the oncoming of cities." As early as May 1861 – before any major battle had been fought – they thrust themselves on general Benjamin F. Butler, whose force occupied the environs of Fort Monroe near Hampton, Virginia. Here was a conundrum. Butler's reckoning was that he couldn't very well send them back to their owners, though they too thronged his headquarters seeking their property. (One of them demanded the return of his chattel under the Fugitive Slave Act, only to have Butler reasonably point out that secession seemed to have made Federal law, and the Constitution, void to those who annulled their compact with it.) Yet Butler couldn't very well emancipate them. In prewar years he had earned a reputation as a slippery fellow, a lawyer and politician and opportunist with wit but not necessarily scruple, as looked to be the case by appearances, where sludge seemed to weight the swinging bags under his eyes and grease to whip his pendulous jowls, and by allegiances, since he had recently left the Democratic Party to become a Republican, and eventually a radical at that. In this matter his cunning served him well. He declared the slaves in his lines "contraband of war," no different than ammunition or cotton or any other property useful to the enemy war effort. Rather than returning them or emancipating them he employed them as cooks and teamsters and camp laborers. Theoretically, the contrabands, as they came to be called, were impounded. Practically and effectively, if they were not free they were not slaves.

The doctrine might have been messy but it was one Lincoln could live with. So could many Republicans in Congress – it underwrote that summer's Confiscation Act, which authorized the seizure of property used to aid the rebellion, as well as the broader Second Confiscation Act of 1862, which authorized the seizure of property belonging to disloyal persons, whether used explicitly in aid of the Confederate war effort or not. Neither confiscation law had strong teeth, and the provisions of the second were particularly rickety, but in granting the power of seizure to the president, Congress provided the ligature for the eventuality of an Emancipation Proclamation. Not many thought of themselves as paving ahead. In the second act's ramshackle course through Congress, and in its shambling provisions and qualifications, were practical compromises that tidied up legal proceedings can make all too neat. Like so much involving the fate of slavery in the War, especially the flurried responses of people and enterprising slaves on the ground, the discussions in Congress were muddled responses to unpredictable events that might have already passed by.[14]

The doctrine was also adept as a political instrument, as many messy doctrines are. Few Northerners were likely to support emancipation as a humanitarian mission, fewer still as a vision for the War. Among the worries was the old one: what would happen to the slaves *after* they were freed? Yet the direct linking of slaves to the Confederate war effort contained a military rationale with fangs that could plunge deep into public opinion and in turn be bared, ferociously, on the enemy. The feeling was growing already, in itself it was the most obvious force of separation and nationalism in the Union, that since slavery was clearly the "something" that caused the War, and clearly, also, the most distinguishing social, economic, and cultural institution separating North and South, it was the thing that needed to be removed if the Union was to be one again. Humanitarian aim or no, attacking the institution was a brute matter of logistics. The Confederacy survived, its armies survived, in large part because slavery – or more precisely, because the manpower provided by slave labor – survived. These realizations remained slow in dawning as long as the military situation tilted toward Union victory. The logic was relentless and ineluctable.

Fluxed and unpredictable were the events moving public opinion: still, the force of public opinion was a fixed fact of power. Lincoln attempted to convey as much to loyalists in the border states determined to hold onto their slave property even as pressure mounted on him, and the debates about slavery's future grew more intense. In March, around the time Congress prohibited Union

Figure 13: Frederick Douglass, *c.* 1879, Public Domain.

commanders from returning any slaves from army camps to anyone claiming ownership, be they loyal or disloyal, he proposed a plan of compensated, voluntary emancipation for the border states. The expense of it, he pointed out to critics, would amount to the bill for three months of the War, which presumably would be shortened. At the same time he reiterated that no one could read hieroglyphs but that something was being written on the wall nevertheless, as the circumstance of war in motion. "It is impossible to foresee," he said in a message to Congress, "all the incidents, which may attend and all the ruin which may follow it." And again, in May, meeting privately with border state representatives, came another plea to accept compensated emancipation framed within a warning of contingency's power: "Will you not embrace it? You cannot if you would be blind to the signs of the times." And again, on July 2, he made the appeal explicit in a letter to representatives of the border states in Congress: "The incidents of the war can not be avoided. If the war continue long, as it must, if the object be not sooner attained, the institution in your states will be extinguished by mere friction and abrasion – by the mere incidents of the war. It will be gone, and you will have nothing valuable in lieu of it."[15]

It so happened that he had written to McClellan on the Peninsula ten days earlier. The general had asked for 50,000 more men.

> If in your frequent mention of responsibility, you have the impression that I blame you for not doing more than you can, please be relieved of such impression. I only beg that in like manner, you will not ask impossibilities of me. If you think you are not strong enough to take Richmond just now, I do not ask you to try just now. Save the Army, material and personal; and I will strengthen it for the offensive again, as fast as I can.

Disaster had struck.[16]

****

In the last week of June, its heels dug in and its back pinned against Richmond, the Confederate army launched a massive assault on McClellan's army that drove it east and then south, away from the capital, to a more modest (and now relatively harmless) position on the banks of the James River. Salvation had seemed hopeless, the cause already lost, and so the attack's cost and audacity might be blithely explained or overlooked entirely. Some 20,000 Confederate casualties, bled out over a series of hard-fought engagements collectively called the Seven Days' battles, brought the horrors of Shiloh's woods to the urbane streets of the capital, where every conceivable resource was improvised to handle the dead, the dying, and the wounded. McClellan's loss was also substantial, some 16,000 killed and wounded, and thus his plea to Lincoln for 50,000 reinforcements. But the loss also included whatever nerve the Young Napoleon kept in his personal reserve. He was beaten. And whatever else might be said about him, he was beaten because he sensed presence in the audacity of his nemesis and was no match for it.

Very few in the American Civil War were. The attack's architect came to dominate the War and its legacy on a scale alike only to Lincoln: Robert E. Lee. The year between his pained resignation from the US Army and subsequent lot-casting with the Confederacy and this, his dazzling pummeling of McClellan outside of Richmond, had not been good. Charged first with organizing the Virginia volunteers, which he managed superbly, he had been commissioned as the third highest-ranking general in the Confederacy (again behind Sidney Johnston) and given command of a small army in western Virginia. That errand was miserable torture. He was then assigned to the Carolina and Georgia Lowcountry, near Savannah, a defensive mission which – by the lights of popular opinion, anyway – also sunk into gloom. Difficulty there was an outcome on which the Lowcountry's languor and loam might have given Lee deeper reason to dwell. His humbled father, Light-Horse Harry Lee, a cavalry hero of the American Revolution and former governor of Virginia, was buried in its soil. Light-Horse Lee's glory did not survive the Revolution, for he was scofflaw and pariah in afteryears, and had cut and run from all connections, including his family – Robert, his youngest son, was 5 years old – and all antagonists. These included many creditors as well as the beefy fists of a many-fingered Baltimore mob, which had beaten him nearly to death because its membership objected to the old general's opposition to the War of 1812. After a period of exile to the West Indies, Light-Horse Harry sailed back to the American shore in 1816 only to die on it, ironically (or perhaps fittingly, depending on one's perspective) on the same Lowcountry plantation where Eli Whitney had invented the cotton gin – the device that had powered the cotton-and-slave empire of the South with which his son had cast his lot.

What we are to make of Robert E. Lee's extraordinary aggressiveness, and how much of it can be legitimately chalked up to Lee's profound experiences with frustration and loneliness, has been a matter of conjecture since the first great modern biography appeared almost a hundred years ago, hagiography though that also was. Lee was a risk-taker, bold but not impulsively reckless, and where others in Confederate gray favored a defensive conservation of resources, Lee preferred concentration that those resources might be unleashed. His was partly a matter of taste; of stance; of posture. But in style was profound substance. It was grand strategy invested with insight into democracies at war, and particularly the pugnacious Southern society sustaining the Confederate war. At once, Lee favored a conventional war but doubted the zeal of

Southerners to maintain an endurance contest. Offsetting this pessimism was the doubt he sensed in the opponent he once served. The Northern home front might buckle if Confederates could, in the short term, make matters violent and costly enough.

Lee's vision was to seize for his army, and then constantly control, the strategic initiative: to force his opponent to react to him. And he thought beyond narrow military circumstances to consider the effects of such an approach reaching past the lines of the armies, in both directions. An aggressive Confederate army was an army whose sheer provocative power, at once, invigorated cultural values long paramount in Southern society even as its wily combativeness might demoralize Northerners conditioned to think of Southerners as the superior martial people. In its assertiveness, in short, the army might develop an unconquerable aura sustaining it at home and afield, in the far reaches of the North. For Lee, as with Lincoln, the opponent was time. The longer went the War, the more likely its length boded a braced-up Northern morale and

Figure 14: Portrait of General Robert E. Lee, Officer of the Confederate Army, Library of Congress Prints & Photographs, Public Domain.

commitment of resources. Conversely, a defensive, reactive stance of endurance would chew Confederate resources and spit them out in a cycle of moil and attrition, grinding up the self-assured bellicosity of its people to pulp. All was dependent on blood.[17]

Lee had been sidelined after the demoralizing experience in the Lowcountry. He was jockeying a desk in Richmond as a military adviser to Davis when McClellan began his slogging advance along the Peninsula. In that position, though, at the right hand of the president, Lee was also something of a harbinger of centralization. The catastrophic reverses of early 1862 had forced on the Confederacy a stunning in-gathering of power. To those among the fire-eating classes who thought of the cause as the pure quest for decentralized republicanism, centralization seemed to corrupt the simple essence of its creation. Yet they were not representative of the dominant mood. The collapse of the western line, the utter desperation of Shiloh, the death of Sidney Johnston; the fall of New Orleans and Union domination of the upper Mississippi River; McClellan's slow but grinding relentless pressure on Richmond: the substance of spirit was dread – death at the hands of the enemy, not corruption and destruction from within, and so the response to shuddering reverses not limited to these was a summoning of a new birth of revolutionary zeal.

This was not quite the popular mania channeled by the fire-eaters at secession and whipped into the passion of the War's first year. The second blooming took on the directed, statist form. Oddly, statism was evident in April in the Confederacy's official approval of localized, independent operations through the Partisan Ranger Act, a contradiction on hasty inspection but actually the embodiment of a deepening, centralizing nationalism. Certainly, in approving the enrollment of partisan rangers the Confederacy had authorized a form of warfare that heretofore it had hesitated to permit, since such warfare bumped up in kinship with the intense localism and perhaps individualist license of guerrilla war. Just as surely the act acknowledged dire straits. Partisans, after all, operated independently, and typically behind the advancing lines of the enemy. The step, hesitant though it was, was no license to dispersal. It could only be the very opposite. It sought to bestir electric idealism and direct it toward the organized, regulated, conventional ends of the state – precisely to contain any diffusion of power or license that might otherwise jeopardize the nation's legitimacy.

Centralization and the legitimacy of the conventional state were the new touchstones of the Confederate revolution. The Ranger Act was one step but not the only one. Nor, manifestly, was it the most comprehensive. The Confederate Congress had opened 1862 by authorizing Davis to suspend the writ of habeas corpus and to declare martial law as he judged necessary. So too did the government begin to demand and energetically impress resources unto itself – food, war materiel, slaves for military and defense labor – and to nationalize the nation's still-fledgling industrial capacities. The most imperative need was manpower. The revolution of 1861 claimed the young and the fanatical in a jamboree of volunteering. They came to war behind drums and banners, but there were not enough of them. Older white Southerners with families, perhaps property, with other claims competing on honor and duty, tended to be nominal Confederates but reluctant rebels. In April, at the same time it passed the Ranger Act, the Confederate Congress authorized conscription. The law drafted men between 18 and 35 years of age, but exempted various classes deemed essential at home and allowed the draft-eligible to buy substitutes if they could be procured. A few months later the upper-age was raised to 45, which in the nineteenth century might be considered on the farther side of middle age.

Although only 82,000 men were forcibly drafted over the life of the Confederacy, conscription was not really the design of the act. Its purpose was to stimulate "volunteering" by the implied shame of impressment and to encourage by similar means the re-enlistment of the happy volunteers who had signed on for a year's service in the war-frantic spring of 1861 – a bowdlerized *levee en masse.* It worked. Allowing for adjustments over the course of the War and for enlistment considerations other than public shaming, the Confederacy mobilized nearly all of its available white manpower – 750,000 men from among a pool of one million. But as with the other developments of centralization, it worked only with constant maintenance and against initial and then widening social and political cleavages. The draft, and particularly the exemption and substitution provisions, would become the Confederate revolution's most volatile internal issue.

No greater caper has been perpetrated on American history than the nostalgia-tinged inventions of the founders of so-called Southern heritage: that the Confederate nation was the last-gasp, lost-cause avatar of decentralized, purely federal government. Theirs are fairy tales. Over time the stalwart machinery for achieving centralization in the Confederacy became arguably more thoroughgoing than the apparatus of the supposed leviathan it fought. Yet nostalgia is not easily shooed off, and neither is the opposite approach, abiding as it does in a pose of know-better righteousness toward Confederate defeat. Ever since that desperate, in-gathering spring of 1862, some writers, a few self-styled as the messengers of history's comeuppance, have seen in centralization an example of the base hypocrisy of the Confederate revolution. Their slings and arrows are better aimed (in truth they probably are aimed) at the fairy tales and the hypocrisy of the postwar tradition-makers and their still-active descendants.[18]

Revolutionary government was to Davis and other nationalists what it was, say, to Robespierre or Saint Just or the members of the Committee of Public Safety. (The Confederacy, incidentally, lacked a guillotine for its internal enemies, but certainly not terror or whipping posts or scaffolds and tree limbs for them.) They did not see themselves as betrayers or tyrants, and certainly not as hypocrites, though the molten tongues of archconservative fire-eaters such as Robert Barnwell Rhett in Charleston often spewed against the cause's treachery to first principles or, more typically and widely, scorched Davis by proxy. Nor did Confederates intend to upturn institutions or customs or even cultural identity. Intensifying efforts aimed at developing Confederate nationalism through literature and education, after all, moved parallel to political and military centralization. And those continued to emphasize the distinctiveness of a Southern people. Nationalists thought of the revolution as a suspension of time, in essence. *Revolutionary* described the nature of the emergency *government* and its measures – temporary – and not the effects of a revolution itself – not, in other words, the intended and permanent consequences of anything it might undertake in crisis. They understood what they were doing as necessary to protect their revolution so that when the crisis passed their nation could emerge in its purest form.[19]

And so Lee in Richmond, at the right hand of Davis, was harbinger. Much else in the war effort besides him was gathering in the capital. Yet if 1862 showed the Confederacy's willingness to centralize, it had made obvious the corollary: it *had* to. Diffuse reluctance and hesitation were still pushback forces to a pulling nationalization, demoralization more so. Suspended between desperation and nationalization was a wound-up torque poised for release. Events would tell its direction. Either the Confederacy would buckle into a whirl of utter collapse. Either that or the coil would spring, somehow, forward.

4

EMANCIPATION: 1862

Freedom, like liberty, could be made the lucidity of purpose, both in a future-looking promise and in a halcyon aftermath. So was it possible for Julia Ward Howe, when the American Civil War began, to sing "mine eyes have seen the glory of the coming of the Lord," to claim to have seen Him "in the watch fires of a hundred circling camps" and even "across the sea, in the beauty of the lilies, where Christ was born," from whence He cometh to this crusade, marching on. And so, too, was it possible for Confederates to believe that Stonewall Jackson, their greatest warrior hero, had peered beyond a nameless, silverline river, at the moment of his death in 1863, to behold a pastoral wood where there was a cradling stillness, underneath the shade of the trees. America – north and south – was a Christ-saturated land before the War, a nation whose people – white and black – despite their shackles of fault and sin, believed in millennial promise.

Of course war on the ground, as combat, was not like that. It could not by itself bring freedom or redemption or lucidity. It was only partly as Clausewitz defined it: it was merely the messy human instrument of politics by other, inhumane means. When men in the ranks beheld it for what it was, and not as the millennial portent of a thousand years of peace and prophetic fulfillment, they could compare it only to "seeing the elephant," a creature most in fact had never and would never lay eyes on. Seeing it close and near was to behold something so mammothly, so hulkingly carnival, that no experience was like it, and no metaphor of placidity or order could capture its booming sensual chaos. Its lucidity *and* its purpose were illusions. One Confederate officer glimpsed it as he beheld the watch fires of the camps for himself. It may have been beautiful but only against distance. Thousands of constellated campfires flickering, for miles around, were "a very fine sight" in the nighttime, he recorded as he muddled in the dark toward his headquarters. But in the blackness he still could not find his way. It was all muddle – massive, awkward, clumsy, improvised muddle.

Its sights overwhelmed the senses, and its ironies toppled reason or at least expectation, though that was a dizzying lesson by hard knocks, taught and learned and unlearned over and over and over again. In the spring of 1862 the Confederacy was near its ignominious, humiliating quicksand collapse – its entire western line caved in; its largest city and most cosmopolitan port at New Orleans gun-boated, battered, captured, and shut off; its coastline blockaded and raided; its capital grimly besieged and going under ... and then the thing tumbled over itself again. By the summer it was the Union behemoth tossed up and thrown over, and the great Confederate armies of east and west not only jaunting again but turned about, loosed upon Union soil, and threatening to end the War just as swiftly with the strokes leaving the Confederacy right-side up.

This war's momentum was its own unpredictability and the certainty of topsy-turvy and of nothing fixed. It was just at that moment of downside turned upward, in the late summer of 1862, that a Northern observer hurried out of Washington on the last train westward, toward danger but driven by curiosity to catch a glimpse of the invincible, invading Robert E. Lee and his Army of Northern Virginia. What he saw near the small town of Frederick in western Maryland shocked him. Passing by was no glittering array. It was a ragged, shabby, menacing host, bereft of uniformity, some without shoes, some without their own shirts or trousers, some escorting property despoiled from the recently twice-manhandled US Army – wagons, ambulances, horses – or appropriated underarm (mainly watermelons) from the local citizenry. The glory shrouding its magnificence was all dust and glistening lice. Its spirit was in its loose swagger and raw physicality, and, he bemused, in the appearance now and then of a toothbrush "pendant from the button-hole."

He saw something else that collided with reason. Among the Confederate army were thousands of black men. Manifestly these were not "soldiers," since Confederates officially forbid such man-given status to African Americans but also denied, philosophically, that God had given black men *capability* to be soldiers. Yet somehow these men did not seem "slaves," either. But they were here, randomly uniformed like their Confederate masters in the ranks, haphazardly armed like them ("rifles, muskets, sabres, bowie-knives, dirks") and "promiscuously mixed up with all the rebel horde." He chalked up his overwhelmed expectations to the hypocrisy of Southern civilization. Talk of possibilities, of emancipation, and of the Union arming black men and even freed slaves was already in the air. Had not Confederates, catching wind of that chatter and fearing already that Spartacus was at home, howled at the murderous brutality of the Union potentially sanctioning such insurrectionary measures? What baseness was this, then, to see more than 3,000 black men in the rebel army – he counted them – perhaps not formally recognized as infantry, but armed and dressed like it; perhaps not bound for the firing line, and instead driving wagons or scouring for food or nursing the sick and wounded, but without question freeing up 3,000 white Confederates for killing duty?

Black Confederates: the notion beguiles our own hindsight certainties. From this distance it can be speculated that most of these slaves (for that is what they were, no matter what they appeared to be) weren't there by choice. Some maybe even took the opportunity to run away. A few might have cast their lot differently. A favored relationship with a master now in the army perhaps had given them privileges in life not easily surrendered, and a certainty with their lot that contingent events could not give them. After all the tide could turn one way as easily as another, in as well as out, with what result or consequence – creating or destroying – no one could know. None are wiser that way than the dispossessed. Whatsoever we make of seeing our own elephant in Frederick, the sight should not be approached naively. If it is true that some "chose" to be there, it is just as true that what we see only illumines the limits of the choice. Even the privileged slave was a slave. And thousands of slaves, tens of thousands more across the Confederacy, were making other decisions.[1]

The War's ghastliest day occurred two weeks after this scene, and in that destruction was birthed emancipation. But it remained hard to see just what emancipation was or meant. Emancipation: freedom *from* control, *independence.* In the America of the nineteenth century, an understanding of independence was still conditioned by the eighteenth century. Americans of today see the word complete, and the concept whole, as independence, but that's because our egalitarian posture has long since outgrown its origins. In the days when the American Revolution was still a living memory, independence was a mentality modified from its root in dependence: as *in-dependence*, or perhaps even better rendered, *un-dependence.* In-dependence was breaking away from traditional relationships defined by measures of power, wealth, rank, status, and inferiority. The negative frame of reference – freedom *from* control – gave meaning then to what today have become positivistic, affirmative, liberating concepts: freedom *of* choice, or freedom *to* pursue opportunity. Our constructions look forward to new chances and new possibilities. Theirs looked backward, toward old relationships or to history, and the breaking away was tangible. Freedom from control was (quite literally) grounded in the economic means to maintain *un-dependence*: a family farm, say, or a trade – a competency, to use another revealingly grubby word that has since shifted meaning.

Black emancipation took its central wartime meaning here, as freedom *from* slavery. So did Confederate independence, as separation *from* the former Union. What those might have meant as *freedom of* or *freedom to* constructions were entirely, electrically, profoundly unknown. And what the Union itself might mean – if it were freed from slavery but remade whole, into the possibility of a new thing – was not even, as yet, an expectation. Freedom did not go marching on. It stumbled.

****

Indeed: Lee was on the move. As impossible as it all seemed just two months earlier, when the Confederate army in Virginia was pinned against Richmond, Lee had turned the war in the east upside down. He had assumed command outside Richmond after Joseph E. Johnston, a competent leader and strategist who nonetheless had lost Davis's confidence (if ever he had it) by his apparent passivity in everything except ill-humored demand for rank and recognition, was incapacitated during the battle of Seven Pines. That otherwise unremarkable contest, fought at the end of May on the outskirts of Richmond, altered little. As yet, awareness of the changeover in command as a potentially liberating development was generally limited to the sardonic or the ironic, such as Johnston himself, who sourly hailed it as deliverance. The "shot that struck me down," he said, was "the very best that has been fired for the Southern cause yet," since Jefferson Davis now employed someone he trusted. Mostly the army seemed marred. So when Lee set the troops to drilling or like an old washerwoman nagged at them about their shambling unruliness, they called him Granny, and when he had them digging ditches and trenches in the rising miasma of summer, they grumbled darkly that he worked them like slaves. Their twinned metaphors of unmanning, allusions of gender and race and dependence, are not to be overlooked. Spirits were anything but martial.

The gripers and the carpers misread their new commander. All the drilling, digging, and nagging was prelude to a revolutionary circumstance, as was a concurrent concentration and augmentation of Confederate firepower. It seemed nearly every available soldier was being trucked to Richmond. Among them were troops brought in from the Shenandoah Valley under the command of Thomas J. Jackson, known widely (and ever since) as Stonewall for his heroic defensive stand a year prior, at Bull Run. Also reputed widely (and ever since) was Jackson's manner, which some read as a marionette's, and some more flatly as a flake's, and at least one as "cracked-brained." His Cromwellian intensity soon became legendary not for standing his men like a stone wall but for the ferocious aggressiveness that would just as soon drive them right through one. In May, Jackson had unleashed his small force in a series of brilliant maneuvers in the Shenandoah that had flummoxed first one, then another, and then a third Federal army. Eventually, he mystified and embarrassed all of them at once – and his blue-light relentlessness burrowed deep into the enemy's weakest point. It was Lincoln's anxious imperative to keep Washington, DC, secured that had led him to detach 40,000 men from McClellan on the Peninsula, to the deterioration of their already strained relations. The jitters generated by Jackson's sudden, surprising offensives in the Valley kept those men more or less right where they were, clutching in and around and near the Federal capital, while McClellan plodded on to Richmond convinced of being double-dealt. Ultimately, some of them would go scurrying into the Valley after Jackson only to get a final thrashing. Assuming they were more useful to McClellan – we must be careful here – those 40,000 men could have plunged overland to Richmond to seal the Confederacy's doom.[2]

Jackson's gashing movements generated dread and multiplied his power. His aggressiveness stunned and confused and sometimes paralyzed his opponents, who suddenly felt themselves in the snares of a hunter. Yet while Jackson was the onsite designer and executive, doing all with an enterprise and decisiveness and lit-up intensity that would transform him from crackpot to the Confederacy's first national warrior-hero, the idea had been Lee's, conceived while he was still manning a desk in Richmond as one of Davis's military advisers. Here was something primal. Maybe it was a dice's throw or a knight's gambit in the short term: maybe it was something else if the life of the Confederacy could be prolonged – a play-for-keeps aggressiveness, a protean energy. As matters stood, with the Confederacy gasping for survival, the combined pressures of circumstance and exigency limited the range of perception. It could hardly be playing for keeps when hardly nothing was to risk because nothing was to lose. And it could hardly be expected to reach fulfillment as a force of its own, as protean energy, when it was a desperate response to boxed-in necessity. But it became a vision of war.

So, too, as first necessities, were the conditions necessary to free this vision – one being the freedom of the visionary. The wounding of Johnston, who did not share it, lifted Lee from desk jockey to commander of the army, though the appointment was anything but unifyingly popular. The other condition was the obvious necessity of freeing Richmond from McClellan's lumbering, suffocating siege guns. Thus the summons to Jackson and his men in the Valley. Thus the concentration of a force larger than any yet fielded in the Confederacy. Thus also the digging and trenching and drilling. And thus, in late June, with Lee now wielding an army approaching 90,000 men, came the violent sledge-hammering that led to McClellan's panicked call

Figure 15: General Jackson's "Chancellorsville" portrait, 1863, Public Domain.

for 50,000 reinforcements and Lincoln's equally urgent reply that his general "not ask impossibilities of me." In a series of battles called the Seven Days, Lee suddenly fell upon McClellan's exposed right flank and flailed the grand Union army southward, like he was lashing a massive drover's lot into the slaughterhouse. Day after day he continued, until a week later the carnage ended with Lee's lusting attempt to drive McClellan into the James River at a place called Malvern Hill. That was a ghastly mistake, not his last. Ever after some would remember wounded multitudes crowning the hill, their clutching and twitching giving the earth a "singular crawling effect." Yet McClellan had been driven away and bulldozed into a strange, paralyzed listlessness. Not only was Richmond saved. The threat of McClellan was gone.

Lee wasn't finished. Six weeks later he shuttled westward out of Richmond and into northern Virginia, near the old Bull Run battlefield, where his long-striding minions encountered and manhandled a Union army gathered from the remnants of the various Federal forces in and around Washington. Three months; two bold maneuvers; the impending siege of Richmond raised; a Second Bull Run; Virginia cleared of enemy threat – not for nothing did Lee re-christen his new-model force the Army of Northern Virginia. But he did not mean to keep it there. To turn back now, from a northern Virginia hard-won and fairly reclaimed, was to diminish his men's swaggering, newfound confidence and their *esprit de corps*. By default, stasis would restore the initiative to the enemy. Stasis might also bleed from the Confederacy a surge of patriotic fervor and upswelling nationalism, for in hothouse fashion Lee and his army – and not Davis and his Congress; not this flag nor that flag nor any regalia of government – had become the emblems of the nation. To go onward was risky, it was aggressive, and it was relentless. It might catalyze Confederate nationalism in the protean bonds of a Confederate way of war.

Entering Maryland, perhaps Pennsylvania, might be *hyper*-aggressive, but it would plant Confederate banners on nominally enemy soil. On September 3, Lee wrote to Davis ostensibly asking leave to do what he in actuality committed to do before Davis could have read his dispatch – cross the Potomac. The president, who had declaimed a mere seventeen months earlier on the Confederacy's supposed passive desire merely "to be let alone," now contemplated his leading general's bold calculus. The costlier burden of offensive warfare was always with the Union, but a move north, Lee argued, would remove the hard hand of war from battered Virginia, a landscape by now pillaged of its farmland, shorn of woodlands, despoiled of livestock, divested of fencing. It would flummox a Northern electorate on the eve of crucial Congressional elections and perhaps even cripple or even disempower the Republicans. A victory in Union country – for what else was there but victory? – might also emancipate Maryland, one of those border slaveholding states still in the Union, from Lincoln's thrall. Maybe most importantly, Confederate victory in Maryland or Pennsylvania might persuade England and other European powers of Confederate legitimacy: it might, yes, persuade them that the arms of the slaveholding South had made a nation. If the British and French governments offered to broker peace, or to provide more tangible military and financial support, Confederate independence was only a matter of time.

Ahead were all these hopeful outcomes, or so Lee projected. But there it was, again. Time – *time*. Lee felt it as Lincoln felt it, as a palpitating, innard pulse swollen under the firm grip of the hands on the clock, as urgency squeezing up audacity. His resolve to go north with his aptly named army is often conceived as an invasion, but it was not really, because Lee had no intention, and no logistical ability, to *stay* above the Potomac. Neither was it a raid, because forage and plunder and temporary terror were decidedly secondary in his conceptions. As Davis read Lee's *ex post facto* request for permission, he might massage his face and rub the black-bagged socket under his neuralgic eye, pondering: All of his general's justifications were potentially true; all of them tactful and politic. Yes. Yes. But Lee's fundamental desire was the one that didn't make it into the letter, though it seeped into consciousness as the invisible frame of it and was manifest in the act of withholding prior notification. If ever blood-water would nourish Confederate nationalism, *now* – after unlooked-for, marvelous, magnificent victories – was the time. The certainty was that the Union army must fight him on northern soil. Lee would draw it out, he would draw it away from its fortified stronghold in Washington, DC, and what would happen then was what he intended to have happen from his first trial in command. "Under ordinary circumstances," Lee had written in his report of the Seven Days, even as the image of a crawling battlefield at Malvern Hill was superimposing itself on the memory of those who witnessed it, "the Federal army should have been destroyed."[3]

****

Elsewhere other armies were moving, too. By happenstance, for one instance, was the aggressive reemergence of Confederate designs west of the Appalachians. This turn of fortune in the fall of 1862 was something of a wonderment. The war in the west after Shiloh had seemingly ground down into a crawling kind of McClellan affair. After Shiloh, Halleck had seized field command from Grant and reduced him to bystanding status, perhaps all the while taking secret delight in the newspaper assaults on his subordinate's "butchery" or more rumormongering about his supposed drunkenness. Grant's fighting methods had required no brains, after all, no science, no sobriety. Yard by yard, mile by mile, scratching at his elbows and entrenching at every stop to avoid the kind of screeching surprise Grant had invited in the woods in April, Halleck furrowed eventually into north Mississippi. There he besieged the important railroad town of Corinth and compelled its surrender in late May. With Grant sitting tight, and Halleck in control of north Mississippi, the defensive line that the lamented Sidney Johnston had established at the beginning of 1862 had been bullied backward and palsied half the year later. All seemed well. The army under Don Carlos Buell, adjuncted to Halleck's forces since Shiloh, was huzzahed and sent eastward, toward Chattanooga, to establish Union control of that important railhead.

The surprise came in what followed, and somewhat *under whom* it followed. Confederate grandiosity might be expected from Beauregard. But the strife of the past year – some brought on by his own magnetic attraction for controversy – had finally shattered Beauregard's nerves. Off he had gone, to water at a spa. Davis replaced him with Braxton Bragg, an old army veteran turned erstwhile sugar planter and like Sidney Johnston before him a loyalist whom Davis trusted. If Beauregard's crutch had been self-regard, what Davis had called his propensity to exalt himself at the expense of others, in Bragg an utter lack of any charismatic presence whatsoever eventually became crippling. More evocative of him was sheer cantankerousness. It had been told on Bragg by contemporaries (probably in jest, but one wonders) that, before the War, serving by necessity as both commander and quartermaster of an isolated army post, he had found himself so disagreeable that he couldn't avoid bickering with himself over whether to obey his own disagreeable orders to supply himself. His distemper was such that a modern-era biographer (or so again it is told, but no one wonders) abandoned the two-volume life of Bragg he intended halfway to the mark because he could not abide another book in Bragg's mephitic company. In more recent times Bragg has been less provoking to writers more sensitive to his genuine strengths, though no one disputes his churlishness, and though his nasty arguments with persons of more consequence than historians were far from apocryphal. At least one subordinate threatened to kill him.

Thus in some respects the surprise. Over the summer, while Union forces consolidated the line they controlled deep in the heart of the western Confederacy, Bragg concentrated various Confederate commands in Mississippi and Alabama and brought them over rickety railroads to Chattanooga. He got there ahead of Buell, whose pace was leisurely, but did not stay. Reinforced by yet another Confederate command in eastern Tennessee, so that his force now included 40,000 men, Bragg, against all odds and maybe unbelief, too, invaded Kentucky.[4]

The military and political rationales, to say nothing of the audacity of the whole thing, had been similar to those Lee advocated in crossing the Potomac – the liberation of Tennessee substituting for the liberation of Virginia; the liberation of the border state Kentucky substituting for Maryland. Yet for that, and importantly, the Confederacy's Maryland and Kentucky offensives were not coordinated invasions. They were not intentionally simultaneous so much as they were separately and situationally opportunistic, and their accidental synchronicity obscured slight but important differences. Bragg expected even more Confederate sympathizers to join his ranks in Kentucky than Lee expected to join his in Maryland. Bragg even brought 15,000 extra muskets with him. There was also the reasonable chance that Bragg might have been able to stay in Kentucky after a hoped-for victory. It was not to be. After installing a Confederate "governor" at Louisville and speechifying there and elsewhere about redeeming the state for the slaveholder's cause, Bragg turned to face Buell, whose Union force had veered northward from Chattanooga in pursuit – still leisurely. The armies collided at Perryville in early October and fought to a nasty tactical draw, after which Bragg abandoned the whole enterprise and fell back into Tennessee, and on the knives that eventually were brought out against him.

He had retreated all the way to Chattanooga, it was true, and just as truly would face the usual recrimination for it. But in defeat Bragg had flipped Confederate fortunes. After a year of dismal failures in the west new prospects were imaginable. Bragg took note of them by rechristening his force the Army of Tennessee, like its eastern counterpart under Lee, an army of place, and like the Army of Northern Virginia, an army named for what it *hoped*, eventually, to recapture and control. From 1862 onward, these were in fact

Figure 16: Braxton Bragg, between 1860 and 1870, Public Domain.

what one writer has called them – the Two Great Rebel Armies. By that was suggested, correctly, that these were more than musket-carrying hordes. They embodied the Confederacy and its ambitions in both the literal and figurative senses, and martial identification with them was a channel through which flowed the broader forces of social and cultural identification. To imagine a people and a nation required a great scale of awareness proportionate to the vast expanse of the territory the Confederacy claimed to hold. Other attachments and affinities required time the Confederacy might already have borrowed against too heavily. Their coordinated offensives in the late summer of 1862 might have been accidental, but both were cultural as well as military endeavors, after a fashion: certainly not deliberate in that way, but present, tantalizing if intangible, as the fettle of heated up, hothouse nationalism.

Accounting for Confederate strategic decisions is virtually impossible without sensing it. After all, there were obvious alternatives to aggressive warfare, and in theory even alternatives to conventional war. Most readily and historically available, for its legacy was profound, was the Fabian example of the American Revolution. The Continental Army under Washington won the Revolution by not losing it, relying both on movement and on time while trading space, to defeat a vastly more powerful British Empire. Washington's genius was in recognizing his intact army as the vessel of revolutionary nationalism. He did not seek the climactic battle but masterfully and deliberately avoided risking one. On the other end of the theoretical continuum was the possibility of abandoning conventional warfare entirely. The Confederate war might be fought by relying solely on partisans and guerrillas. Here too were lustrous examples from the old Revolution and even Confederate heroes either already in the grave, such as Turner Ashby in Virginia, or still in the saddle, such as John Hunt Morgan and Nathan Bedford Forrest. (It was Forrest, incidentally, who menaced Bragg with a death threat.) Not merely those of name but countless others in local areas called by whatever name – bushwhackers, guerrillas, free-lances, marauders, brigands, banditti – theoretically might have turned the War into a red-limed bog of bloodletting from which Union armies could never possibly hope to emerge victorious.

The Confederates embraced none of those alternatives. They chose to fight conventionally and often aggressively. There is no manual – no minutes of any summit in which the Confederate high command gathered to debate the merits of one approach or the other. Their choice was not deliberate so much as responsive, improvised, and nearly reflexive. Yet as an emerging pattern of adaption to circumstance, aggressive conventional war is more telling of a cohering Confederate identity than less so. Among the more prosaic reasons for convention was its symmetry with Confederate purpose. Defending territory was a means of establishing nationhood in the eyes of the Western world and of conserving slavery, which an unconventional war or even a Fabian one most likely would have frayed or destroyed by its essential lack of concern for institutions.

And yet a chain of assumptions should not coffle the obvious advantages of conventional thinking to an endorsement of inevitability, as happens with some writers: the Confederacy had to fight conventionally but could not muster the numbers or resources to win conventionally, therefore it was doomed at the outset, as Lee said it was at the end, by the Union's overwhelming numbers and resources. Reality is more potent, because it takes into account the Confederate purpose as well as the Confederate imagination, because it accounts for a vision that was very much modern and forward-looking, not hidebound and doomed. Through the substance of its armies, and through the style of fighting in its armies, would the very *idea* of a Confederate people be born. Success in boldness, in calculated risk, in offensive war to protect and defend, portended to become the sustaining spirit of the nation, a *felt thing*, recoiling to spiral higher and higher again into new levels of ardor and fealty after each audacious stroke as the very life force of liberation and liberty. Its conventional war and its armies of place – the Army of Northern Virginia; the Army of Tennessee – were the means of conservation *and* liberation.

What the Confederacy yet lacked after almost two years of putative existence was a fully developed internal sense of itself as a nation: a people both set apart and bound together. As soldiers likened the stunning experience of battle to the awe of seeing an elephant, so the organizing of a nation had been its own kind of awkward strangeness, neither linear nor natural. The antebellum South lacked a native literature; it lacked urbanity. The region's sense of itself was more ephemeral and peripheral than coherent or internal. Had it been formed in 1860, Lee's army would have been the second-largest city in the Confederacy after New Orleans, and Bragg's the third. Each army's campsite would have been the region's largest inland city if both St. Louis and Baltimore – slaveholding and Southern-tinged, but still part of the Union – are excluded. While the antebellum South did not lack for improvements, its roads and railroads were essentially extractive; they were transactive without quite being integral. The region's terminals pulled toward its perimeter, to ports such as Charleston or Mobile or Savannah or Wilmington. The antebellum South existed not because most of the people living there said or thought it did, but because *outsiders*, and especially those living in the North who conceived of imperative difference because their own lives were becoming vastly and rapidly different, said or thought it did. One esoteric dynamic of the Confederate double invasion of 1862 was the imaginative effect of discovering *outside-ness* for themselves. To "leave" somewhere was to step beyond and set it off. Separation from it created a place to go back to.

If all those words about it are fair, if something elusive called the South didn't yet exist before the War, something inchoate called *Southern* did, and because white Southerners (like Northerners) said or thought it did. They lived neither as narrowly nor as provincially as historians sometimes have made them live. Experience was bounded and centered, certainly, on family, kinship, and neighborhood. Many had never been farther than the county courthouse, fewer still had left their own states. (Arguably, and powerfully given their marginalization outside the mental image of "Southerners" that exists to this day, more of the South's slaves had seen more of it, thanks to an internal commerce in human beings that trafficked more than one million African Americans from east to west in the antebellum period.) A typical white Southerner was not a planter, the archetypical glove-wearing, pistol-dueling, horse-backed cotton cavalier of manse and mythology. He was a strong-wristed yeoman who maintained a family farm *without* the benefit of slave labor. Shared connection was in these modest households, though – the intimate configurations, the patterns of everyday living, were largely the same and familiar in one homestead as in another, in one community as in another, replicated across the region's cornfields as well as its cotton fields. These configurations might often be ineffable, lived everyday without reflection, yet they were tied to a set of common assumptions and tactile habits sometimes conjured indefinitely as "a way of life."

The planter's columned porticoes are today still symbolic of it: but the ethics governing life in the South were spread far beyond the slaveholding classes, staked deeper into society than on the foundations of plantation estates. The Big House held many mansions – *all* white Southerners knew and felt the shaping force of slavery in their lives – because by law and custom, white men were possessed of the right to control the worlds, large or small, magnificent or modest, marked off at their doorsteps. He was connected, elbow-to-elbow with his neighbor, to a primal authority, a mastery of his family and hearth and threshold, and to the expectation that he would protect and defend that right. This they did do, often violently, at the cost of gouged eyes, cauliflowered ears, tattoo-purpling scars, or knife-maimed appendages, and they were protected by formal and informal community sanction when they did it. The right and its assertion *was* whiteness.

The Two Great Rebel Armies were heaped-together combinations of these households and these neighborhoods. At the most basic level of mobilization, the infantry company, men tended to be raised and enlisted together from their own immediate locales and brought forward into the armies. Both armies might themselves be strange, sense-shaking behemoths, but if so it was because they were the white South mammothly larger than most had ever seen it. And these were the men, as householders and fathers and husbands and sons, who fought in the Confederate army, this was the man turned soldier and elbow-to-elbow in the ranks, slaveholder or farmer, who believed or was expected to, as W. J. Cash once phrased it unforgettably, that "nothing living could cross him and get away with it." The Confederates fought a conventional war not because they had no other choices. They chose it ultimately because the other choices couldn't sustain all the social and cultural institutions and assumptions the Confederacy was created to conserve. To submit tamely or patiently to enemy occupation of their neighborhoods – for either a Fabian war or a guerrilla war required it – would have been a degradation that Southern white men, holding dominion over their households, maintaining mastery over their slaves, told themselves never to permit tamely without a blow. They might have slid impromptu into aggressive war, but aggressive war became one of those reticular connections by which the Confederacy legitimated itself among its own people. It, too, was a felt thing, proxy for the honor bound up in the imperative, lethal defense of family, household, neighborhood, and whiteness, the spokes radiating to and from slavery's hub.[5]

Soon they would celebrate it, because no other method promised to free the vital lifeblood and the sheer physicality of assertion necessary to give those institutions being as the nation, housed in the mansions of government, living in the movements of its armies. Slavery created the South. Nothing but war was capable of creating Confederates.

****

"Too cautious and weak under grave responsibility," "wanting in moral firmness," "likely to be timid and irresolute in action": such had been McClellan's evaluation of Lee when Lee assumed command opposite the Army of the Potomac in front of Richmond. They were delusional as deployed against Lee. Had McClellan been capable of honest self-scrutiny they might have been revelatory or even liberating. They seem in any case the words of a man screwing up his willpower to face a challenge too big for him. After the humbling downthrow of the Seven Days – a sledgehammering defeat that he called a "change of base," not a retreat – McClellan began another letter, this one by now predictable for its authorial misapprehensions. When Lincoln rode by boat in early July to visit the army at Harrison's Landing, sheltered forty kilometers southeast of Richmond on the James River, McClellan handed it to him.

The Harrison's Landing Letter was not correspondence: it was a conservative proclamation disguised as memorandum. "You have been fully informed, that the Rebel army is in our front, with the purpose of overwhelming us" – McClellan began it as the beaten man he was. And beaten on two fronts, for with the chance to end the War at Richmond gone, so also did revolutionary circumstances threaten to overwhelm the Union's conservative war. He continued: "This rebellion has assumed the character of war: as such it should be regarded; and it should be conducted upon the highest principles known to Christian civilization. It should not be a War looking to the subjugation of the people of any state in any event." In that category – subjugation – McClellan stacked every conceivable evil of radicalism by revolution. The grave danger to American liberty seemed not to be the resilience of the Confederacy but the measures taken to subdue it. We must not, McClellan lectured, war on civilians. We must not consider the execution of traitors or confiscate property. Most of all we must never, not for a moment, contemplate the "forcible abolition of slavery." This was the *true* way, the *true* system, the *true* constitutional and conservative policy – truth that superseded the merely correct and merely political. His approach was "pervaded by the influences of Christianity and freedom," and verifiable because "it would receive the support of almost all truly [that word again] loyal men, would deeply impress the rebel masses and all foreign nations, and it might be humbly hoped that it would commend itself to the favor of the Almighty."[6]

Lincoln read his general's manifesto and quietly, without comment, pocketed it. Most of it was a prospectus for a lost cause, and what weight its words held was in their accrual in the word-horde, heaped upon *cautious, timid, and irresolute*, that Lincoln was piling up against him. No sooner, in fact, had McClellan begun composing it than Lincoln appointed another general, John Pope, to gather up the piecemeal Union forces in northern Virginia and form them into a new army. McClellan rightly suspected the new force was meant to absorb and supplant his. That eventuality never quite came to pass because this was the army Lee shattered in late August at Second Bull Run. But Pope's appointment had signaled a clear change of circumstances and a different prospectus for Union victory. Pope allowed his men to poach food and firewood and much else considered "private property" from civilians. He prescribed exile for those in his lines who refused to take an oath of allegiance. He codified summary execution of guerrillas infesting northern Virginia. Not any guerrillas or civilian spies were actually shot, and thanks to Lee, who called Pope a "miscreant" who needed to be "suppressed," Pope's army didn't exist long enough to subjugate much of anything under the new syllabus of hard war. More to the point, however, was that Lincoln had allowed Pope's orders to stand.

Pope, unlike generals Frémont and Hunter before him, had not said anything directly about slavery. McClellan had said something, but the soundings in his letter, while masquerading as counsel, were not much different than what Lincoln had been hearing for months from his border-state constituency. It was on returning from Harrison's Landing that Lincoln met with border congressmen and again plead the cause for gradual, compensated emancipation. The question was not merely an abstract matter of emancipation, Lincoln told them, as he had begun to tell others. It was a question of *warfare*. Whether or not the government touched slavery directly, the War required harsher measures. The way of conservative war – the views of McClellan – could not save the Union. "This government," Lincoln wrote one correspondent, "cannot much longer play a game in which it stakes all, and its enemies stake nothing." Hard war was not a matter of retribution but of recognizing that conciliation and emancipation were stark and mutually exclusive alternatives leading to irreconcilable ends.

"I shall do nothing in malice," he wrote to another. "What I deal with is too vast for malicious dealing."[7]

Such was the frame of his plea to the border-state congressional delegation on July 12. Harsher means would inevitably waste slavery away, even where it was protected, whether or not undertaken in enmity. Better for the Union states of the border to let it go voluntarily and be compensated – better, in an odd medley of motive, for their self-interest to mesh with and grow into an intentional act, a generosity of spirit – than to meanly lose slavery by friction, by abrasion, by intractable circumstance but also by their own intractable narrowness of greed and fear. They must act, for the War would most certainly act on them. But Lincoln could not get them to do, or to see. As with McClellan, then, so the congressional contingent: no, never. Emancipation would radically alter society, they protested. It would lengthen the War by driving Unionist slaveholders into rebellion. No, never.

Of course, for slaves, and for African Americans in the north and other abolitionists, compensated emancipation was distinctly narrow-minded itself, *ungenerous*, and all the more because Lincoln paired it with colonization. Meeting with a delegation of free black leaders some time later, in August, Lincoln called slavery the "greatest wrong ever inflicted on any people." Great wrong that it also was, racism's virulence in America remained an intractable fact too vast to be dealt with otherwise than by removing free slaves and free blacks to other shores. "But for your race among us," he told them, "there could not be war." To Frederick Douglass this stance was "canting hypocrisy," which scapegoated the cause of the War – slavery – on the backs of black Americans who were slavery's victims. For massively different reasons, then, when word emerged of what Lincoln had said to the black delegation, Douglass and others denounced Lincoln's vision of emancipation just as the border-state conservatives had refused it a month earlier. Yet both conservatives and radicals had understood distinctly in their rejections that emancipation went far beyond forcing the Confederacy to risk something. It was potentially the whole shooting match, playing for keeps, a new game explicitly *on all sides*, risking everything.[8]

In one other matter did the different delegations meeting with Lincoln that summer share alike, and that was their mutual if partial ignorance. Lincoln had already made up his mind that the gravest danger to American liberty was the resilience of the Confederacy and the conservative war that prolonged its life. And while he had talked of emancipation as a possibility or even a probability, he had already all but decided upon a formal proclamation. "We must free the slaves, or be ourselves subdued," Lincoln said to two members of his cabinet during a carriage ride on July 13, mere hours after his meeting with border-state conservatives. A little more than a week after that, on July 22, he revealed to the full cabinet his intention to issue, *now*, an Emancipation Proclamation. Those gathered were divided on the merits, as was Northern opinion, but William Seward, the secretary of state, objected strenuously over timing. An immediate proclamation would appear desperate – it would sound across the land as "our last *shriek*," he said, "on the retreat." As long as it seemed that Lee was the master in Virginia, as long as Union democracy perceived the western war as a secondary, slogging progression by which momentum trickled in beads of sweat and blood, an Emancipation Proclamation would be greeted as the dregs squirting from the government's empty cause. Only a victory would give emancipation moral force and only a victory would give it legitimacy. It was taken almost as given that the victory would have to come in the east, against Lee.[9]

And so into Lincoln's pocket, alongside McClellan's Harrison's Landing Letter, had gone the Emancipation Proclamation. The pairing of pocketed proclamations proved fitting in more than one way, for McClellan had written something else that the border state congressmen also mentioned, and which shaped all vicissitudes, including colonization, in this the summer of debating hard war. "A declaration of radical views, especially upon slavery," McClellan had predicted, "will rapidly disintegrate our present Armies." Whatever the designs or ideals of the president, whatever the movement to harsher, revolutionary means, wherefore emancipation and colonization, this was perhaps an accurate assessment. And it helps explain something of Lincoln's motives as well as his tactics, even if it did not absolve him of words Douglass held against him for long years after the War and which still sting his legacy today. Lincoln may not have been any more persuaded about colonization's feasibility than the fiery critic who called it "charlatanism or the statesmanship of a backwoods lawyer." But as a policy alternative coupled with emancipation it cushioned public opinion for the coming shock of black freedom. Of all the facts memorable about his meeting with the delegation of African Americans in August, perhaps none is more revealing than the invited presence, and him soon scribbling and publishing, of a newspaper reporter.[10]

Lincoln still needed his armies. In point of fact he was just now embarked on a massive effort to enroll 300,000 additional men to serve for three years. Emancipation might bring dissolution in another form, then, that of his volunteers, who might huzzah for Union and die by tens of thousands for it yet might just throw down their weapons if repurposed as the Noble Martyrs of Abolition. Union soldiers had long since been a long way ahead of their leaders, in belief and in practice, on the matter of hard war – they were eager to lay aside the constraints of conciliation. But slavery: slavery was another thing entirely. Would they fight to liberate slaves? Would they fight to change, rather than preserve, the Union? For that was the ultimate revolutionary circumstance at work. Whatever the ambiguity of meaning in American liberty, the traditional definition had clearly accepted slavery and racism within it. Any move against slavery was to change the War and change the Union, no matter how emancipation might be framed or justified. Any move against slavery was a potentially devastating admission that the Union as it was, celebrated and gloried as it was, had proven too frail to be saved.

The logic flowed differently for Lincoln. The unwillingness to move against slavery stymied the nation, circumscribed its measures, diminished its might – diminished *it*. Realizing the nation's power was no simple matter of gathering force unto the cause. What would hold the armies together, after all – what would keep the volunteers in the ranks, as the embodiment and instrument of the gathered cause – would require an idea they sanctioned, or could be brought to, either fully or tacitly. Ending slavery was necessary to save the Union. Freeing the full measure of the Union was necessary to ending slavery. For Lincoln the proposition was self-evident: his pregnant utterance of July 13 – "We must free the slaves, or be ourselves subdued" – was a potent fusing of physical might unleashed and ingathering idealistic, metaphysical force. But just now it was a potential void of form and substance, precisely because McClellan's give-pause prediction about disintegration in the ranks suggested questions without answers.

Nor were these questions empty of irony as July became August, and August became early September. The torment of uncertainties, hanging about like a sopping summer curtain of thunderclouds, and the threat of outpouring martial dissolution, were here-and-now present in the wearied army Lincoln had given to John Pope in the confidence that he could give the country its transformative victory over Lee. It had been smashed instead on the old Bull Run battlefield in late August. Here it was sloughing back into Washington on the heels of its humiliation. Only one man was at hand who could keep the Army together, whip it back into shape, and get the volunteers in it to stand and fight. And he was McClellan.

Cautious, timid, wanting in moral firmness – if those words came before Lincoln as he pondered his command options they were on the points of Lee's bayonets, for Lee was, indeed, on the move. In long afteryears, history has taken on the hue of taunter's ink for McClellan, especially for these, his words that seem so worthy of ridicule. Lee had proven quite the very opposite. Yet some writers have misconstrued how and why: Lee took bold risks, so they say, because he knew well the cowering defensiveness of his various opposing generals, McClellan first among the feeble. There is something to that, but not everything. Reappointing McClellan to command was the only sensible option Lincoln could have chosen. And it was not his cowering defensiveness that Lee preyed upon, or at least not only timidity. Seeing something other than irresolution in McClellan, seeing in-between *something* and *everything* to reveal the logic of Lincoln's choice as well as the genius of Lee, requires a temporary removal from the momentous accelerating circumstances of the late summer of 1862. From the crows-eye is a view which reveals enriching perspectives of continuity.

On the one hand, from July of 1862, when Lincoln first superseded McClellan with Pope, until Gettysburg, the following July, a period concurrent with Lee's passion-fired first year in command, Lincoln sorted through three diffident McClellan replacements. Pope, of course, was the "miscreant" whom Lee tossed aside at Second Bull Run, and his bombastic imbecility was the immediate reason for

McClellan's return. Ambrose E. Burnside, who took command of the army when Lincoln sacked McClellan for good in the fall of 1862, nearly threw it away, in December, in a futile frontal assault at Fredericksburg. Lee's defensive position there, halfway between Washington and Richmond, was stronger than Burnside's moral courage *not* to attempt it. The attack cost Burnside more than 13,000 casualties but inflicted fewer than half as many on Lee. When Burnside overcompensated for that disaster in January, 1863, by directing an aborted winter maneuver abysmally typical of a sinking, sludge-mired war effort, Lincoln fired him, too. His replacement, Joseph Hooker, restored the army's luster and even startled Lee with an aggressive initial blow in the opening moves of the spring campaign four months later. Yet Hooker, too, was equivocation masked in braggadocio. At Chancellorsville, in May of 1863, in what became the hallmark of spectacularly inconceivable Confederate victories, Lee first paralyzed "Fighting Joe" by counter-punching furiously. He then divided his grossly outnumbered army directly in Hooker's stunned front and sent most of it with Stonewall Jackson on an all-day, twelve-mile march through thicket, forest, and bramble. When they emerged in the evening on Hooker's exposed flank like demon-fairies of the darkening woodlands, they surprised Hooker's legions and wrecked them.

Union generalship in the east left something to be desired, surely, though kneejerk reactions and firings were also the hothouse fruit of Washington's close-range glare, and inseparable from the palpitating crisis-sense of public opinion. So, *something*. Lee could and did prey on weaker opponents who lacked in nerve what they disguised in vanity. But not *everything*. The clarity of a crows-eye perspective seems even more revealing in what it exposes in Lee: a pattern of brilliant audacity, and a style that was authentic – defining – regardless of opponent. War fed Lee adrenaline, and its anticipations, which might very well have risen in him kinesthetically as he felt for his opponent's timidity, made him vital. Fredericksburg, for instance, was a beautiful foolishness that he tasted with relish. As he peered over the field, Lee remarked that "it is well that war is so terrible – we should grow too fond of it!" He did not wait or rely upon his opponent's mistakes so much as he stirred to create the conditions that led to them. His daring, almost reckless gambles north of the Potomac in the fall of 1862 were especially brazen, and as distant from McClellan's profile of an irresolute, wavering master of ambivalence as perhaps it was possible to be.[11]

The sources of Lee's aggression were several – but a sly one slips in the finesse of some puzzling words about McClellan attributed to him after the War. These must be handled carefully but they are worth considering. Strangely, almost credulously, maybe laughably or even apocryphally, Lee was supposed to have claimed that McClellan was the ablest "by all odds" of the Union generals to face him. Quite clearly, McClellan was *not* Lee's best opponent. Lee's remarks might hint at the guile or deception of the authors who originally reported them, but something in them is suggestive of the guile and self-deception that spare few human beings (in McClellan, at least, they were surface qualities), and something in them is suggestive of something true in Lee. They might be interpreted, for instance, as the tactic of a shrewd Fabius operating in the fog of the postwar. By the time of Lee's supposed assessment, after all, the fighting was ended. McClellan had been discredited, and McClellan's approach to Union victory had been systematically demolished. Like most white Southerners after defeat, Lee feared that a hard peace might have been aroused and legitimated by a hard war. "Radical reconstruction" might include any or all of hangings, confiscations, and – the sum of horrors – the empowerment and equality of their former slaves. McClellan's reputation might have been beclouded in the North, but for humiliated white Southerners aghast in loss, he remained a vivid face of still-strong Northern conservatism. Withal he remained prominent in the Democratic Party, by which vehicle a conservative, conciliatory peace in Reconstruction might yet come. Lee, in short, might have been patronizing.[12]

But to hear only begrudging rationalization or shrewd diplomacy in Lee's supposed postwar rumination is to possess only a cynic's ears. McClellan was a civilized general – Lee had conveyed that loaded compliment in other contexts at least. Yet maybe more subtly, the compliment was not really about McClellan or really a compliment. Instead it seems an awkward revelation of the primal source of Lee's soul-genius. McClellan liberated Lee to fight the very war his being animated within him. He allowed

Lee to act with all of his imaginative power unleashed. Lee could sense not just *creation* but legitimacy through McClellan. For even though McClellan cowered behind a messianic persona inflected by profound self-doubt, he was no blunderer and no bumbler. What Lincoln (and others, then and since) had called over-caution, of a persuasion shaped by the avoidance of mistakes, was also, in other shades and lights, the enviable precision of military art: to avoid mistakes was also the highest form of classicism. Lee's regard of him was not self-deceiving so much as it might have been self-aware, for Lee, too, was a classicist, and a good one, when necessity forced him into a similar posture late in the War. But in the summer of 1862, and for some time after, Lee imagined himself against the foil of the classical form. His creator's vision of what might be newly possible was released against the rules and structural forms governing his opponent's choices, with his instinct for boldness liberated yet honed against his enemy's strategic discipline and precision.

Not in Pope, and not later in Burnside, not later in Hooker, were medians of ability and temperament combined as they were combined in McClellan. That is not to say McClellan possessed daring or was steeled to hard-driving relentlessness. It is to say, suggestively, that while possibly Lee was no less capable of casuistry and self-deception than was McClellan, he *needed* McClellan because McClellan's mastery of classicism accentuated the purity of his art. McClellan was good enough to punish Lee for the risks that so vitally were the passion of his form and style, if those risks became mistakes. What genius could possibly be reckoned to those who fattened reputations on the imbecility of others? What risk was there to animate, to tantalize, when outcome was assured because banal, inanimate fatuity was assured? And it is also to say a second thing, in descent from the perspective of crow's flight to the matters as they were on the ground, in the late summer of 1862: that with Lee's dangerous host entering Maryland, Lincoln needed McClellan badly, too.

The rebel horde that crossed the Potomac River without impressing its curious spectator at Frederick was something less than itself, whatever its menacing notoriety. Thousands of them fell out of the ranks long before Lee crossed them, unable because ill-clad, ill-fed, or ill-rested, or, in the case of scores of them who believed defending home meant remaining home, unwilling. Lee pushed them onward anyway, though probably he tallied only 55,000 effectives. At Frederick he divided even these into three wings – the second bold risk of the campaign, if an offensive on enemy ground with half an army is considered the first one – and prepared to continue into Pennsylvania. Operational plans were confided in a document numbered Special Orders 191, copies made and distributed, and the ghosting gray cavalcade was off again, on the move again, soon after. Meanwhile McClellan had done what McClellan was recalled to do, some said with bestirring energy. He reorganized the battered-up Union forces, rekindled suppressed spirits, and turned them right back around to go after Lee. The Army of the Potomac arrived at Frederick town just three days after Lee left it. And there, tossed among the dizzying litter and hoof-and-foot debris of the abandoned Confederate campsites, wrapped around three (as yet unsmoked) cigars, was a paper – "with which," as McClellan gleed when it was authenticated, "if I cannot whip Bobbie Lee, I will be willing to go home." It was a copy of Special Orders 191.

The so-called Lost Order was an unlooked-for surprise, and in later years it kept a busy afterlife to appear as the avatar of fate and chance in novels, as the black swan or flapping butterfly in history books, or more muscularly as the bony club of contention among recriminating Confederates in their memoirs. In the immediate present it was the proximate fact that led to battle. Lee knew of its loss, and knew of McClellan's good fortune, within hours. Incredibly, he refused to retreat (the third bold risk) but chose instead to reconstitute his divided wings near a village called Sharpsburg. There he brazenly ensconced himself with the Potomac at his back (the fourth: if McClellan broke his lines, there was nowhere to go). Lee could not be the aggressor but he seemed determined to be the instigator: he virtually dared McClellan to attack him, and on September 17, McClellan did. From dawn to dusk, the armies punished one another on a landscape of rural America so placidly ordinary that its simplicity of place has become evocative, even iconic, of the blood shed there: the West Woods, Dunker Church, the Cornfield, Bloody Lane, Burnside's Bridge. Corpses lay harvested in the Cornfield, which changed scything hands some thirteen times, and piles were stacked in Bloody Lane,

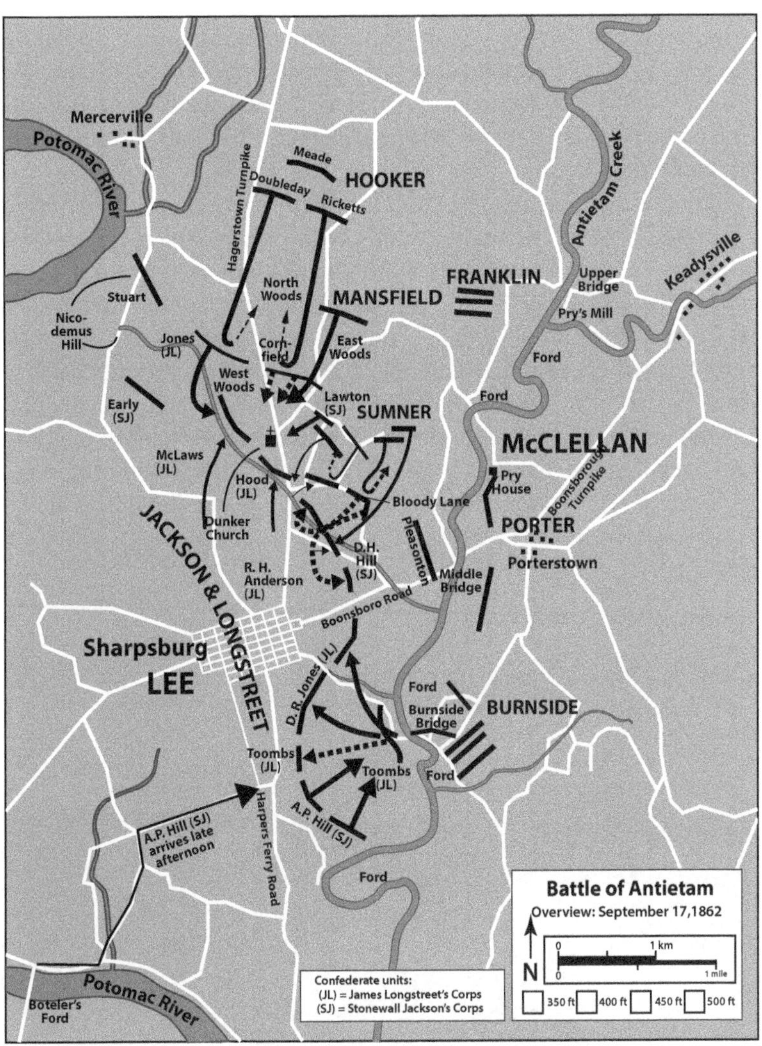

Map 6: The Battle of Antietam, September 17, 1862.

which in actual purpose was a farmer's shortcut between market roads so that the locals could avoid the tolls. McClellan's pressure was cautious and disjointed throughout the day but effectively constant. By dusk he had driven Lee to the wall. Only the climactic arrival of the last remnant of Lee's reconcentrating army, on the jog, and by happenstance at the one point of the battlefield where McClellan threatened to wreck Lee's flank and roll his army backwards into the Potomac, saved the Confederates from probable destruction.

The battle of Antietam – so-called for the battlefield creek that separated foes – remains the single bloodiest in American history. Almost 23,000 Americans, about 12,500 of them Union, and more than 10,300 of them Confederate, were killed or wounded or were otherwise missing. The grueling calculus of that arithmetic transformed every single battlefield from the Revolution, the War of 1812, and the Mexican War into one vast American cemetery, for more men were strewn on the farmland near Sharpsburg than had been laid low in all of the country's previous wars put together. Unimaginably, the next day, Lee did not budge but dared McClellan

Figure 17: Bodies on the battlefield at Antietam, by Alexander Gardner, 1862, Public Domain.

to attack him again. Yet McClellan had had enough. He might, in fact, have ended things the day before even with the timely appearance of Lee's last reinforcements – he withheld 25,000 fresh men. He was going to use them. He almost used them. He nearly put them in at the end. But as he was about to order it, or so we're told, he was reminded to avoid mistakes. "Remember, General," said the leader of that reserve to McClellan, "I command the last reserve of the last army of the Republic."[13]

****

These were not the last men of the last Army of the Republic, or in fact of either republic, as another year would show, and another year after that, too. But what they were fighting for, and what they were dying for, was a purpose in constant flux. In the balance of preservation and creation the foes were alike. So, too, were enemies alike in their embrace of improvisation. The continuous act of adjustment was as awkward and halting and experimental north of the Potomac as it was southward. Our case is new, Lincoln would say at the end of 1862 – but he had said it essentially to those border Unionists who would not or could not think newly about slavery, emancipation, and possibility. He completed the point by adding "we must think anew, and act anew." And so he did. Five days after the victory at Antietam, hardly decisive, but good enough to avoid the whiff of desperation that Seward counseled him to avoid in July, Lincoln issued a preliminary Emancipation Proclamation. As revolutionary as such an act portended to be, its issuance in preliminary form was the ballast of preservation. Lincoln allowed Confederates one hundred days of grace to lay down their arms before emancipation was effective. If they surrendered the Union would be at peace, at one, with slavery intact.[14]

And if they did not – surely the prohibitively likely outcome – slaves in *areas still in rebellion* would be *declared* free. That was hardly emancipation, since by definition areas in rebellion were areas where slaves were slaves. Emancipation would come by military fiat, on paper, through Lincoln's power as commander-in-chief of the nation's armed forces. Its authority in the near term was strictly moral and symbolic, underscored because its enactive day was not lost on anyone. When January 1, 1863 dawned one hundred days later, either the War would be over and the Union preserved mostly as it was or the War would become a promise toward something new, a new idea, and something of a second American Revolution. For it would no longer be a war to preserve and conserve, but a war for an Idea. What had been an abstraction – the Union as liberty – would become reified in the cause of Union arms. Or mostly so.

There was one element not strictly symbolic, one thing with fangs, one thing that was hard war's answer to the feared dissolution of Union armies if black liberation was made an equal aim of the fighting. The Emancipation Proclamation legalized and formalized the enlistment of black soldiers into the Union armies. These would be drawn either from the North's smallish population of free blacks or from the much larger and always growing population of runaway slaves who previously had been designated "contraband." Such a new concentration of power would burn and dynamically feed on its after-burn by the very linkage of Union and emancipation, because it would constantly gather unto itself the slaves freed under the advance of Union arms. No one doubted the radicalism of the provision, or the real fact of it, least of all Confederates who immediately accused Lincoln of fomenting atrocity and massive slave rebellion. In time, the black soldiery became the revolutionary lever of emancipation. In time, too, Confederates would prove to be the fomenters of the atrocities they feared. Both in fact and in aspiration, from January 1, onward, Union armies would be armies of liberation.

Such was the crux of Lincoln's trouble with conservative and especially Democratic politicians, who had feared new meant radical. It was the crux of the trouble with many of his generals. Now came a series of strokes by which Lincoln sought to reconcile the instrument of victory to his vision of it. McClellan he had sacked once already – at a time when the president was committed to emancipation but before he was ready to be committed publicly. Now he sacked McClellan again. The Young Napoleon had failed to do anything in the aftermath of Antietam except complain: to his boss, about fatigued and sore-tongued horses, and, to his wife, about his boss. To Mrs. McClellan the general portrayed himself immodestly. "Those in whose judgment I rely," he wrote, "tell me that I fought [Antietam] splendidly and that it was a masterpiece of

Figure 18: Black soldiers (1863–1865), Public Domain.

art." An underappreciating Lincoln thought of metaphorical tools other than a painter's brush. He was tired, he told an associate, of boring into McClellan's deep-grained pat "with an augur too dull to take hold." Shrewdly, Lincoln waited until the conclusion of 1862's Congressional elections to send McClellan home, and thither McClellan went, but not permanently. The elections had revealed deep fissures on the Northern home front, especially over the progress of the War and its new linkage to emancipation, if indeed they were not a rebuke to Republicans. The polls were perhaps portent. When the national election cycle next turned, in two years' time for the presidency, it was McClellan, the champion of conservation and preservation, who would be sent forth as Lincoln's Democratic challenger.

Nevertheless, off he went to New Jersey, and he was not alone in going home. Buell might have "won" at Perryville but had done so as McClellan had "won" at Antietam. He was fired two weeks after the battle for the sluggish, McClellanesque way he had failed to follow Bragg's retreat into Tennessee. Lincoln replaced him with William S. Rosecrans, on whom, as the fall of 1862 closed on winter, the jury of public urgency remained in deliberations. On the one hand was Rosecrans's own case of the slows – he met telegrams goading him to action and threatening his firing with headstrong, bluff-calling replies. On the other was his important victory over Bragg's army at the Battle of Stones River, just outside Nashville, which opened on December 31, 1862, paused solemnly to observe New Year's Day, and concluded in blast and bombast on January 2, 1863. Maybe Rosecrans was no McClellan and no Buell after all. He had won Stones River and acted there with a resolute coolness that proved his insensibility to more than the paper threats dispatched from Washington. (The details are graphic: his chief of staff, riding alongside Rosecrans in a particularly ghoulish part of the battlefield, was decapitated by a cannonball. Sopped in blood and brains, Rosecrans rode on, unperturbed.) It was true that no one confused Stones River for a masterwork. But coming as it did just two weeks after Burnside's imbecile loss at Fredericksburg in the east, it saved more than Rosecrans his job. "I can never forget, whilst I remember anything," Lincoln wrote to him, that "you gave us a hard-earned victory, which had there been a defeat instead, the nation could hardly have lived over."[15]

What that nation was, and whether there was one, was precisely in the pit of Lincoln's urgency. What opened in the fall with the preliminary issuance of the Emancipation Proclamation and the twin firings of McClellan and Buell was not in anywise a new moment of inaugural promise. Instead it begat another long season of beleaguered malaise and fear as Lincoln's Union felt its way toward and into the relentless unforeseen, into the shifts of war. A harder, more aggressive war, augured by the firings of conservative generals, was one area in which there might be enough consensus and even, if the attitudes of Union soldiers are any guide, a boots-on-the-ground demand. But a harder war to preserve the Union and destroy slavery – which everyone understood would *remake* the Union, whatever became of the black men and women who had been slaves in it – was another matter.

Against this, Lincoln's impatience in the spring and summer of 1862 appeared to be so much anxious fidgeting. Morale drifted with the autumn leaves, and by winter the Union cause and the spirit sustaining it seemed bare and bereft, aged like boughs shaking against the cold. In the east, of course, only more dullness and stiff-necked ineptitude in the Army of the Potomac followed McClellan's removal. In the west, Stones River was the bloodiest battle of the War by ratio of numbers engaged, even excepting the brains of Rosecrans's chief of staff. Still, even at this hindsight distance, it is possible to detect in the tone of Lincoln's missive to Rosecrans – in fact the tone is hard to miss – that the joy of victory consisted in relief that it was not defeat. If a victory it was, it hardly seems to have felt like one.

On felt things, indeed, did public opinion move; on felt things did democratic war efforts depend. Lincoln himself seems to have been feeling his way toward something, boring, as it were, toward an idea yet to take hold. When the president sought to render the Union and its cause from abstraction to reality, he typically chose tactile nouns, such as *country* or *government*, which seemed earthy, physical, substantive, material: *things* to be preserved. Yet he had said to Rosecrans something else. "The nation," he had written, could not have lived beyond another defeat. Whether that is true is impossible to know. What can't be gainsaid is Lincoln's jittery, edgy sense of the country's discontent. *Nation* had not been kept too fain in his word-horde. It was metaphysical – fluid, dynamic, more than a country, more than its people, more than a government, more than those living in it but also those dead and yet to be born in it, yet somehow the sum of all of them, the spirit of all of them, the idea connecting all of them: the mystic chord he had summoned to close his inaugural address, elusively immaterial because it could be touched only by the "better angels of our nature." What Rosecrans had preserved, rather oddly, was perhaps less the Union than the chance of thinking and acting in new life. On felt things and things felt in common did nations emerge and endure.

5

BLOODFIELD: 1863

Magnificent failure was not an ambition nurtured by either cause in *chronos*, in what the ancient Greeks called chronological, sequential time. When events augured misfortune, as they so often did during the American Civil War, the jumbled, jammed together exigencies of the present occasioned grievance and gut-churning uncertainty – it was *chronos* lashing both sides with the vile possibility of losing. But the ancients had comprehended time in a second register. As *kairos*, time existed independently of the lattice of events: it was not measured or counted, but felt; not separated and sequenced, but whole. One sensed *kairos* like the weather, neither as subject to it nor as master of it, so much as being in it continuously, immeasurably. For the Gospel writers it was the vastness of God's time and God's moment. In *kairos* were past and present and future diminished as discrete elements and intensified by unbroken integration, and by awesome, profound blue-sky continuity. Thus it was with Freud, who experienced time as distance and nearness at the Acropolis, or Montaigne, who apperceived time as separation and unity in Paris, or when famously Gibbon, sitting among the ruins and suddenly overcome by awe of the ancient, felt time suddenly come near and depart again in the vesper light. There he saw the decline and fall of Rome.

Just so could magnificent failure *in* time – so odiously haltered to unpredictable events – be transfigured *over* time. *Kairos* is where the sense of the epic works, where the mythic works, and where the sacred works. Unavoidably but sometimes unfortunately, it is also where the duality of history works. The past is dead but among us. Many an unsentimental particularist of the American Civil War has walked the Antietam or Shiloh battlefields and *felt* what happened there, as Gibbon did Rome. Many a Southern writer confronting Faulkner's imperative to tell about the South found its maw somehow, someway, in the War – a past that wasn't dead, as Faulkner had it in *Requiem for a Nun,* but not even past. To this day there remain those Southerners for whom it hasn't happened yet, for whom "it's all now," because "yesterday won't be over until tomorrow and tomorrow began ten thousand years ago."[1]

It was the past, yes. But *it* was particularly transcendence in the moment that remains in memory the watershed of the American Civil War: Pickett's Charge. For white Southerners of the War era and beyond, the risk-almost-everything attack that Lee launched disastrously at Gettysburg, on the afternoon of July 3, 1863, became the War's seminal event. Something called "the South" was created in the devastation of its failure, and in the story white Southerners came to tell of and for themselves about it. Over time the tales of defeat at Gettysburg became substitutionary for their account of defeat in the War, and over time their defeat in the War passed into a kind of creation mythology known as the Lost Cause. By it was defeat in the War transmuted into a sublime, redeeming triumph. Through it, *the South's* cultural nationalism became proxy for *Confederate* nationhood. Southerners of the Lost Cause came to tell and believe that the Confederacy was doomed from the beginning and that they knew it was, just as Pickett's Charge was hopeless and they knew it was, and so came to believe that they had not fought for any worldly interest or anything material. Their cause was in higher ideals – virtue, courage, honor, duty – vindicated precisely because they were doomed and yet fought anyway. The myth made the white Southerners who survived the stillbirth of their sovereign political entity into a people. And at Gettysburg had their fathers gathered, primogenitors all, arrayed in lines of gray and butternut in the rippling summer afternoon of July 3, a host under the heat-swelled banners of the cause, the heroic, the sacred, and the transcendent in *its* moment, gathered to make and be made.

Gettysburg created a people of defeat. Gettysburg created also a people of victory. The mythopoeia of the Union's triumph was not in the repulse of the Confederate charge, which though dramatic was hardly Thermopylae, but as the founding ground of a "new birth of freedom" in Lincoln's Gettysburg Address. On November 19, 1863 – the weather had changed countenances since the sulfurous summer boil and returned as the bracing late autumn, cold and chill but clear – Lincoln journeyed to the battlefield to deliver a "few appropriate remarks" at the dedication of its national cemetery. The day kept all elements of the epic-heroic. For more than two hours prior to Lincoln's elegy, one of the great orators of the era, Edward Everett, held forth after the fashion of the nineteenth century's Greek revival. His eulogy of the Union dead sought to capture in the after-stillness of Gettysburg the distance and nearness of Marathon. (Homer, greatest of bards, had asked a goddess muse to sing the rage of Achilles, of the murderous, merciless hurling down of souls to the underworld and bodies to the carrion-field for feasting dogs and gorging birds. Everett asked more humbly of his 15,000 auditors to lend him indulgence and sympathy.) Lincoln's effort extracted long hours of preparation but was spoken in a matter of minutes. Some missed it entirely.

Lincoln's attempt was to bind the war dead to affinity with every living heart and hearthstone, and to devote the living to the "unfinished work" of saving the Union so that "government of the people, by the people, and for the people shall not perish from the earth." The Union was itself, in those same remarks, rededicated to a "new birth of freedom" in the promise of emancipation. To dedicate was not merely a matter of establishing this newly conceived nation in *chronos* time. It was to fix its rebirth in *kairos*, as both the enduring promise of the founding fathers, in the living force of the Declaration of Independence four score and seven years before, as the legacy endowed at Gettysburg for generations of Americans yet unborn. Lincoln had first touched those themes in his 1861 inaugural address. He vainly hoped then to swell a chorus of Union, conservation, preservation, and peace. At Gettysburg the mystic chords of memory were translated anew, the great war and its epic battlefield elevated, its patriot graves hallowed and now fully dedicated to a Union transformed in the "proposition that all men are created equal."[2]

In large measure, maybe the last and fullest measure, that mythos has become America's transcendent story of its victory, and Gettysburg a people's ancient capital. The thunderous contemporary exaltations accompanying victory should not be gainsaid. After two years of failures in the War's vital eastern theater, Gettysburg was the Union's first undisputed, untarnished major triumph. But too much can be made of it, and too much has. In the narrowest of military senses, Gettysburg did not yield richer bounty than the stunning capture of Vicksburg, on the Mississippi River, by the once-reviled, suddenly revealed Ulysses S. Grant, which occurred simultaneously (some said poetically) on the 4th of July. Gettysburg did not mean more than the reversal – this time proving final – of Confederate fortunes in the Tennessee country: again under the direction of Grant, a man in advent, coming on horseback. It may not have meant more than the sheer slow trauma of one nation increasingly applying its impersonal industrial and financial might to destroy the resources and asphyxiate the will of the other. All the same, these are rearview judgments only clearer by hindsight. For contemporaries with no way to know they were only half the way through, all remained to be seen. As always for them was the ill-shaped, unwieldy, combustibly, and chronically volatile *now*.

Even after Gettysburg, long after Vicksburg, events retained a radical contingency, and they continued to move with intrusive, in-breaking power, their impacts more cutting than layering, and jagged with a force sheer to interrupt. No one knew displacement better than the residents of Vicksburg, who hovelled like rats under town in hillside caves when Grant's siege guns opened daily. No one knew disruption better than slaves, whose resistance became more assertive in symbiotic connection to its momentum, or disaffected murderous rioters in New York City, or fearsome guerrillas and marauders and deserters from Missouri to Mississippi to Maryland, or radically dissident politicians north and south, or the women who mobbed for bread in Richmond, or Confederate soldiers so enraged by the sight of black men with guns in the Union army that massacre was honor and retribution. War was cruelty unrefined, as William Tecumseh Sherman said it was. He did not say war is hell, as if hell were a gated realm one could visit and return – but said war is all hell, out of bounds. Its visitations went everywhere.

Home was at war and war was at home. None knew more of it than the residents of Gettysburg. When the battle was over the armies simply left it: distended corpses of humans and blackened feet and hands and heads and trunks of humans, rotting horseflesh and broken mulebone and the bowels and brains and shattered teeth of horseflesh and manflesh, cratered-out farms furrowed by fuse and shot hollowed by shell and shovel, smashed orchards, broken boulders clefted into rock-shards, woodspikes snapped from shattered fences and trees and wagons, ash and cinder, bootsole and sack, campgrounds hallowed in the urine and dung of the tens of thousands, the staggering reek of offal, the discomposing carrion-stench of the dead. They left all of it. Even in November many of those patriot graves Lincoln attempted to dedicate to a new birth of freedom were undug – the dead still lying, quite literally, among the living.

After a fashion, the detritus of war is still here, for the War in *kairos* time is also messy. Lincoln had said, compellingly, that it was all unfinished work, the nation's founding ideal a *proposition* always living, always fragile and contingent, because always proffered for assent or dissent. If Gettysburg created two

Figure 19: The dead at Gettysburg, by Timothy H. O'Sullivan, 1863, Public Domain.

peoples – a people of victory, a people of defeat – it became the seminal moment of American consciousness because it occurred as the battle of one war only to spawn a second, succeeding war between *nations* of Defeat and Victory. That war does not always seem with us. But it is of us. Their peoples are no longer affiliated necessarily by regions of north or south or even east or west, and they are no longer contestants on the battlefields of *chronos* time. Yet they remain grappled in conflict in other spaces where the outcome is still very much in the balance, and yesterday won't be over until tomorrow. It was neither Lincoln nor Gibbon nor Faulkner nor Montaigne who captured that proposition's displacement first or best, though all knew something of war, but Joyce, who knew something too. He saw clean in the slop the first relics and ruins and monuments – what to do with it all? – and rendered redolently as *bluddle filth* in *Finnegans Wake* what he put plainly in his conversation: There is no word for it. A battlefield was temporary. Its aftermath was scree and turmoil. "When the battle is over and the field is covered in blood, it is no longer a battlefield," he said, "but a bloodfield."[3]

****

To read U. S. Grant's *Memoirs* is to encounter a man supremely unconcerned with the metaphysics of war. They are today regarded as among the War era's best writings (the bar is low; but in Lincoln, Whitman, and, yes, Grant, quality is classically high – the memoirs were published by Mark Twain). His style is declarative, earthbound, and frontal. He regarded the Mexican War "as one of the most unjust ever waged by a stronger against a weaker nation." He rated Robert E. Lee highly but not supremely and thought his cause "one of the worst for which a people ever fought, and one for which there was the least excuse." He regarded himself, in hindsight the colonel commanding in battle for the first time in 1861, as both different and the same as the man writing in remembrance almost twenty-five years later. Grant took his men up a hill expecting to face Confederates on the other side, his heart climbing as he climbed and pumping "higher and higher" until "it was in my throat." At the crest, it fell – "my heart resumed its place" – for the enemy had scampered off and was gone. "It occurred to me at once that [he] had been as much afraid of me as I had been of him," he wrote. Grant forgot neither the pounding anxiety of inexperience nor the lesson the experience taught.[4]

Grant's pragmatism lacked Lincoln's searching, transcendent wisdom. He was a man who looked to apply lessons and not to teach them. But like Lincoln he was a discriminating reader and no simpleton. The augur, dull as it might sound, was like Lincoln's an apt metaphorical tool for his approach to problems. He bored at intractabilities as a way of experimenting with them – much like emancipation in Lincoln's case – and minded neither ridicule nor the failure of means if the ends were worthy and intact. Grant was also one of the combat figures who survived Lincoln's great conservative purging of the fall of 1862. This was perhaps because Lincoln sensed something about their affinity. The haranguing hue and cry over Grant's seeming bluntness of compassion and martial imagination had followed Grant and harassed Lincoln ever since Shiloh. How much skill was required to toss meat into a mincer? Yet Grant's prowess was not merely in putting his men in position to fight. Ultimately, it was in *desiring* them there, and of risking mistakes rather than avoiding them. Lincoln grasped this about his general at the handle.

The simplicity in Lincoln's sentiment obscures a creative vitality in Grant's impulse. To privilege and envision what might become in the use of the instrument of prowess – that was a form of imagination beyond the vision of many of his Union peers, a profundity in the prosaics of *making* war as he went about it. In the conservative mode, ends and means were integrally connected. For the ends to be legitimate the means must be also. Grant instead fixed on objective, on ends, not means, and sought a way there even if it meant taking many paths.

Still, by early 1863 it appeared that *earthbound* applied to Grant not as a quality or a character trait, but as a series of problems, all literal, that might just bury him. By the late summer of 1862, while McClellan chased Lee in Maryland and Buell lumbered after Bragg in Kentucky, Grant had been restored to field command near Corinth, Mississippi. Halleck had been summoned east to succeed McClellan as general-in-chief of all the Union armies, there to antagonize his subordinates from afar. Grant could not do much at all for most of the fall other than occupy space – the territory under his command was too vast for the 50,000 men under him to assume an offensive posture. So occupy space Grant did, avoiding actions of substance other than inciting an unnecessary controversy in December by expelling Jews from his lines. It says something about Grant's obsessive need to fiddle with problems that he lost his balance when he didn't have one to obsess him – as in this rather oddly spiteful act, which in any event Lincoln overturned. His episodes with the whiskey glass were more immediately consequential. According to those making the claims, his boozings were epic benders, and they occurred not just when Grant was lonely, but when he was bored and when nothing else seemed to be tempting his curiosity save tinkering with the state of his consciousness.

What he waited for, in a sense, was for the War to catch up, and for various elements of affinity to meet and join together in a combination that would restore a kind of fortune for the offensive. Soon they did. The massively bloody battles of 1862 no longer seemed outliers against Shiloh, and the old guard did not seem capable of aggressive generalship. Halleck even played an unintentional part by proving unable to do much in Washington other than reveal himself extraordinarily capable of rubbing people the wrong way. Competent with standard labors of administration, he kept the armies supplied and informed, but he could not get the generals commanding them to operate with a view larger than their own bailiwicks. Lincoln's eventual disappointed but cutting estimation foretold the remarks of one German in the next century who deemed his general-in-chief "scarcely any longer even a postman": Halleck was not much of a grand strategist but was indeed "a first-rate clerk." All those elements moved toward a synergy in Grant's favor. What brought them together, finally, was the vitally real and apparent linking of tools and instruments. By the late fall of 1862, Lincoln was experimenting toward emancipation as a means to end the War, while Grant began nubbing toward a prize that perhaps more than any other, *both* by the means and the ends of its capture, made emancipation real: Vicksburg, Mississippi.[5]

Vicksburg was a military problem on the order of emancipation's political and social one. Crowned high on the bluffs overlooking the Mississippi River, about halfway between Memphis and New Orleans, the town was the inland emporium of the state's Delta

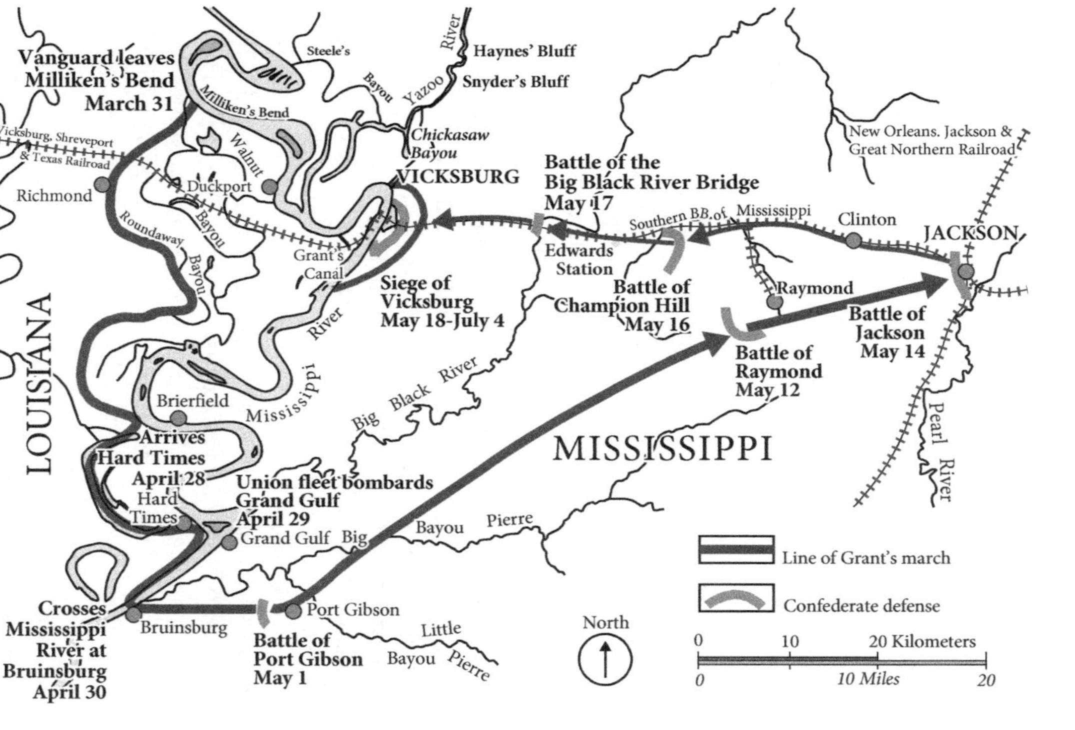

Map 7: The Vicksburg Campaign, 1863.

region. A generation earlier, in 1835, Vicksburg's civic fathers had rather infamously lynched a pack of rogues and vagabonds whom the locals suspected of fomenting disquiet among their slaves. These days one could hardly have said much to distinguish Vicksburg from the grog-shopped, dust-filled, pot-holed, hog-strewn streets of mercantile America. Its service was to the steamboat traffic plying up and down the river and to the local planters and merchants who traded in cotton and grocery and household goods. (Two of these were Jefferson Davis and his brother Joseph, whose antebellum plantation was south of the town.) And yet by early 1863 Vicksburg had become the hinge of national and territorial integrity to both sides. New Orleans was already in Union hands. So was Memphis. But between New Orleans and Memphis, a stretch of more than 300 nautical miles, it was as if Confederates had thrown up mighty locks to either side and walled off the waters.

As long as Vicksburg remained in Confederate control, the Union was kept from using the Mississippi below Memphis, or from using it above New Orleans. Between those choke points Confederates retained the unmolested ability to move back and forth from the states of the trans-Mississippi Confederacy. Soldiers and internal supplies passed over the river and back as if on dry land, but so did the Confederacy's cotton and European trade, which increasingly was circuited around an ever-tightening Atlantic blockade via Mexico and Texas. The moving chattels included thousands of slaves whom jittery planters on the eastern side of the river wanted crossed over, in safety, to the west. Two years had elapsed since Winfield Scott proposed squeezing the Confederacy to death by slow constriction, by securing vital arteries and holding them vitally, with the Mississippi as a principal necessity. He had been jeered and ignored then for the supposed banalities of his Anaconda Plan. Though not fitted precisely to Scott's grand idea, which sought to avoid hard war, Vicksburg's military importance was precisely Anacondian.

The material, logistical considerations nevertheless have a fusty quality about them. Something more elemental about the whole thing remained intangible but *felt*. At Vicksburg, rather starkly, and requiring no great imagination then or now to grasp, was the aspirational Confederacy halved together. At Vicksburg also were the aspirational halves of the continental Union winched into separation. That point should not be passed over: a prosaic understanding would miss the Mississippi River coursing indomitably in the imagination of nineteenth-century America as both the real and visionary power of the future United States. From Jefferson, who purchased the Louisiana territory in 1803 as the bequest of his Declaration of Independence, to William Tecumseh Sherman, who viewed the Mississippi as the fundament of everlasting American progress and harmony, to Mark Twain, who rendered through it the masterpiece of a people's literature in *The Adventures of Huckleberry Finn*, the river was the running pulsing coronary lifeblood of American character. It was liberty, freedom, emancipation, whatever those might be given to mean, now or in the future, as when the great Delta bluesmen of the early twentieth century, forefathers of American and British rock music, sang of rambling, and of being steady rolling men. Without the Mississippi the nation could not live. As long as it was choked, and Vicksburg Confederate, the Father of Waters lapped up in the middle of North America as its big muddy sea.

On a map, taking Vicksburg might seem simple enough, but the water and dirt on the ground defied simplicity. The high river bluffs made futile any direct naval bombardment such as had blown up Memphis and New Orleans or Fort Henry. Plunging fire from Vicksburg's guns threatened to smash any flotilla out of the water. Attacking landward was no easier, which Grant discovered the first time he had a go at it in the late fall of 1862. The marshy low ground north of the town, along with strong high-ground Confederate positions, brought a river-borne expedition under Sherman to grief at Chickasaw Bluffs on December 29. Grant's supporting force, moving overland along the Mississippi Central railroad, was harassed mercilessly by Confederate cavalry and local partisans and guerrillas snapping at his lengthening communications. They soon destroyed his base of supplies. Without safe means of provender – in previous campaigns he had been able to use the surety of supplying himself by river – Grant turned around and marched right back, headed for Memphis.

What, then, might *work*? In the winter and early spring of 1863, while in the east Lincoln was asking the same question about his high command and niggling along from one failed general to another – first McClellan, then Burnside at Fredericksburg, then Hooker

Figure 20: Ulysses Simpson Grant, by Edgar Guy Fawx, 1864, Public Domain.

at Chancellorsville – Grant began to putter. He tried anything, from the merely risky to the ridiculous to the preposterous. He literally *tried* boring, though with tools larger than augurs. He moved flotillas inland on the Mississippi side, above Vicksburg, along the Yazoo River or the mossed-up, murky bayous and creeks deep enough (or so the engineers said) to float them. He thought of displacing the water of the Mississippi into the shallower inland lakes and bayous of Louisiana, flooding the latter and permitting gunboats to get below Vicksburg in safety, and thereby freeing him to attack from the south. And then there was the aforementioned boring: digging a canal across a bend in the Mississippi opposite Vicksburg, which theoretically would allow him to ship and land his army below Vicksburg without coming in range of the city's guns, or maybe, hypothetically, at least according to a few more breathless army engineers, even moving so much water that the Mississippi would change course. In that case, Vicksburg would be high and dry, rent from its river moorings and transformed by elbow grease into a dusty, dried-up Snopesian hamlet, and Grant wouldn't need anything more than a few shovels. Or so it was said.

Grant later claimed that the motive force in these failures was the healthy activity in all of them. He didn't anticipate the success of any one of them and didn't look for the stupendous triumph of the theoretical leap. He just didn't want his men dawdling all winter. In fact, Grant had hoped something might turn up, whatever his assertions to the contrary. He had long since understood what Lincoln exhausted himself trying to drill down into McClellan as democracy at war. He must *act*. So this was action or at least it was activity. Accomplishment, when it came finally, was in the pulp. In mid-April Grant chose what until then appeared to be the riskiest course of all. Twice he ran fleets of gunboats and transports downriver into the teeth of the Vicksburg guns. Doing so seemed a lesser risk than not doing it, and maybe even reduced against the backdrop of seven failed demonstrations of going about war any other way. The backdrop of the attempts, both made in the night, was darkness turned livid, and a terrifying, plunging cacophony of shot and shell, flame and sonic fury, which pummeled the starlight and battered the senses. But only two transport ships were lost, and little damage was done to the gunboats – the fleets passed. Afterwards, Grant marched his army southward, safely opposite Vicksburg on the Louisiana side, without recourse to man-made floods or canals. It joined up with the transports below and was ferried across without contest to Bruinsburg, on the Mississippi side, about sixty-five kilometers south of Vicksburg.

Lincoln would say that he thought that *this* was the breaking through, and on getting his army "on dry ground on the same side of river with the enemy," Grant felt a "degree of relief scarcely ever equalled" himself. All that seemingly remained was for him to assault Vicksburg and be done with it. But Grant didn't. Tinkering had taught him something else – which lessons of generalship he planned to apply, as before, not via ideological or messianic fiat but by necessity, in precisely the same way Lincoln was coming to learn the presidency. Though Illinoisians in an era smaller than it seems to us now, and which might actually have expected their acquaintance, Lincoln and Grant didn't know one another. In 1863 they met at the Mississippi and were twained, as it were: Lincoln's deliberate, careful experimenting with emancipation, Grant's methodical noodling with the means and mechanics of war, the one to the other becoming mutually necessary, and mutually revolutionizing.

Neither undertook his mission in pursuit of grand theory or everlasting glory but in a kind of humility necessary to the survival of the Union. "I do not remember that you and I ever met personally," Lincoln later wrote Grant, after Vicksburg had fallen to Union forces. He never had any faith, he said, that the failed expeditions would succeed. But he did not consider them mistakes. He only considered grossly mistaken what Grant had chosen to do once he was at Bruinsburg, after he had got to the Mississippi side. For Grant did not turn toward Vicksburg, as he might have. In choosing another path he helped revolutionize means and ends. "I now wish to make the personal acknowledgement," Lincoln said to him, "that you were right, and I was wrong."[6]

****

Before one can fully understand the seminal battlegrounds of the summer of 1863, one must understand them embedded within – for they produced – a cosmic mythos of national remembrance. One cannot comprehend the lastingness of the American Civil War otherwise. Especially is this true of memory and the Confederacy. Like most belief systems, the Lost Cause mythology of the after-war was as lissome as it needed to be to privilege credence above consistency. Nothing was more striking in it than the development of two discordant litanies that over time were invoked together as a single liturgy. The principal tenet of the Lost Cause gave white Southerners and their descendants the salving assurance that defeat was inevitable, was unavoidable, was doom. Yet they believed also that they should have won. The dualism's subtlety was too tremorous to acknowledge openly or boldly: Confronting it would have meant cultural dissonance. But it was there. The same print culture that pressed off the books and memoirs and magazines and poetry of the Lost Cause also produced plenty of blame-casting, apologia, stilted justification, scapegoating, and accusatory bickering among ex-Confederate leaders (very seldom admission of mistaken selves) for failures and blunders that shouldn't have mattered if defeat were foregone. Running side to side with this rancor was a certain counter-factual wish-belief that never quite made its way to innocent whimsy. *What if* was the mythology's liminal hope, and *if only* its essential, everlasting life. What if Special Orders 191 had not been lost before Antietam? What if – if only – the arch-heroic Stonewall Jackson had been at Gettysburg?

Some even conjured a speculation on the grand scale. What if Lee had been the Confederate president? If only that leader had been anyone other than the chapfallen Jefferson Davis. Hadn't this son of the Confederate dawn kicked away in his pride the victory of a righteous cause? Some were saying it during the War, and certainly, by the winter and spring of 1863, the Confederacy was as close as it would come to glory. Lee, fresh off his demolition of Burnside at Fredericksburg, had routed Hooker in the woods near Chancellorsville in May. Bragg, who had been pushed back after New Year's at Stones River, nevertheless held Chattanooga, and Tennessee was at least in play. In Mississippi, Vicksburg was still in Confederate hands. If star-crossed vanity existed there it might be with the enemy and his fruitless attempts to take it. The Confederate force holding the town was almost 20,000 strong and commanded by John C. Pemberton, a native of Pennsylvania and former army captain who had married South and cast his lot with his wife's high-toned family. Davis liked him for his advantageous marriage but may well have projected Pemberton's unshakable loyalty from his own antebellum experience with Northern politicians, those so-called doughfaces whose principles were, like Pemberton's, irredeemably Southern.

Matters might not exactly be said to be looking up, then, yet neither were they bleak, and by comparison with the state of things a year or so before or even with the dread and weary discontent weighted just then on the Union cause, they could have been worse. The Confederacy seemed primed for its independence.

In modified form the imagined usurpation of Davis sometimes appears as the conjecture of historians who posit a switching of presidents – Lincoln in Richmond, Davis in Washington. (White Southerners did at least draw their hypothetical line at the contemptible.) The game is played to emphasize differences of leadership and maybe an alternative outcome. It's true that Davis lacked Lincoln's dexterity and his political acumen, that Davis was prickly in matters touching honor and authority and often seemed to govern from aloft in whatever chair he occupied, even as a husband. By comparison with his leather-skinned opposite, Davis was indeed easily distempered. Time or infatuation could earn his trust – Davis's most successful subordinates knew the tact of managing *him*. For some traducers then and now the office seems to have shrunk him. The game is nevertheless a bit of the historian's thimblerig, since the impossible of fact is dubious also as counter-fact. The differences between presidents are clearer by the known outcome, and for the same reason similarities are obscured. Lincoln's homespun style was not Davis's dour stiffness, for instance, but it was discreditable to the many contemporaries who mocked him. To some others it was intolerable, chafing abrasion. Many thought him massively unequal to his task.

At least one distinction is far beyond the ken of counter-factual conjecturing. The Confederacy possessed no solid institutions apart from its military. Its politics, in the absence of formal parties to contain fissures and discipline discord, were riven by invective and faction. It lacked a sturdy economy to underwrite the costs of its war-making, and as a result even by 1863 inflation ran at 10 or 15 percent per month and ravaged its currency. Its refugee population was already so large as to swell its towns and irrupt its smallish cities into Dickensian slums where the poor took livery, the diseased and wounded convalescence, and the artful dodger whatever he could from whomever he could get it. Transportation networks were overworked, so were civil services, so were civil servants. The Confederate nation's new industrial classes included many white women and even children hired to mills and munitions factories or tanneries or machine shops that had not existed in 1860. They were churning goods but close to a breaking point, too. When civilians could lay hands on meat they often could not get the $60 for a bag of salt to preserve it.

All went for the war effort. In one notably widespread spasm of discontent, in the spring of 1863, rioting women in several Confederate cities mobbed bakeries and smashed up storefronts in desperation for bread and relief. The most notorious occurred in Richmond, the by-now bloated Confederate capital, and was dispersed by Davis himself. He stood in a cart among a summoned militia, watch in hand, and after tossing his pocket money into the crowd and informing them he'd given them all he had, also informed them that in five minutes the militia would open fire. Home they went, sullenly, here in Richmond as elsewhere in other disturbed cities, if only in bitter consideration of the home they lived in. Any civilian leader would have been beleaguered under such challenges, though Davis's militant two-handed paternalism in Richmond suggested the strain under these and other stress reactions threatening outright fracture. The Confederate draft, ongoing since 1862, was deeply resented, and of course draft-dodging more popular. A high-handed system of requisition by which the authorities impounded foodstuffs and draft animals for the armies tested the stoutest patriots. Most dangerously, a growing class sentiment hardened under privations and proliferated by word-of-mouth into an especially quick-cutting byword. This was a rich man's war, some said, *and a poor man's fight.*

There is just the hint that the strains were more febrile because these conditions were known weaknesses at the outset. Yet in 1863 some perceived Confederate advantages were agitating as well, with signs of collapsing into doubts. It had seemed impossible, for instance, that the Union navy could blockade 5,500 kilometers of Confederate coastline, and more or less it was for the first two years of the War. The blockade had begun to tell even as Davis was tossing his loose change into the Richmond streets. Its impacts were comprehensive and debilitating, denying the imports necessary to sustain the cause (medicines, munitions, and the like) and the exports that might float Confederate credit overseas.

Another perceived advantage had been the presence of four million slaves whose grinding exertions on plantations and farms, on roads and forts and defense works, in industry, and even in the army, freed white men for military duty. Only forced labor made possible mass Confederate mobilization. Yet recalcitrance on the part of slaves *and* their masters had become troublesome. Under combined pressures – self-interest, the threat of emancipation, the necessary absence of white men now in the army who otherwise would have been local security – slaveowners were less willing to risk their human property with the cause. And slaves did seem more assertive at home while white men were away. They were even more assertive in running away themselves. There was no escaping this vise of fear. If slaves remained at home they began to appear in nightmares as the enemy within, an embedded fifth column of Union and self-emancipation. If slaves ran away and joined the Union army under what Confederates thought of as the Emancipation Proclamation's black rubric, they could destroy the Confederacy as revolutionary black regiments marching in the enemy's hosts without.

So not all was as appeared in Confederate fortunes. Neither victory nor leadership were matters of Davis switching seats with Lincoln, or even Davis with anyone. The Union was an industrializing, urbanizing nation before the War and would remain one after it, regardless of outcome. Lincoln governed within that society's *adjustment* to war. The Confederacy not only required victory to establish nationhood, but in its experience, fundamentally, the impulses of romantic nationalism were inseparable from the destabilizing impulses of industrial nationalization. An agrarian economy, society, and culture, toned distinctly before the War by localism, by hierarchy, and by rural sensibilities of scale and pace, was transitioning in the hastening vortex of industrial, urbanizing, and technological forces. Its human and material resources were taken, tallied, planned, bureaucratized, managed, and distributed within an incorporating machinery even more decisively centralizing than the leviathan it opposed. Davis thus governed astride war's *dislocations*.

Justly, then, it might be said that the Confederacy was lost twice. Defeated in war, it was also vulnerable to its own mythology of the afterwar – and utterly overcome by it in the gilded age of the 1880s and 1890s. By the time the children who inherited the Lost Cause from their fathers and mothers governed remembrance, the mythology had transposed the antebellum South into the place of the wartime Confederacy and conflated the hierarchal, local, and agricultural slave society for the modernizing one that fought the War. To the original foundations of belief – that Confederate defeat was inevitable and due, mechanistically, deterministically, to the overwhelming might of an industrial enemy – the Lost Cause had by then also built up a third that over time became its fundamental dogma. The mythos now made central the claim that slavery had nothing to do with the Confederate cause. Their fathers had not seceded to protect it nor fought to preserve it (despite the unmistakably direct affirmations of the fathers that, in point of fact, they had). They had risen – valiantly: in defense of the constitutional right – to confront the overwhelming numbers and resources of their doom. The cause was all the more peerless, selfless, and glorious *because* they knew they could not win.

And not until then, in the 1880s, was Davis given his seat in the mythology's pantheon of heroes. Long had it housed Lee as its sainted figure and other generals as luminous beings. The Valkyries held Davis at the gates, blamed as he had been for the defeat that the mythology had nevertheless always insisted was unavoidable. His admission was eased by memory's excision of the industrial, urban, centralized Confederacy and the very real and threatening tensions within it that he had been tasked to govern. The dislocations of war were silenced, erased, forgotten. Never had a more unified society striven more organically in shared sacrifice to a nobler cause. Davis, by then an old man bearded, positioned himself as that substituted society's apologist and philosopher in his own memoir, a phlegmatic colossus of distended, defensive detail and sprawl which appeared in 1881 and at 1,500 pages surely tested the industrial capacities of its publisher and its readers alike. Few bothered. (Oscar Wilde called *The Rise and Fall of the Confederate Government* a masterwork but didn't actually read it, either: he was touring America at the time and thought well about how best to fill the lecture halls of the South.) Throngs now came to greet Davis, to fete him, and at train stops and reunions across the South, in crowds nearly as swollen as the memoir they bought but never cracked, to speed him toward apotheosis.

In one element – defensiveness – were the philosopher and his mythology at unity. In another – dislocation – did the philosopher's experience as Confederate president move from the anomies of wartime into those of an enduring identity in Southern cultural nationalism. In time, over time, into the twentieth century and beyond, defensiveness was to become the Lost Cause's deathless feature, taking form within the various negative comparisons by which the ever-defeated region suffered against the progressive innovations and rising strength of a victorious, always-advancing United States: the impoverished South identified by Franklin D. Roosevelt, the backward Bozart South ridiculed by H. L. Mencken (for its supposed vacuity in the *beaux artes*), the time-captive South conceived by W. J. Cash, the blighted, bigoted South that nevertheless produced Zora Neale Hurston and Alice Walker and Ernest Gaines, the guilty South marked for redemption by the civil rights marchers of the 1960s. Against these, *fed* by these negative comparisons, did the Lost Cause live on beyond the memory of any participant or offspring, beyond any necessary connection to the War, until its disposition became an ongoing cultural war against declension. In its cognitive orientation to reality – a posture of attitude *against*, besieged by the decline without – it came to be embedded in a regional pathology of white consciousness. In its deepest recesses it moved into yearning for time that never was.

The Union victors never made a formal doctrine of their inevitable victory, the way, say, the Lost Cause formalized defeat

Figure 21: Jefferson Davis, by William R. Howell, 1875, Public Domain.

as a necessary belief. Their mythology never acquired a name, unless it was *history*. Over time, the great contingency of winning, the great possibility of losing, always central to experience and Lincoln's decision-making in the War – central to the War's original name as the War of the Rebellion – lost its urgency. Silent acceptance of victory simply *accreted*, especially into the twentieth century, the generations that had not fought the War comfortable and confident that the known outcome was assured. By then, in an America reunited in apartheid, the victor's mythology was even hued by strange affinity with the mythos of the defeated: slaves, and race, had nothing to do with it. One needed no questions about the outcome of the War because one needed no questions about national sovereignty and one no longer needed questions about race. The victory's linkage of Union with emancipation became less urgent, then less present, then not required. Emancipation was unfastened from its frontal necessity to become a celebrant's shibboleth, and the mythology of victory detached from the grittiest of its imperatives to become a nation-state's hollowed-out triumphalism.[7]

This was, of course, not entirely the cause that Lincoln presided over. In 1863 the Union war effort was no more unified than it had been previously and, if anything, showed signs of fraying desperately. As with Davis, Lincoln was harried with tensions, dissent, and formal resistance. He did not face the same corrosive force of inflation – the Union ultimately financed its way using taxes and bonds underwritten by a strong wartime economy, and ultimately succeeded in keeping a governor on the spiral. (For the war, the Union encountered inflation at a rate of 80 percent– the Confederacy, 9,000 percent.) Nor were there food shortages or indeed major shortages of any kind, except perhaps volunteer manpower. The Union fed its own, clothed its own, transported and armed its own, and in fact by the end of the war was even exporting wheat and other produce. Putting off the ever-present distress over casualties and costs, coming from all sides, the divisions challenging Lincoln's leadership were instead over matters of trespass on freedom and conscience for dissidents.

Two especially were turbulent and longstanding. Lincoln's occasional suspensions of the writ of *habeus corpus* had emerged early in the War as a discordant issue but had broadened since then into more expansive outrage. The protestants would have said that was because Lincoln had expanded his outrages. Although it has been demonstrated that suspensions were limited and targeted, opponents seized the club and boxed him with it: he was a tyrant and his administration a conspiracy to wrest from them their civil liberties. The emotional valence of these fears, and their reach, are best comprehended by recalling their resonance in the Slave Power conspiracy of the antebellum era, when many Northerners were converted to antislavery precisely because they feared Southerners intended to do the same by the extension of slavery. The other matter was the Union draft, instituted in 1862 shortly after the Confederacy adopted conscription, but no more popular in the North for being only lately resorted to, and for similar reasons. Tensions over it finally exploded into deadly rioting in New York City less than two weeks after the Union victories at Gettysburg and Vicksburg – one might have thought the lyrics were being composed instead. Marauding cabals of draft-weary whites, agitated by local labor pressures, marked free blacks for maiming and some for murder, set parts of the city on fire, and incinerated entirely the Colored Orphans Asylum. (In this element, the rioting seemed to reprise the spasms of violence loosed against free blacks in several Northern cities the summer before, when vigilantes took Lincoln's comments about colonization as permission.) The mobs were finally put down by a division dispatched directly from the Gettysburg battlefield.[8]

New York City's designing mayhem attests that by 1863 all forms and shapes of dispeace had been altered decisively. Existent anger was impossible now to separate from the augury of black emancipation. And it was impossible to calculate apart from the new configurations of hard war. Victory needed both, integrally. That reckoning was as readily made in farm homes and humble machine shops and groceries as in white-columned Washington or mob-roving streets, and it was murderously fissiparous. Many Democrats in the North, in their best moods ambivalent about the conservative approach that Lincoln now disparaged as war "with elder-stalk squirts, charged with rosewater," may have been a minority power, but they used cunning tactics and packed a fearsome political punch, especially in Illinois, Indiana, Ohio, and other states of the middle west. If Union victory meant anything more than restoration, by bludgeoning means bloodier than conservation, if it meant social revolution as well as political disruption, if winning the War meant conscription to fight it and suppressing *their* civil liberties in it, the War was not merely wrong. It was diabolical. Though these opponents, like Confederates, were ultimately beaten, and with Confederates became ethnic in a people of defeat, northern critics did not misapprehend what was at stake. They opposed it, whether they maimed in the streets of New York or thrusted elbows and pushed side and shoulder in bad-tempered, volatile protest meetings in Ohio. This hard war, this emancipationist war, could never be worth escalating costs in blood, treasure, and the cheapening into shoddy of white supremacy and white democracy.[9]

Lincoln, then, had problems of his own, and they did not include the luxury of considering the dyslexic postwar mythologies of victory and defeat. He might have been bumfuzzled by their trajectory, had he lived to experience it, though perhaps not by the retreat from emancipation. To him emancipation and Union, together, was *unfinished work*, as easily ended, suspended, reversed, or even displaced, as completed. He might or might not have been puzzled by the most insidious conceit in the postwar cosmology. This occurred in the joists where race met in the myths to insist, in the one, that slavery had nothing to do with their lost cause, and, in the other, that national sovereignty and Union victory were always assured. If emancipation was no longer a central issue in either cause, neither, then, were African Americans central to America.

The Lost Cause and Union triumphalism will always be separated as myths by the unalterable fact in both of Union victory. But, tellingly, both adjusted for race. There remain persistent canards emphasizing familial white reconciliation, a familial sameness, a kinship in *We*, some told even today. One insists Lincoln owned slaves – he did not: he ever was antislavery to his very marrow; another, that he was kin, a blood-relative, to the grand antebellum architect of secession, John C. Calhoun – he was not; and still others, some out and out flimflams, such as that he was particularly chummy with George E. Pickett, the man who lent his name to the birthing moment of the Lost Cause in Pickett's Charge. As this one goes, Lincoln stopped by the Pickett residence to check up on things when Richmond fell in fire and ash during the last days of

Figure 22: Abraham Lincoln, November 8, 1863, Public Domain.

the War. Lincoln probably knew Pickett before the War or knew of him, and Lincoln was in Richmond after its fall. He was certainly not there to drop in on Mrs. Pickett, as one of the great romantic mythologizers of the postwar – Mrs. Pickett – later claimed he did. He was instead mobbed in the streets by African Americans whose emancipation his cause had just secured, with Union, some of whom called him the Messiah, and at least one of whom knelt in front of him. "Don't kneel to me," Lincoln implored, teary-eyed. "That is not right. You must kneel to God only, and thank Him for the liberty you will enjoy hereafter." After that he went to the Confederate White House and sat, smiling, in Jefferson Davis's vacant chair.[10]

****

Just as there is a first necessity in understanding the battlegrounds of the summer of 1863 as inseparable from the bloodfields they became in memory, there is profit, also necessity, in viewing the summer's military events on the whole. Gettysburg, Lee's colossal gamble and failure in Pickett's Charge, the fall of Vicksburg, and the severing of the Confederacy into halves breached by a now free-flowing Mississippi River were of one great act, set against a sweeping backcloth. Together they embraced all the disordering circumstances of war-making in 1863, social and political and most of all military, even if war-making was not driven by any one or two of them in particular. Grant's dramatic rescue of Chattanooga in late November, a consummate but not inevitable denouement, was rather a *catastrophe* in the classical sense: a profound overturning, a disaster for the Confederacy but godsend for Union. At year's end, Lincoln would travel to Gettysburg to talk about Union and emancipation in a way very different than he had talked about either at year's beginning, because, as he would say, "the signs look better. The Father of Waters again goes unvexed to the sea."[11]

In May, against a very different sense of possibility, when the signs looked better for Confederates than they would at the end, Davis summoned a series of war councils in Richmond. Davis would have preferred not to have been heading any council at any point, of course, coveting as he originally did a field command. Nevertheless he was the Confederacy's responsible grand strategist. In electing Davis to a full presidential term of six years beginning in February, 1862 – his first year was provisional – Confederates understood they were handing their war over to him, very likely to its end point. Their fortunes thus far had been volatile. By the spring of 1863, the nation was both increasingly driven by the impersonal forces of industrial nationalization to establish home rule *and* riven by them – at growing political, social, and economic costs to those who ruled at home. Vicksburg was imperiled. But if the cause was fraying it was by no means rent. Bragg still held Chattanooga. Lee had just consummated a magnificent victory at Chancellorsville, despite its losses the greatest of all Confederate triumphs. The councilors met several times and considered the stars in their courses. What next?

Gettysburg was the lodestar decision, and in two senses, the campaign was not a one-off. One was fundamental in an approach to war that Lee championed and that Davis acceded to, gradually – if his precise role in shaping it is one of those ink-sated arguments of historians, Davis's responsibility for managing and supporting it cannot be. Lee's aggressiveness sought to control the initiative. He wanted his enemies to react to his pressure, perhaps to paralyze them by audacity. Most notoriously and recently, and with stunning emphasis, his tendency had been repeated in the springtime wilderness at Chancellorsville. What was true at battle-scale was true in grander strategy. Lee did not believe the Confederacy could win by allowing the enemy to apply its pressure. This was a telling, mayhap damning, judgment not entirely shared by Davis: telling as considered against the supreme question of initiative, since it was incumbent always on the Union to be first-willing to offer war; damning against the *idée fixe* of the postwar Lost Cause, which glorified an unconquerable spirit. Lee was probably not different than most Confederates who thought the War would be over within the term of Davis's presidency. He may have doubted whether Confederate nationalism was indomitable enough to sustain for even that long the processes of nationalization or the pitch-and-pull fever of patriotism.

Those were matters of the heart and mind, and somewhat too of the stomach and the gravedigger's shovel. There was also the matter of the gut. His battlefield triumphs had been famed but frustrating, beginning with the Seven Days and carried right through to both Fredericksburg and Chancellorsville, where his vanquished enemies had nevertheless been able to put the Rappahannock River between their withdrawal and a potentially devastating Confederate finishing stroke. Lee wanted desperately a decisive victory. Even after Antietam, itself a following-through movement after Second Bull Run, Lee had withdrawn with the intent to reenter Maryland straightaway – and he actually tried to go back, like a boxed-out fighter on an eight-count, until it was abundantly clear that his tattered army was too staggered to return. In its technical aspects, Lee's desire to move north again after Chancellorsville was an individual campaign, but viewed more broadly, the campaign's endgame at Gettysburg six weeks later was the culmination of a series of his campaigns, and a single vision of destruction and creation. *These*, of course, are matters of the pen – matters of the historian's gut, and of a certain school of thought disputed or readily qualified by other historians. Nowhere did Lee make this instinct or ambition so entirely plain that it is indisputable, save in one pinked intimation about the Seven Days.

Yet he sought in 1863 what he sought in the summer and late fall of 1862. At the height now of his powers, of Confederate national power, of the power of the Army of Northern Virginia, Lee wanted to destroy the Army of the Potomac.

The other sense in which Gettysburg was an embracive campaign is not in dispute. It is a matter of record, decided so by Davis and his councils of war. The deliberations began in Richmond on May 15, even as the mourning shrouds of infinite sadness were the capital's bunting, for Stonewall Jackson had died of his Chancellorsville wounds days before. (More precisely, he died not by the mistaken Confederate volley that cost him an arm but by the pneumonia that attacked him after a surgeon cut it off.) The state of things required discussion on the grand scale. Rosecrans had not done much threatening in middle Tennessee since Stones River. Hooker, too, was checked into a kind of torpor after Chancellorsville. But in Grant and the situation Grant had created, the Confederate high command minded a Union general who learned his lessons. In April, improbably, he had run the Vicksburg guns and gotten his army across the Mississippi. But then, equally amazingly, even astonishingly, he had not turned on Vicksburg as virtually everyone expected. He had gone east and north instead, to Jackson, the Mississippi capital, where he drove off a disorganized Confederate force gathering to aid Pemberton and his army. Once Grant had captured and burned parts of Jackson he turned back around on Vicksburg to come at it from the east, the only feasible landward approach. Worried though not harried by the Confederate threat still behind him, he pinned Vicksburg and Pemberton's army within against the great river.

Grant's daring was almost as surprising and risky as the stroke of Lee's boldness at Chancellorsville. By itself, divorced from results, this was a new force to consider. Grant could only accomplish his maneuver (and did, to the wonderment of his own president) by disconnecting his line of supply via the Mississippi River. He fed his men there and back again from Jackson without one. Months before, in December, during the first go he had taken overland at Vicksburg, Confederate cavalry had wearied him into an abrupt, ignominious retreat by demolishing his supplies and forcing him to forage his way home. Yet in turning around and doubling back Grant had also gotten a view of the question he had not taken before. There was enough in Mississippi to feed his army, man and beast. Now he applied the lesson, cagily, and the whole matter from Grant's relentless cunning on down to the impending crisis at Vicksburg was a disconcerting new thing, an enshadowment on the cause as foreboding as the black-veiled dirges sung for Stonewall Jackson. Grant could stay at Vicksburg just as long as he liked. He had reconnected his army to its supplies via the river and laid siege. Pemberton was not strong enough to drive him or release the pressure.

Davis asked his assembled leadership for options. Vicksburg could not be given up. One option might be to hold steady in Virginia, while Hooker was still quiescent, and where defensive lines were much easier to maintain, to concentrate Confederate firepower for a relief blow on the Mississippi. This was to raise the siege of Vicksburg, on a grand scale, as Richmond had been saved a year before. And this the debaters debated. Some variation might be worked by which Bragg might be reinforced in Chattanooga for an offensive thrust in Tennessee, which if successful might force Grant to release Vicksburg to help Rosecrans. Even better: Lee himself might be sent west to lead either movement. Vicksburg simply could not be given up. Why not deploy the Confederacy's best general to its weakest point? The debaters debated this also. Or – *or* – might the Confederacy's foremost general be reinforced in Virginia, reequipped, be given the Confederacy's best available resources, in a theater of war he knew well, against opponents he knew well, under a vision of war he was most committed to, and with those advantages go north again to fulfill Confederate fortune? Here was the Gettysburg campaign as conceived quite literally a grand one. Raising the siege of Vicksburg, and all its relief meant for matters west of the Appalachians, from Chattanooga to the Mississippi River, fell within the umbrella of a bold movement in the welkin east, at least as a justification for its risks.

Debated this was, too, and decided. Lee would move north, into Pennsylvania, maybe as far as the Susquehanna River, maybe farther. That movement would threaten the Union capital, as the Antietam campaign had meant to threaten Washington nine months before, and might again force Hooker or some other Union general (if again Lincoln fired the one he now employed) into rashness. When battle was offered Lee would again decisively defeat the Army of the Potomac. From Davis's perspective, the presidential seats would stay exactly where they were but the tables would turn. To save *his* capital and *his* cause, Lincoln might have to recall *his* best general, Grant, and have to concentrate all *his* firepower, to defend Washington much in the way that Davis and his Confederates were now contemplating the defense of Vicksburg. Not everyone involved in the decision agreed with the logic or the possibility. Later schismatics include the historians who wonder whether Davis was too much in his general's thrall, for a mystique of invincibility had already come to surround Lee. Lee had not only expressed diffidence bordering on declination to serve elsewhere other than Virginia, with the army he built, but forcefully advocated the dubious proposition(s) that an invasion east would release the pressure west if Mississippi's dreaded summer weather didn't cripple Grant's army first. That success was a prospect borne out of Lee's preference and carried along by awe of his heroic sagacity was precisely what the plan's most vocal critic, the Postmaster John H. Reagan, worried about.[12]

Just as the campaign that would culminate in Pickett's Charge began in some rancor and disagreement, it would end that way, too. With close to 80,000 men striding with him in the Army of Northern Virginia (this time accompanied by as many as 10,000 army slaves), Lee moved out in early June, taking the traditional route west and north through the Shenandoah Valley. By late June he was into Maryland and Pennsylvania. Hooker followed but not urgently. In fact, Hooker suggested that he go on into Richmond rather than follow, since Lee had left the door open, a suggestion that Lincoln regarded with cocked eyebrow. The idea seemed to him both a rearing of Fighting Joe's ambivalence to come again to grips with Lee and an imbecilic insensitivity to allowing a massive Confederate army free-ranging pillage throughout the North. Lincoln fired him, as he had sacked four others, and appointed in Hooker's stead a native Pennsylvanian and military careerist, George G. Meade, who did indeed follow urgently. In July the two armies collided accidently in the southern Pennsylvania town of Gettysburg, unremarkable as a burg but militarily notable because, like a hub on a wheel, at township center were brought together several roads spoking to and from more important somewhere elses.

For three days Lee and Meade did battle, each army coiling its strength as the fighting intensified – both had become unspooled and hydra-headed while on the move – Lee on the offensive, the Army of the Potomac holding a strong, hook-like position, curved at its northernmost end around two hills, shanked in the center on high ground known locally (now ill-foretelling) as Cemetery Ridge, and at its southernmost end anchored on two other hills. The battle's first two days, on the opening days of July, exhausted all save the ritual of death. Massive and ghastly fighting engaged 80,000 men on either side in parts of the field ever since called by gore-pasted names such as the Slaughter Pen and Devil's Den. They resolved nothing. Meade didn't move. Lee couldn't move him. His attacks had reached as far as the center of the Union line on Cemetery Ridge – the problem was less in getting there than in staying there, as a subordinate put it. To the soundness of Meade's ground was added the advantage of interior lines: he could move reinforcements from one area to another relatively quickly along the tangents his position offered him.

Like the clattering of tin cans tied to Lee's invading wagon trains, the disputatious tones that sounded first in the Richmond war councils came clinking into the Pennsylvania countryside. There had been finger-pointing and blame-casting already, to become long years later even more strident in the pages of postwar Confederate memoir. Lee was angry with his still-absent cavalry commander, J. E. B. Stuart, for taking indiscretions with loose orders. He may have been frustrated with other commanders for *not taking* advantage of discretionary orders. His attacks thus far had been uncoordinated, effective when pushed but clumsy and club-footed, the same primal error as at the Seven Days, exactly a year earlier, when, had "ordinary circumstances" prevailed and his army acted in concert, the enemy "should have been destroyed." A bad fall from his horse aggravated these frustrations and the sufferings of a summer illness. Whatever the reason or combination of them, Lee was not the general who at Fredericksburg had peered coolly at the enemy across from him in a kind of reverie for war. He was notably snappish. He looked now to see Meade still there, after two pain-punishing days, still there, holding strong ground across the way, maybe not unlike McClellan looked to him a year earlier at the tail end of the Seven Days, sitting atop Malvern Hill.

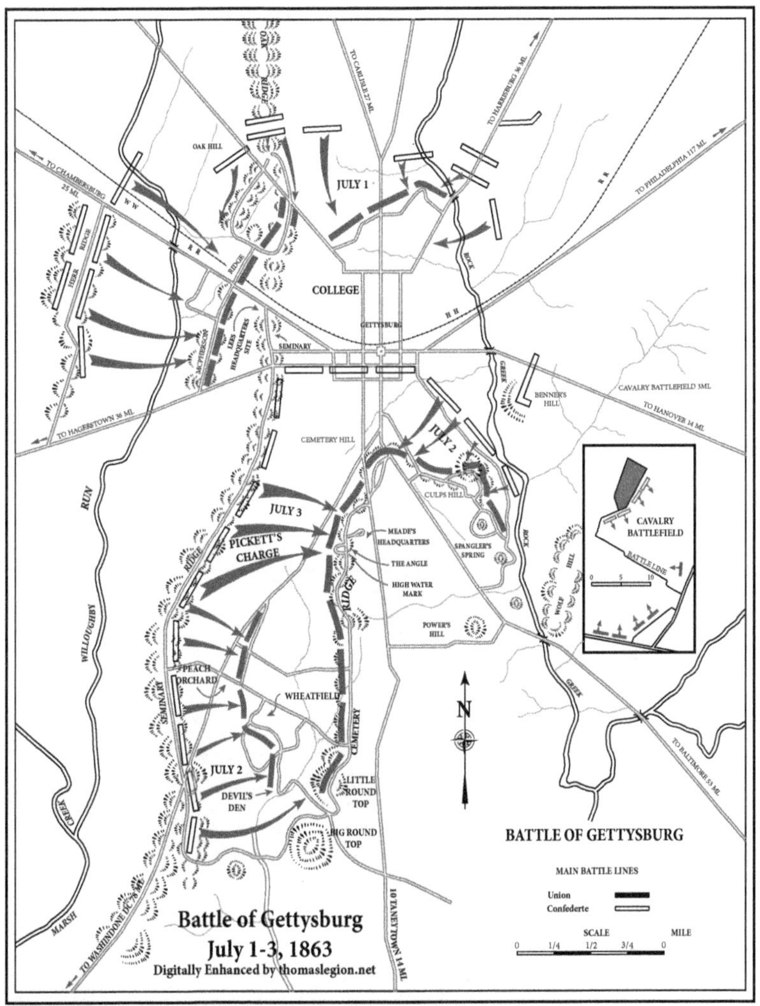

Map 8: The Battle of Gettysburg, July 1–3, 1863

His instinct was to hunt the killing blow. On the night following the second day's fighting and into the morning of July 3, Lee envisioned the Confederate tomorrow: he proposed to gather his strength, the last of his fresh soldiery and nearly one-quarter of his army, and send it across a kilometer of open ground, directly into the center of a Union line positioned on a high ridgeline and supported right and left by enfilading artillery. If he pierced the Union line, all of it would be over. He was confronted by his top subordinate, James Longstreet, who had been privy in Richmond and who claimed, in his own rattling memoir, to have been a voice of caution there. Lee and Longstreet now strove bitterly over the plan. "The fifteen thousand men who could make [a] successful assault over that field," Longstreet reported himself saying to Lee, "[have] never been arrayed for battle." It would proceed, Lee responded. Lee had said something like that from the very first day, when Longstreet, as if apprehending calamity, urged him to maneuver Meade out of his position and into attacking him. No, Lee snapped: "If the enemy is there tomorrow I will attack him."[13]

Figure 23: Lieutenant General James Longstreet, Public Domain.

The dispute between Lee and Longstreet became the most infamous of Lost Cause controversies, especially after Lee's death in 1870, and remains worthy of an extended note because it reveals a tantalizing glimpse behind Lee's mask – what Grant later called Lee's "impassable face" – of politesse and reserve. Longstreet observed that Lee was "excited and off his balance" at Gettysburg but more searingly that he had labored in aberrance "until enough blood was shed to appease him." He would also insist that his own pique was manifest because he agreed to the grand campaign only after Lee had given assurances that Confederates would fight its major battle to come on the defensive. By 1863 the War had taught most generals its lesson: Advances in weaponry and engineering made a good defensive position almost impossible to take and a middling one only certain in its costliness. Quite correctly, historians have cast doubt on Longstreet's self-interested assertion that Lee gave him a *promise* – inferentially, an appeal to extract consent from a subordinate. Some in fact have accused Longstreet the memoirist of making it all up, to dodge blame for his own shoddy battlefield performance, for one thing, and for another to duck the bruising incantations of the high priests of the Lost Cause. These curates of postwar Confederate memory turned the circumstances of Longstreet's conversion to the Republican Party after the War into a heretical transgression so black that his battlefield diffidence became original sin. Blaming Longstreet for the seminal loss at Gettysburg, by implication Confederate defeat in the War, became a scapegoating ritual vital in the creation of their mythology: they could have won *if only* they had not been betrayed.[14]

Yet there seems something at least equally strange, something not quite right, with Lee's self-evident, manifest *id*-desire for offensive war running headlong into his more protective personality traits, crenellated as these were within a certain withholding quality whether called dignity or restraint or reluctance. Lee withheld even his own war memoirs, choosing instead after defeat to write a vindication of his father. Even given understandable reasons to lie, it seems hardly plausible that Longstreet told one outright. It seems at least possible that in war councils cutting right to the quick of Lee's vision, a vision being debated at the moment of its fulfillment, with his top subordinate among those purportedly advocating a defensive course of action Lee could not foresee *but also was not predisposed to accept*, Lee might have fallen into a listening reserve or a genteel posture of agreeably silent non-agreement that Longstreet might have interpreted as assent. He need not have confronted Longstreet in those several Richmond war councils because he knew he already had the votes and whatever permission might be required. We cannot know.

Lee's only concession to the odds of the moment on July 3 was a gargantuan cannonade concentrated on the point of attack. Massively ineffectual, even indifferent, the barrage detonated a hum that reverberated throughout the afternoon, beyond the echoes of a gaping roar. It was spent after ninety minutes and succeeded mainly in alerting Meade and the Union army to what was coming and where. The gallant thing called Pickett's Charge ended in half an hour, in disaster. Only about 12,000 men were fielded for it, not the 15,000 Lee thought he was sending. Half of those were killed, wounded, or captured. The survivors muddled back to Confederate lines, some dazed and confused, some carrying pieces of themselves, some whole, all of them jittery. The *beau vivant* Pickett, a ringlet-haired, perfumed Virginian who oversaw it on the field and was himself shattered by the experience, might have lent his name to it, but technical command belonged to the man who didn't want it, Longstreet. Lee met the survivors as if a poise thieved had been returned to him. He sued them to regroup against a potentially devastating counterattack but did not conceal the obvious. Nothing of magnificence resonated about what had just happened to them. "It is all my fault," Lee said again, and again. "All good men must rally."

He was more reluctant to admit defeat to his opponent. Lee stayed at Gettysburg the next day just as he had refused to vacate the field at Antietam, chumming for a Union counterattack that might redeem the horror of his error. There was no chance of that from Meade, new to command and sufferer of more than 25,000 casualties, though Lincoln wanted a finishing blow so very badly that in his telegraphed messages to the new general he became off his balance himself. Leaving war-scree on the field, including the dead and wounded approaching 28,000 of his own, Lee abandoned Pennsylvania on the night of July 4, and returned, for good, to Virginia. His retreat marked the end of an offensive campaign that as a matter of truth he had launched nine months prior – not in the summer of 1863, as rigid, brittle fact (and most history books) has recorded it, but in the autumn of the previous year, at Antietam.

Death, too, had come to a vision. In later years Lee would be transfigured in the Lost Cause mythos into something like the Christ, whose obedience to foreordained failure and inevitable loss became the modal example of virtues the cause would make deathless – honor, duty, sacrifice, endurance, truth, ultimate victory – but which was, nevertheless and always, lost (or betrayed) in the present time. It says something vitally important about that mythos that Lee's plaintive mantra after the failure of Pickett's Charge – *it is all my fault* – was never repeated in it. It says something as vitally crucial that he was just as reluctant to admit defeat to himself when it was clear there would be no immediate Union counterattack. After midnight, sitting in his tent with loss in the stillness and the memory of a "sad, sad day to us," Lee thought he should have won: "If [Pickett's men] had been supported as they were to have been – but, for some reason not yet fully explained to me, were not – we would have held the position and the day would have been ours. Too bad! Too Bad! OH! TOO BAD!"[15]

****

Gettysburg was not a turning point any more than Antietam was, nor was it high tide, nor was the Confederacy in twilight. In all of these conceptions and popular metaphors are tacit certainties. All of them presume an ability to forecast what contemporaries could not tell, any more than they could predict the weather. As Lincoln would say wisely – Lincoln, who had experienced the switchblade vicissitudes of war so that its ruts lay cleaving in his face – events might portend, trends might be discernible. Where they might go was beyond the vision of men. "No prediction in regard to it," Lincoln said about the War's outcome in his Second Inaugural, a speech he believed he would not be reelected to deliver, "is ventured." Matters had changed, merely.[16]

Gettysburg alone brought no emancipation from uncertainty, and no certainty in either emancipation or Union victory or in the staying power of their combination as war aims. Northern public opinion might recoil in horror and deprecation at reports – true –

that Lee's army had captured free blacks while in Pennsylvania, and marking them as runaway chattel by skin color, driven them southward to slavery. Yet those reports were simultaneous with the deadly riots in New York City, and almost so with the circulation in the North of a new word, *miscegenation*, that owed its coinage to emancipation and its spread to the War's dissident partisans. These dissidents, especially Democrats, sought to stoke fears that black freedom would lead to lusty race mixing and an inevitable devolution of civilization. For them, Lee could take with him all the supposed runaways he wanted.

On the other hand were events with impacts cutting other ways, not least of them, but not only, the twin victories at Gettysburg and Vicksburg. In South Carolina, two weeks later and concurrently with the New York riots, a Union force attempted to storm Battery Wagner, a Confederate citadel protecting the harbor at Charleston. The assault was led by the 54th Massachusetts Infantry, a unit composed of black soldiers and commanded by white officers, including the abolitionist Colonel Robert Gould Shaw. The attack was a bloody failure and its aftermath callous. Hundreds of black and white Union corpses were tossed by the Confederate victors into sandy mass graves, the bullet-mutilated, sputum-coated body of Shaw among them for his impudence in leading black men in arms against the master race. (The consequent pummeling of Battery Wagner by the Union navy over the next several months exposed the graves, and the stench, a reeking tarpaulin overspreading all, hastened its abandonment.) At Milliken's Bend, in Mississippi, scarcely a month before Vicksburg fell to Grant, black Union soldiers fought with conspicuous valor, as they had at Wagner, but won. Many were former slaves who were only recently recruited and hardly armed.

These were distending matters of *chronos* and its pressing ambivalences. Among other elements of a hardening war of destruction, what had been smashed at Battery Wagner and at Milliken's Bend was the error of racial theory. Black men supposedly without the natural capacities to fight with courage and discipline and valor as soldiers, black men as fit to be mobbed in the streets of New York or collared by Confederates in the countryside as runaway slaves, not only could fight nobly in the Union army but did. As a result, both the Union's openness to using them and efforts to enroll them accelerated. By the end of the War almost 10 percent of Union soldiery, about 180,000 men, were African Americans. In a concession to deep prejudice the black regiments were commanded by white officers. But four out of every five men in them were former slaves.

Haltingly, anxiously, was black legitimacy surfacing, and with it a question of whether the emerging truth would hang together as self-evident. The emancipation of slaves required the emancipation of the military means necessary to win the War, and the emancipation of military means required the emancipation of slaves. The grand twinning might be freed from the assumptions of conservative war, yet it was improvised, affirmed by need but insecure beyond the moment. On the answer and not on pomp or triumphalism or messianic mission, and certainly not on the inevitability of victory but rather very much rubbed up against fears and doubts and the earthbound ever-presence of possible defeat, was the future set.

One key was affinity. Frederick Douglass, the West's most famous runaway slave, and now perhaps abolition's most prominent leader, had all but predicted it. Once black men were allowed to fight, a common respect for them as soldiers would explode the myths that shackled all of them, black and white. Beyond combat ability Douglass had a second competence and far-reaching consequence in mind. Nothing was more secure in the republican ethic of self-government than the idea of the citizen-soldier. The same characteristics associated in America with men as soldiers were thought to qualify men as citizens. Yet nothing was more cognate to the idea of radical abolitionism than securing political and civil rights as a coeval condition of freedom. Thus had Lincoln, as far as he had moved personally, pandered to the intractable fact of white supremacy by promoting colonization in the summer of 1862. Even as late as 1863, when emancipation had been coupled with the enlistment of black soldiers, the government attempted (but failed) to plant a small colony in Haiti. By then, just as Douglass had hoped, the cascading effects of emancipation and hard war destroyed colonization as both a program and an idea.

It wasn't exactly certain what was left in its place, but then again affinity was not settled in place, either. It moved and grew, and strengthened through combat, especially as outraged reports

Figure 24: Fort Pillow Massacre (April 12, 1864), Kurz and Alison, Chicago, 1885, Public Domain.

spread of black soldiers specially maltreated as prisoners of war or even murdered and mutilated by Confederates flying the black flag. Some of these reports circulated to uncertain veracity as early as Milliken's Bend but were accepted, because true, at such places as Fort Pillow in Tennessee, where in 1864 Confederates shot scores of surrendered black soldiers in cold blood. The Fort Pillow Massacre has generated controversy right down to the present day, partly because the Confederate in command, Nathan Bedford Forrest, has become something of a historical cipher for American racial violence. As a matter of policy, whether carried out in fact, Confederates claimed the summary right to execute or enslave captured black soldiers as insurrectionists. They considered use of a black soldiery nothing so much as a diabolical design to foment rebellion and massacre and rape among the fifth column on their plantations and farms at home. Lincoln responded with the Order of Retaliation (only two weeks after the New York City riots), which proscribed tit-for-tat treatment. This, too, was a galling equality. Black Union soldiers must be treated as prisoners of war for white Confederate soldiers to be treated likewise.

Empathy developed beyond combat experiences. The longer Union soldiers remained in the field, the more they saw of the South, the more they saw of slavery, its persons, its conditions, its cruel punishments, the more they came to bitter perception of the plantation system as the pith of anti-democratic arrogance – and that the slaves on them were like unto their comrades suffering in Confederate prisons. Affinity in this way was perhaps unexpected. A growing solidarity with slaves reified how they interpreted the pain and trauma and suffering of their own experiences as soldiers. Recognizable in the authenticity of a slave's struggle for freedom, in its dirty, daily realness, was something of their own rugged endurance, and a common cause. The last armies to invade the American South – the British, in the War of 1812 – experienced this strange fellowship, too. And it was double-barreled because paired with a separating force of repulsion, as anti-affinity, as mercilessness toward their enemies. The forces of attraction and repulsion grew in response to how vigorously they were resisted and how deeply they were dreaded by Confederates. By 1864, as emancipation and hard war reached its expressive climax, the Union armies knew precisely how, and where, to strike, for they had known their enemies previously as themselves. They drove hardest at the places they knew as the rawest.[17]

A climactic point was still a long year away. The conclusion of the great summer campaign was actually in the fall, four months following the important Union victories of July, at Chattanooga. As Vicksburg was key to the Mississippi River, Chattanooga, a small industrial city and an important railhead that Braxton Bragg had used to engineer his invasion of Kentucky in 1862, was vital to the area between river and the Appalachian Mountains. Possession of it allowed access to points west (or the middle-border, in Bragg's case), and, for the Union cause, also opened up the possibility of an eviscerating drive southward, into Georgia and Alabama. The immediate emergency requiring attention at Chattanooga was also the one unlooked for – the most spectacular victory ever recorded by the Army of Tennessee. Bragg's game but woebegone army, which had been shouldered out of middle Tennessee and into Chattanooga by Rosecrans after Stones River, had only recently been pushed from Chattanooga and into north Georgia. All had seemed of a piece with the Union's summer of fortune before fortune turned again.

In September, Rosecrans began moving from Chattanooga into Georgia, heading for the even more vital hub of Atlanta. Bragg met him at a place called Chickamauga on September 19, and opened a battle of now-typical length and ferocity. Its moment was a year and a day from Antietam, and its aspect the confused wilderness slug at Shiloh. By now the casualties were also a massive norm, second only to the war-carnage at Gettysburg. Yet Chickamauga was an epic contest sung by far fewer bards, perhaps because there were fewer left of them, even though the results were stunning. Bragg broke Rosecrans and chased him all the way back to Chattanooga. Just what was owed to Bragg's skill is a matter of debate, though certainly nothing was owing to tact. It was just afterwards that Nathan Bedford Forrest threatened to kill him, one of many disputes at a Confederate headquarters flush in bickering before victory, and which soon forced Jefferson Davis into a laborious, rickety, roundabout trip to appease in person. At least as significant to Confederate success was enemy blunder. A mistaken maneuver in the Union lines opened a gap for thousands of shrieking Confederates to pour through, which they did, immediately – led by the divisions just-arrived under Longstreet, who had hectored his way into Tennessee in a belated attempt to salvage one of the western options discarded in May. Only the steadying fighting of the Union rear guard on September 20 saved Rosecrans from an ignominious destruction.

Likely it also saved the Union attempt in the Deep South from collapse. Rosecrans fled all the way back to Chattanooga. There Bragg locked him in from towering, imposing positions overlooking the city on Lookout Mountain and the 120-meter climb of Missionary Ridge. Rosecrans, Lincoln said, seemed wobbled by the whole turnabout, much as Hooker at Chancellorsville – "confused and stunned ... like a duck hit on the head." Grant was straightaway summoned from the Mississippi to face a prospect in some ways as daunting to relieve as Vicksburg had been to besiege. Wanting, urgently, was a reliable chain of supplies. Without it man was scavenger and beast was carrion: more than 10,000 draft animals and horses had already died of starvation. In due course, the Union army secured a so-called cracker line, the army's resilience and experience solving stubborn problems and predictable Confederate dysfunctions jointly nicking away at Bragg's significant advantages. Grant soon rationed his forces effectively, but the main thing was his simple, steadying presence as a leader more obstinately immovable than any obstacle in front of him. "He habitually wears an expression as if had determined to drive his head through a brick wall," one observer would say upon meeting him, "and was about to do it."

No wobbled duck, he, but the final breakout at the battle of Missionary Ridge amazed the most stalwart veterans. On November 25, Grant's soldiers turned what was supposed to be a limited demonstration, a diversion in the center to relieve pressure on the flanks, where the main attempt to raise the siege was taking place, into a full-throated, go-for-broke charge. In theory this was an assault more reckless than Lee's misbegotten attempt at Gettysburg, and Grant had not considered its possibility for a moment. A full-frontal attack faced, uphill, three successive lines of Confederate entrenchments bulwarked as impregnably as any partition of the earth could be. But there had not really been any contemplation on the ground. Upon reaching the first line Union soldiers realized the Confederate positions commanded their own in such a way that going back was as suicidal as going on. So they went up. And perhaps for that reason – desperation unadorned as nothing to lose – their assault succeeded in taking Missionary Ridge, and in overwhelming Bragg's army so spectacularly that its subsequent retreat into north Georgia, though shy of panicked, was conclusive. Chattanooga belonged for good to the Union.[18]

The consequences of Chattanooga mattered for portents beyond the military moment. Lincoln had found his general. Or perhaps, in keeping with his refusal to be cowed by uncertainty, the general had found him. In Grant was the embodiment of the last affinity, the linkage of hard war and emancipation *as both means and ends*, or, put differently, the decoupling of old assumptions of war from these new means necessary to win it. If waging war meant moving the Mississippi River, he would try it. If it meant abandoning supply lines, he would do it. If it meant demolition he would also do that. Harsher war was not new in 1863. But in 1863 it had been explicitly tied to emancipation, and now the momentum of both was quite literally expressive in Grant's movements. The freedom of pursuing one, hard war, was in the freedom of pursuing the other, emancipation. Both previously had halted and started,

started and halted, stuttered, stalled, spinned out, advanced and retreated. Now they were one, moving. New means meant no necessary assumptions.

As with the war effort so its author, for Lincoln had moved – was moving – toward the fullest connections piecemeal. His fashion had long been to work out his major ideas on paper scraps, sometimes slotting them in the inner band of his top hat until he could pull them into coherence. By late 1863, as he had found in hard war the promise of saving the Union and in Grant the sure promise of hard war, he had also found the voice of affinity in the full measure of emancipation. Freedom for the slave was freedom for the free, neither possible without the other, neither possible outside of Union, and saving the Union impossible without the armed service of black and white. Douglass, fearing "the danger of a slaveholding peace," had first visited him officially in the White House that August, and pressed the matter. He came also with a demand that black soldiers – to that point, among other discriminations, paid less than white soldiers – be treated equally. Douglass was not treated civilly himself, at least not by the crowd of white men queued and anxious to plow the president for an office or a favor. Most black men who had been to the White House before him were the slaves who helped build it or been slaves and servants to presidents in it. "Yes, damn it," one of the waiting muttered as Douglass was escorted by, "I knew they would let the nigger through." But he was cordially greeted by Lincoln. A second meeting two weeks later convinced Douglass of Lincoln's "deep moral conviction against slavery" and the president's commitment to emancipation. Their essential compatibility was ensured when Lincoln made it a point of calling him "my friend Douglass."[19]

Around this time as well, in August 1863, Lincoln sent a letter to be read to a political meeting in Springfield, Illinois. Lincoln had been looking for a public opportunity, in a fitting setting, to reconcile means and ends with purpose and consensus. He wanted badly this one, and to return home to deliver it in person. The summer's press made a trip impossible. His Springfield letter was nevertheless the fullest expression of his talents as politician and statesman come to strength. Its craftsmanship, sweat-dripped, took weeks. Its purposes were manifold, its maneuverings artful and frankly partisan yet guided by a clear moral linkage of Union and emancipation. He bucked up Republicans, confronted insurgent Democrats, and challenged a more generalized opinion, even among supporters, opposed to black equality via emancipation and the black Union soldiery.

Lincoln's only request to his messenger was that his letter be read out "very slowly." "But to be plain, you are dissatisfied with me about the negro," Lincoln wrote. "You dislike the emancipation proclamation; and perhaps, would have it retracted." Long years earlier in Illinois, stumping the state during famous debates with the other Douglas who had figured so prominently in his life, Lincoln had scorned his rival for moral indifference. Stephen A. Douglas said then that he didn't care whether slavery was voted up or down in the territories but cared merely for the principle of popular sovereignty. Yet just a year ago, during the fall elections of 1862, Lincoln had borrowed his rival's technique in his public letter to Horace Greeley by saying he didn't care more for slavery than he did for Union. He had even pandered to that sentiment for much the same reason that Douglas had pandered in 1858 to popular sovereignty – because purpose could not be brought to consensus, because means staggered in a blurred crusade toward uncertain ends.

Now, in master-strokes of guile and reproach, Lincoln turned volatile Northern public opinion to advantage by making opposition to emancipation an indifference still purposeful as an instrument in saving the Union, while slyly inserting the higher virtues of democratic citizenship as the possession – and the memory – of the scorned. "You say you will not fight to free negroes. Some of them seem willing to fight for you; but, no matter. Fight you, then, exclusively to save the Union." Peace would come. It "does not appear so distant as it once did ... And then, there will be some black men who can remember that, with silent tongue, and clenched teeth, and steady eye, they have helped mankind on this great consummation; while, I fear, there will be some white ones, unable to forget that, with malignant heart, and deceitful speech, they have strove to hinder it."

Nearly three months afterwards, once its townspeople cleared and cleaned and burned and buried much but not nearly all of its overwhelming detritus, Lincoln conspicuously took at Gettysburg the public opportunity he missed at Springfield. His message of

Figure 25: Clement Vallandigham, between 1855 and 1865, Public Domain.

Union, emancipation, and memory was as sweat-dripped, the same, if sung at salvific cadences to a purer unity. Yet he feared later that he failed in the Gettysburg Address. "That speech won't *scour*," he said. It was all propositional, after all, and contingent, and like war a question of time. There was always in that, there always would be in that – in propositions; in unfinished work; in words; in time – the prospect of magnificent failure. The War's bitter divisions, its petty and gargantuan brutalities, *its murderous fissiparousness*, seemed less a fellowship with the epic-heroic than it did a Manichean apocalypse in which words might be little noted, nor long remembered, and where memory itself would be in perpetual contest between the living and the dead. "If they stake their lives for us," Lincoln had said of former slaves and black soldiers in the Springfield letter, "they must be prompted by the strongest motive – even the promise of freedom. And the promise being made, must be kept." Nothing could be assured in a struggle living between peoples. The promise must be kept – but for how long?[20]

6

ON HOME GROUND: 1864

To the sea – after three pitiless years of war, Lincoln could say, enduringly, that the Mississippi River ran freely to empty itself, as for ages, into the sea. But for Confederates by 1864 the watery parts of the world were possessed of antediluvian disquiet. They had dared to hope. Across the Mississippi were states the Confederate nation had claimed as its own, and territories tithed to visions of the world's greatest slaveholding republic overspreading, as a white-cotton empire, to the Pacific Ocean. To look across the great Father of Waters to the west, now, was to see only deceit in the pale glare of a pale dream. So too had they peered over the Atlantic waters, eastward, in their aspiration of alliance with the great European powers. Recognition by Great Britain and by France had been one of the factors involved in the Confederate choice to wage war as they had waged it, on the theory that the ability to carry out conventional warfare was the measure of national legitimacy. Confederate diplomacy had even acquired complex elements of international finance, propaganda, and espionage since 1861 – limited, like all things Confederate, by resources, but commensurate with a modernizing nation's fully contemporary and fully modern ambitions.

Yet neither was there hope over the mother-water. By 1864 Union envoys held the initiative in trans-Atlantic diplomacy, and its navy, a floating force Lincoln had recently christened as "Uncle Sam's Web-feet," held the Atlantic coastline. The image was one of the worst of Lincoln's folk-conceits of democratic phrasing, propelled inversely by the humbling realization that his maritime force was actually something of an imperial marvel. More or less it had been built from scratch. In 1861 the national navy consisted of forty-two serviceable ships, all wooden. By 1864, underwritten not just by the industrial and financial might to build it, but the technological and logistical innovation to make it a fearsomely modernizing institution, the Union outfitted some 85,000 seamen, almost 10,000 of whom were black, serving on more than 650 vessels of all kinds. A host of these were armored and steam-powered, and the force itself was versatile enough to be present, as Lincoln said, "at all the watery margins": vigorous to support massive logistical and supply operations, nimble for amphibious incursions along the coastline, especially in the Carolinas and Georgia, stout to stand its own against Confederate coastal fortifications. Most augustly, the Union leviathan had done what many Americans and not a few international observers thought impossible at the War's opening: it had successfully walled off the Confederacy from the sea.

Fixed and becoming ever more binding by the end of 1862, the blockade could not be lifted by force, not by the Confederacy alone. Any effective Confederate response was constrained by limitations and realities. Its maritime and riverine war, its international trade, too, relied on an improvised, pieced-up fleet of warships, commerce raiders, rams, and blockade runners. Some had been impounded from Southern ports early in the War and reoutfitted for naval service, and some were built or repurposed in regional shipyards riveted to efforts in national industrialization. Some were purchased or constructed overseas in fervently pro-Confederate ports such as Liverpool. Desperate necessity mothered occasionally arresting moments, among them the dramatic appearance of the *CSS Virginia* off Hampton Roads, where in 1862 astonished witnesses watched her duel the *USS Monitor* in the world's first clash – a tactical draw – of ironclad warships. In 1864 Confederates even deployed the world's first submarine, a hand-cranked, eight-manned contraption called the *H.L. Hunley*, which managed to sink a Union blockader outside Charleston before mysteriously plunging to the harbor floor. The *Hunley's* career in rust and barnacle was fit metaphor. The Union's blockade became disruptive and corrosive over time, more damaging in the deterioration brought on Confederate transportation and communication infrastructure than in denial of imported war materiel. Yet strangely more profound was a deepening, darkening effect of quarantine and oblivion, of being "shut out from the world," as a Confederate naval officer put it in his memoirs.[1]

Only in retrospect do the Confederacy's grandest hopes of becoming a great global civilization seem chuffed-up or hallucinatory, or in some modern writing of the ironic mode, vainglory fully deserving of its reckoning. They had indeed been bold to declare their ambition at secession. Their brashness should not be mistaken for impetuosity. This was so because the true international measure of the American Civil War would be taken not on the preservation or destruction of Union nor even on emancipation, but on the preservation of cotton. The wealth of its fibers was the mesh of fantasy – one poet likened it to the "Haschich of the West" – for capitalists and imperialists everywhere on the earth. The one or two million pounds grown by American slaves in 1800 had multiplied, with empire, into millions on millions of pounds cultivated, baled, and shipped from the South before the War, and reached two billion pounds alone in 1860. Southerners boasted boorishly of it, calling cotton king, and felt no compunction tying slavery to it as an essential (if, they also argued, humane) retainer. But neither are little to wonder. Slavery *was* civilization, "the greatest material interest of the world" sustaining the monarch of the world's commerce. They distinguished their exceptionalism in their human chattel and the wealth and progress it brought upon the earth.[2]

The humanitarian renown that had accompanied abolition of slavery throughout the British Empire in 1833 was not prestige enough to dissuade the real possibility of England leading, for cotton's sake, a broader European recognition of the Confederacy. England's ruling classes were still mindful of the European revolutions of 1848, its genteel elements sympathetic to an American plantation order that ballasted messy democratizing impulses and flattered and aped after the manner of its own. Most imperatively, the vast bulk of Southern cotton was exported to Great Britain. King Cotton's endowments sustained the merchants of Liverpool and the mills of Lancashire, a daily-bread reality attracting pro-Confederate sentiment among the working classes as well. It made the mercantile and industrial wealth of the empire. Its British reach was such that Confederates voluntarily and aggressively embargoed their crop throughout 1861, intending to force recognition by the pressure of economic anxiety and the looming potential of pot-banging disturbance among the masses not unlike what would come to plague their own social order by the middle of the War. For a time Confederates were fond of citing such personages as William E. Gladstone, who had pronounced famously in Newcastle in 1862 that British recognition was inevitable.

But all that was before the Union had overcome its own initially awkward and juvenile attempts at international diplomacy, before news reached across the water of Antietam, before emancipation, before the triumphal Union successes of 1863 and the reopening of the Mississippi River, and before the clutching grip of the blockade all but choked the Confederacy. In the last three years of the War, only half a million bales of exported cotton could be gotten through. Not coincidentally it was also before pressures of imperial supply were relieved when new sources of cotton were opened in India and Egypt. Now the blockade, like emancipation, was only a fit demonstration of the growing power and potential of the Union to make so what it claimed in the posture of saying so. If the measure of a nation was in actualizing its commitments by the force of its arms, and the force of its arms was only an extension of its will to be, one of the American contestants was proving its legitimacy, the other its frailty. By the power gathering to the one, the other might very well be wiped from the face of the deep.

The issue of the American Civil War in 1864 came down to its most basic, insular element, the essence of the people's contest Lincoln had articulated three years before. It was a question of home rule, on home ground – of whether the people of either side would continue to choose to war. For all that had seemed propitious in recent Union victories, their meaning was subject to interpretation, referendum, and ratification in a forthcoming national election. No poll was more vital. Lincoln and the Republicans would carry with them successes, perhaps, yet also the boggling physical, material, and emotional costs since the last presidential election and secession, in 1860. They now carried the question of Union inseparable from emancipation, encumbered under the exhausting burden of endurance: the question of how much more would have to be given being inseparable from how long unfathomable giving must continue. And for all that had darkened Confederate hopes in 1863 and confined them utterly on themselves, turned them inward to consider their ambitions but also the astounding sacrifices of asserting themselves as a separate people, not all was lost to them as long as value and cost were also, for their adversaries, functions of time.

Confederates no longer possessed the capability to assert their nationality in swaggering, offensive warfare. That truth diminished them in more ways than military fact. They as yet maintained the defensive prowess to force their opponents to confront their own self-contained, exacting questions of democracy. There was, in truth, as last leverage, the vague realpolitik of the one alliance remaining to them – the peculiar confederacy between them and their own slaves. No formal compact was proposed in this, or not yet, anyway. It was instead an irregular relation embedded in the larger relations of war and race and democracy, and one Confederates might ply as the tool of their independence. For in 1864 the most important election in American history would be conducted northward on Lincoln's proposition that the Union was to be consummated only through hard war and emancipation. Confederates could hope to resist long enough, and bloodily enough, to force the people of Union to choose peace: that, in effect, an independent Confederacy was the least of all American evils because it was better than reunion with emancipation. If the choice was between vastness of sacrifice for a democracy that must absorb and take unto itself, as one within it, indivisible, the fulfillment of emancipation, or a Union that would spare itself further sacrifices *and* the ongoing toil and commitment to confirming them in the legacy of emancipation, the choice might very well be to bid adieu to the Confederacy and to let go of both the black and white of the South alike.

The procrustean connections between black and white were manifestly *not* in what slaves and Confederates could achieve together. Their twinship was in the menace each posed to their adversaries, thrown together as double threats in necessary combination. Confederates still possessed the firepower to kill and maim in horrifyingly gruesome numbers. Slaves as free men might force on the Union unwilling, ongoing sacrifices to live up to the commitments of emancipation. Here, then, did the Confederacy retain a last initiative, and their own, last best hope on the earth.

****

Absent limited encounters such as a brief affray near a stream called Mine Run in the fall of 1863, absent routine skirmishing or forceful reconnaissance, the war in the east had remained relatively quiet, as if paused, since Gettysburg. Quiescence did not mean stasis. Much had changed. Profoundly, Lee understood the he would fight the upcoming 1864 campaign from a defensive pose. He understood as well the War's bottom-barreling grind on Confederate resources, particularly that skimmed kegs of all kinds, from food barrels to musket barrels, were also turning up lighter on leadership. The devastating attrition among his officers, the constant need to "obtain proper commanders," was a crippling factor that Lee had identified the year before, in the reserve that so often was the husk of his urgency, as a "difficulty." On two extraordinary occasions in the bloodbath to follow he would reveal desperation in all of its nudity.[3]

It was true also that the Army of the Potomac proposed to make him fight defensively. This was Grant's doing. Like the fabled killer angel wending his way to an appointment in Samarra, Grant's intermittent pilgrimage had steadily traveled him eastward, from Shiloh to Vicksburg to Chattanooga. Finally, in the late winter of 1864, he arrived in Washington, DC, as general-in-chief of Union armies. Somehow it all seemed so natural that promotion and accession would follow the relief of Chattanooga, but not quite so. Nothing about 1864 would be undertaken – nothing – without an eye beaded on the fall election. Lincoln might have spared Grant to fight but not to run for president. Upon discreet inquiry, Grant revealed that he had no such ambitions, and with that delicate business arranged and his promotion secured, he arrived in March just as discreetly. His Washington hotelier, used to plenty of pomp and bombast as servant to the capital's peddlers of power, had merely checked his disheveled wayfarer into an upstairs room before a predictable horror-of-horrors discovery, and then situated the republic's general-in-chief splendidly, in a suite.

Nominally Grant's authority would now extend everywhere, including beyond the Mississippi west, where in 1861 he had commanded a small force for the first time in battle at a place called Belmont. Functionally, his control would extend through the Army of the Potomac. He proposed to make his headquarters not at a desk in Washington, as Halleck his tormenter and elbow-scratching predecessor had done, and certainly not in his rooms at Willard's Hotel ("miraculous in meanness; contemptible in cuisine") but in the field. George Gordon Meade, the Pennsylvanian who led the Army to victory at Gettysburg on the shortest of notice after Hooker's inglorious sacking, would retain only a technical command. A "damned old goggle-eyed snapping turtle" in the oft-quoted because unforgettably authentic description of one soldier, Meade held that position until the end of the War, only to thereafter and into history be squeezed between carapace and plastron.

With Grant came a grand vision of coordinated war, a strategy of constant pressure everywhere constantly applied, all along the continental line east to west. The sprawling Confederate armies were to be subdued and tied down all at once. Lincoln's translation of the strategic concept became another of his famous barnyardisms as "if a man can't skin he must hold a leg while somebody else does." In more practical terms, the Union armies would seek engagement with their adversaries. They would slaughter the Confederacy by attacking its forces, not its places, and by not allowing Confederates to move reinforcements from a quiet theater to a threatened one. All would be threatened, all the time, and blooded. Lincoln nevertheless had discarded enough generals whose vision extended no further than their own tent flaps to doubt even the tanner's son he just appointed. If the Union war effort was anything thus far, it was uncoordinated and piecemeal. "I repeat to you," Lincoln said to Grant during the long course of the grand campaign to follow, a campaign that featured a too-familiar share of bumbling and uncoordinated shambling despite Grant's sanguine plans, "it will neither be done nor attempted unless you watch it every day, and hour, and force it."[4]

Grant's best-known quotation – "I propose to fight it out on this line if it takes all summer" – came in response to his massive, squeamishly costly engagements with Lee in northern Virginia. As a summary of resolve in the face of dangerous adversity it became the idiom of the 1864 campaign. Yet at the time the phrase might have worked equally well as a response to a general skepticism about Grant's chances against Lee and, together with those prospects, the War. For Grant, in one fundamentally critical sense, was not only intent on moving forward along his line of attack but also, always, looking back. Over his shoulder constantly was the matter of Lincoln's electoral chances, the president's own raw urgency over them, and a divided Northern home front. Where Grant went, there Lincoln's reelection went also. And just how much Lee sought the very same terms might be hidden in the creases of the proposition's Churchillian mantle. To be north of Richmond, on this line, all summer, fighting it out, was precisely his goal. "We must destroy this army of Grant's before he gets to the James River," Lee told one of his generals. "If he gets there, it will become a siege, and then it will be a mere question of time." For him defensive war was only *in extremis*. Keeping Grant in stasis, away from Richmond, was by default a strategy bound to the fall election as well.[5]

Many pages have been written about Lee and Grant, on many themes. One of the most enduring themes is tied to a trope of national reconciliation that certainly captures something about the spirit of their meeting at Appomattox, at the end, in 1865. The representative figures of bitter enmity met there in mutual understanding, as it goes. Lee, though he said he "would rather die a thousand deaths," came to surrender his army in dignity rather than allow it to dissolve into the woods and become the core of a guerrilla insurgency even more lastingly violent, remorseless, and revolutionary. Grant received his foe in dignity, imposing lenient terms of healing and national uplift rather than a conquering vengeance, which might produce humiliation and the same insurgent result. Those notions can bleed in a bathos of melodrama. The terms after all were instrumental. Grant and Lee did not meet one another as equals, or as fighting brothers, and neither did Grant greet Lee awestruck – he esteemed Joseph E. Johnston as the better foe. His magnanimity was authentic *because* it was accompanied by wariness, an Achilles sitting with his Priam, and his charity did not forfend a devastatingly honest appraisal, explicit in his memoirs, that Lee fought for one of the worst of all devised causes. And incontestably more tragic than the hypothetical guerrilla insurgency prevented by Lee's surrender was the real and longer-lasting white Southern resistance layered subtly into the sentimentality of reconciliation. For Lee never reciprocated, not quite anyway.

This is not the popular view, and its nuance is perhaps blunted in the necessity of making plainer than it actually operated within other, just feelings of mutual understanding. But enmity remained. Anyone not familiar with the cultural language of the nineteenth-century South would see pathos but not essential meaning in Lee's hardly extemporaneous – indeed: *well chosen* – words about dying a thousand deaths. His keeping of the "perfectly impassable face" that Grant could not peer beyond was an expression of meaning as well. Lee could not have fully reciprocated without unmasking his dishonor. A man of honor condescended to give gifts below. He could only receive them on equal terms. Death, even a thousand deaths, was better than accepting a gift – in this case, and especially, the gift of Grant's magnanimity – from a lesser who presumed such haughty condescension. Lee's dubious postwar appraisal of George B. McClellan, not Grant, as the best of his opponents was exactly cognate with that lost language. His unwillingness to give Grant his due eventually became something more lastingly duplicitous. It developed into an underlying, insidious leitmotif in the War that ended at Appomattox but was not reconciled or settled there. In insisting on equality for themselves, but in refusing to give it on equal terms to those deemed lesser – the claims of African Americans to equality were not-to-be-brooked assumptions in the American South long into the twentieth century – the unwillingness, a posture of resistance, has ever passed for honor. It has never quite left the people of defeat.[6]

Lee's obstinacy was of course also a rationalization, a nudging away from the thrust and twist of Grant's sword buried in his quick. By gutting him of his creative initiative, Grant defeated him in exactly the way he might have done it to himself. When the weather cleared in the spring of 1864, Grant unleashed a two-month offensive that became as animalistic as any conventional campaign of the War. Day after day, beginning on May 5, when Lee attempted to crush Grant on the march in a mass of tangled forest canopy called the Wilderness, the frenzied armies tore at one another like great clutching therianthropes, neither quite seeming to know whether it was predator or prey. Lee had chosen

Figure 26: Robert E. Lee, by Michael Miley, 1870, Public Domain.

the battlefield carefully. The woods camouflaged the disparity of the armies – Grant marched with 115,00 men, Lee met him with 65,000 – and neutralized the Union army's superior artillery. In this same confused bramble a year before, the Army of Northern Virginia had routed Hooker at Chancellorsville: not that anyone needed hospitality more ghoulishly reminiscent than the luminous skulls of last year's dead, flesh-and-bone having been washed out of shallow graves by tempest or rooted and devoured by huge forest boars and carrion fowl. A harrow-dream even reached from beyond the afterlife of memory when Longstreet, who had returned to Virginia after his foray west with Bragg's army, was accidentally wounded by his own men near the spot where Stonewall Jackson had fallen a year earlier, in exactly the same way. (Had Longstreet not survived this mischance the confreres of the Lost Cause surely would have exhumed him to pick him clean anyway.)

There is probably truth to disputed stories that Grant collapsed in his cot on the second night of the Wilderness and cried, either from stress or distress. Like Shiloh, the Wilderness was a boscage Pandemonium, the inferno of American savagery every bit the shrieking polis of national character as Thoreau's Walden Woods. The blows were devastating, and repeated. In two days Lee inflicted 17,500 casualties, and Grant at least 10,000, fewer than the trilogy of carnage at Gettysburg, but horrific beyond an already brutal reality or, seemingly, imagination. Enough tears were to be shed with or without Grant's. Not disputed was a confrontation with one frantic subordinate whose cries exclaimed Lee's brilliance and countenance implored a dolorous, Hooker-like retreat. "I am heartily tired of hearing what Lee is going to do," Grant snapped. "Some of you always seem to think he is going to turn a double somersault and land on our rear and on both our flanks at the same time. Go back to your command, and try to think of what we are going to do ourselves, instead of what Lee is going to do." There would be no turning back, as he had said to Lincoln. He kept going, sidling eastward, trying to get around Lee's right flank and into leverage.

Lee was every inch as resourceful on the defensive as he was formidable on the offensive, and chose positions with an engineer's eye for the maximum advantage. By now, in what was called the Overland Campaign, the enterprise of combat prefigured warfare to come in the next century. Both armies used sophisticated entrenchments, emplacements, and fortifications emphasizing technical prowess and capability above so-called natural valor and courage. Overland's other modern feature was its pounding relentlessness. First for two weeks at Spotsylvania Courthouse, then again to the left at the North Anna river, and then to the left again, at Cold Harbor, always to Grant's left but always steadily southward to the James River, the armies mauled one another. They broke only to move to Grant's left and wrestle again in a kind of odd juxtaposition between professionalized prowess and the jugular frontier instinct of "no holts barred," a backwoods Americanism epitomizing the frenzy of Spotsylvania, where stabbing and clubbing, eye-gouging, scratching, biting, and even hair-pulling prevailed. Lee himself, twice, made his way toward the front intending to lead charges across some of the campaign's most savagely contested ground. These desperate offers of self-sacrifice were rejected out-of-hand by soldiers ("General Lee go back! General Lee to the rear!") who offered up themselves in his stead. Neither desperation nor suicide were one-sided. By early June Grant had perhaps grown frustrated by his opponent's skill in parrying him, or the campaign's always-to-the-leftedness, or both. On June 3, at Cold Harbor (so named for an old traveler's hostel that traded on its wayside convenience with a decided lack of hospitality) Grant launched a Somme-like assault which he later confessed to regret. His columns attacked frontally. They were mown down by the thousands in a matter of an hour.

It had been a month, and both armies had been carved in half. Some 65,000 Union soldiers were killed and wounded, at the cost of almost 35,000 Confederates. No campaign in American history has before or since equaled Overland's slaughter. Never before had the War been that *daily*, that constantly, grindingly bloody or costly, for either side. Yet Grant's losses, approximately the size of Lee's whole army, might be replaced. Lee could ill afford anything other than maximum human efficiency above and below ground. The Union commander was no mere butcher, as had been said about him in 1862 by Northern enemies, and which was also the rebuke lurking first in Lee's private correspondence and then revealed openly, at surrender, when Lee assured the Army of Northern Virginia that it simply had been overwhelmed by numbers and resources. Grant had applied his arithmetic unwaveringly as at Cold Harbor, yet many times also cleverly. Lee's own successes, such as they had been, were in combination with mistakes of his own that he had been extemporaneously keen enough to amend.[7]

Grant's last move was his shrewdest. On June 12, he lunged suddenly for the James, then over the James, for Petersburg, thirty kilometers south of Richmond. This was a decisive shift from the strategy of skinning Lee's army, or even holding a leg, to one of clenching at Lee's stomach. Petersburg, fed by five railroads, was a vital railway and riverine supply hub. If Grant took Petersburg, Lee would be forced to abandon Richmond but also abandon all conventional means of feeding and supplying his army. Grant disguised the move brilliantly – Lee, normally preternaturally sensile to the choices of his opponents, was kept in the dark for almost four days. Only at the brink did the Army of Northern Virginia arrive in front of Petersburg to prevent Grant from seizing it outright. A siege was not what Grant wanted but what he had, and not what Lee wanted, either. Yet if Lee could hold out until November, if Grant couldn't break through before the presidential election, siege might make for stalemate. Verily for both, each looking over a shoulder, it was a matter of time.

****

The most communal experience of the American Civil War was suffering, pain its most egalitarian instrumentality. Death became its most democratic agent. Had it been possible in 1861 for white Americans to foresee what war would cost, or to know the depth of suffering's penetrations, they would rather obviously never have resorted to it. They would have compromised on slavery in keeping with a long if nervous precedent. The effects of death spared no feature and no layer of American life, and virtually no institution. Its scale and diffusion ruptured the assumptions of both civic and domestic convention, and, for many, produced an anomalous sense of disconnection, alienation, and anonymity. Death's most dislocating feature was perhaps its strangest. For all it rent asunder, it seemed such a profound feature of everyday life that life itself was pallid existence within it, the prisoner's routine, the psalmist's miry clay, the slough of despond.

The American Civil War's casualty figures can seem perversely quaint or (even more perversely) barbarically premodern in an age that deals death in the tens of millions and delivers its weapons via seemingly autonomous technologies. Yet the 750,000 war dead – perhaps as many as 850,000: we simply do not know – represented 2 percent of the American population in 1860. One million more, or 3 percent, were wounded. By percentage those figures are not inconsistent with the destroying World Wars of the twentieth century. Two or three basic reasons explain the holocaust. In the decades before secession, the expansion of weaponry and technology converted death's erstwhile cache into a feretory. The new arsenals housed rifled musketry of expanded range and accuracy; the new artillery caissons were stocked with macabre varieties of fuse, casing, and shell capable of carnal and sonic mayhem beyond the range of eyesight. Yet battlefield tactics were slow to adjust, with adaptations limited not so much by encrusted tradition as by insurmountable problems of communication, coordination, and maneuver. The major armies fought one another in closed-order formations of rank and row that massed ever more deadly firepower on the parallel masses of their opponents. These tactics were suitable in the age of the smoothbore volley, which compensated in concentrated power for what it could not deliver in efficiency. Prior to the 1850s, an effective musket volley was limited to 45 or 50 meters, and that perhaps on a windless day. Rifled technology and the Minié ball doubled or tripled mutilation's reach for even the greenhorn soldier, while a technician, such as the Confederate at Spotsylvania Courthouse who felled a Union general from 900 meters away, might have felt like a sharper in an arcade game.[8]

The vilest, most lethal of killers was far more devastating. Disease carried off twice as many as did weapons, and it took under great swaths of men whether convalescing from combat wounds, as was the case with the pneumonia that killed Stonewall Jackson, or recuperating in camps and bivouacs between campaigns. Fevers, poxes, fluxes – dysentery, diarrhea – were not only common but often fatal and did not by any means empty a catalog of contractible bodily chaos that also offered the parasitical and the fungal (lice, ringworm), the bronchial (pleurisy), or the venal-*cum*-mortal (syphilis). Sanitary practices in hospitals or in camps were atrocious by any measure because only the scarcest minds were opened to the germ theory of disease. Water supplies were easily contaminated, cholera but the worst of many fears. The most infamous example, Sweetwater Creek at Andersonville Prison in Georgia, was atypical since its black humors served an overcrowded prison camp, yet illustrative because it was a shared water source for tens of thousands of filthy men. The stream ran through an open-air stockade of some ten hectares in which as many as 30,000 Union prisoners were crammed at any one time – almost one-third of those who went into Andersonville never came out of it. Hospitals were sometimes no better, medicine often worse than the disease. Harried surgeons hustled from one operation to the next, one gash and stitch to the next, one amputation to the next, having neither time nor knowledge, one patient to the next, to sterilize the instruments of healing. Nursing, professionalized dramatically during the War, was likely as not a simple act of merciful, godly companionship.

Much like the "elephant" of the battlefield experience was shatteringly displacing, a soldier's life in camp, especially under these circumstances, required social adjustments common to both sides. The soldiering men of the American Civil War were on average older than those of the modern era – the hypothetically typical soldier of both armies was an unmarried, 25-year-old, native-born grunt decamped from the family farm. (A Union soldier was decidedly more likely to have been foreign-born: almost 500,000 of the 2 million men in the Union army were immigrants.) Nonetheless they were nurtured within a culture overspread by the domestic pieties of the Victorian era. Leaving home was an act of discomfiture even for the most ardent of patriotic volunteers. For married men with their own families (if not "average" then certainly so very common as to be unremarkable) it could be accompanied by a wrenching ambivalence that only the shaming threat of conscription might jostle. The other exacting adjustment was to the tedium and boredom of it all. Most of the War, the breadth and depth of its unrelenting vastness, after all, was fought in camp, against war's monotony, against banality, against rote and rotten food, against lice, against the dull day today and the yawning dull day after that.[9]

There is no denying the still-salient view that for many soldiers the War became as much about their comrades as it did their causes. The common terror of battle, and of touching elbows alongside one another facing sudden, violent death, was a transcendent, catalytic bonding experience – lifelong, even if the life alongside was instantaneously extinguished. The various ways that men passed through the utter blankness of shared ennui in camp, and the various ways by which they sought to compensate for it by replicating or at least mimicking as many of the rhythms and features of the domestic family life left behind, also were responsible for their bonds. Their relationships and affections were fraternal and often paternal, and sometimes they were quasi-maternal. For some they were sexual. Something of the lastingness of fellowship, something of the enduring physical and requisite psychological need for touching elbows, as it were, is evident in the hugely subscribed veterans' organizations of the postwar. The Grand Army of the Republic, the largest Union association, and tellingly by 1890 open to black veterans by rule but often segregated in practice, reached half a million members. (The organization's purpose was political as well as social. Veterans drew government pensions that by then accounted for more than 40 percent of the national budget.) The United Confederate Veterans in the same period enrolled as many as 160,000 members, between a third and a quarter of all surviving Confederates.

In local chapter meetings and civic memorial parades and immense encampments at national reunions, including the dual encampments of Union and Confederate veterans at Gettysburg in 1913, the mythic battle's semi-centennial, and again in 1938 at its 75th anniversary, the old soldiers were seeking. As young men of the rank and file they had been abruptly snatched away from domestic life. As veterans they were often adrift in the massive economic and social sea-change that flushed over postwar industrial America. The America of their elder years no longer resembled the country they had volunteered to preserve, as Union soldiers, or, as Confederates, the America they would have restored to its original vision. The physically maimed were so common that Southern states not known for social welfare paid for prosthetic arms and legs. Eventually these entitlements evolved into valuable state pensions that made the widowed ex-Confederate, no matter how ancient or indeed upright, a prized suitor well into the twentieth century. The damaged were a common sight, too, in the streets or at courthouse squares, at the doors or in the windows of rehabilitative soldiers' homes, at asylums for the maniacal, at facilities for the elderly infirm. Ravaged by post-traumatic stress, they often felt cut off and set aside unless among compeers. Their nostalgia – defined purest as a *painful* longing for home – was acute, and their fraternal organizations were most certainly not the play of old soldiers fading away. They were now mimicking the domestic rhythms and features of the camp life left behind them, for many wanted, many desperately, the initial immersive experience of their youth.[10]

For all of that, their connections home, as soldiers, were never completely severed, and the degree to which they were able to convey the authenticity of their war has perhaps been unequalled before or since. Union soldiers were overwhelmingly literate, Confederate soldiers somewhat less so, and besides the thousands upon thousands of letters going back and forth between home and camp (none censored) were the hundreds of newspapers and magazines of a remarkably vibrant if nosy reading culture. All were political and partisan in the constructions they might give to their war news, which was held to dubious standards of accuracy. A few were illustrated. The young art of photography was the most affective medium of communication, also the newest, and the revolutionary contributions of the discipline's most renowned practitioner, Mathew Brady, rode sidelong with the traveling darkrooms that he sent to record the War's eastern battlefields in the immediate aftermath. These bloodfields framed a vision of grim desolation in black and white – they remain haunting. Nevertheless, there was no thought of suppression. Brady opened his first public exhibition in New York only a month after Antietam, concurrent with autumn elections that turned out disastrously for Republicans. For both sides, the War was vitally democratic in what was known about it, how it was known, and by how many. The grinding tedium was among them all, everyday.

Just so, suffering was transmissive, vicariously but also quite literally. A widely circulated conventional estimate places the

Figure 27: Confederate prisoners at Gettysburg, Library of Congress, Public Domain.

number of civilian war dead at 50,000, although that figure is absurdly low and figures to change, rather drastically. It accounts only for Southern civilians and is, in the truest of senses, a guess. The *rex ultimus* of all war-killers did not spare those at home. Ravenous diseases moved along far-spreading vectors impossible to halt at mobilization or quarantine within the tented cities of the plain, be they soldiers' camps or the Union's improvised "contraband" camps set up to care for the massive influxes of runaway slaves. (These particularly were places of "extreme destitution and suffering.") One wretched casualty was none other than Lincoln's young son Willie, who contracted typhoid in 1862 via water sources contaminated by the Army of the Potomac. His death plunged Lincoln into an impenetrable darkness and Mary Todd Lincoln into near madness. Most assuredly, the traditional wages of sin and war – starvation and malnutrition, siege-gun bombardments, the hardships and calamities among thousands of displaced refugees, rapine and murder, mere randomness, accident, or proximite mischief like that meted on aged Judith Henry, cannonballed in the very first battle of the War at Bull Run – also levied shares. Comparatively few Southern civilians were intentional targets of Union warfare, whatever the unpredictable savagery of guerrilla operations or the stories that accompanied the legendary terror of Sherman's March. The final tally, when and if it comes, must also consider what can only be deemed thousands of slaves killed by Confederates through exposure or exhaustion as conscripted labor or, in incidents of the Confederacy's own organized terror, executed locally as suspected insurrectionaries.

By modern standards the civilian mortuary also seems like a parochial concern. Still, if the military conflict was not dissimilar to a twentieth-century World War fought in America alone, the toll on civilians was a war all unto itself. Actually it was three of them, since the (guessed) civilian death toll was at least equivalent to the combined military deaths in the three major American wars coming before. Americans, quite clearly, must cope. Yet they could not, not fully. No aspect of dying, a social ritual of vast importance in the nineteenth century, was spared a scything. The ideal Victorian died at home, in bed, in circumstances far more quietly intimate and peaceful than the hurtling pandemonium that blew up the widow Henry. One died known, surrounded by family, not anonymously, not alone, shoved in a hole in some far-off field or flicked into a mass grave alongside scores of unidentified others like lint swept away into a dustpan. And most importantly, one died whole in spirit, with a confession of faith, with suitable parting words of stricture, scripture, or inspiration. One was not supposed to die in twisted spasms, writhing, unintelligible in pain. One was not supposed to die in pieces, not headless, one died whole in body, not as a trunk with no arms or as legs with no trunk: how, then, to face the Resurrection?

Ten thousands of ten thousands did. The American Civil War exposed the death ideal for the ritual of piety it was, for the unequal way it had attempted to organize meaning. Putting convention back together again was beyond the capacity of the war generation. Putting any convention in its place would have been: for what *possibly* could death on this scale mean? Like everything else

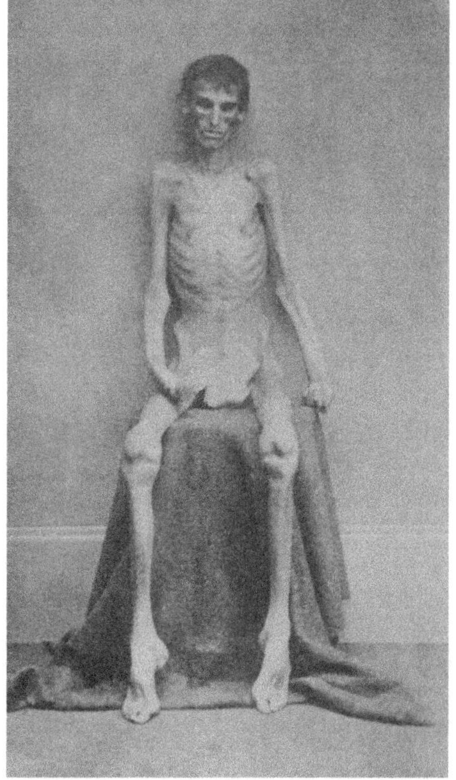

Figure 28: A Union prisoner of war at Andersonville, Public Domain.

obliterated in the War, the duties and pieties of Victorian convention were simply not to scale with the magnitude of the suffering.[11]

It remained to be decided whether democracy was.

****

The responsibility of defending the rest of the Confederacy from the Union's armies was not for Lee but for Davis. These were several, all grasping separately at once, and there was less of the Confederacy left either physically or materially to come to grips with them. In virtually every vital logistical aspect of war-making, but especially in manpower, Confederate resources were taxed or failing – conscription (never popular) was now expanded to adolescents as young as 17 and men as old as 50. Mobilizing them would not solve the equally pressing matters of arming, clothing, and feeding them, or of succoring them in the sure-to-come necessities of hospital ward and cemetery hole.

The matter would, then, be one of acute choices. Grant had placed 10,000 men in the Shenandoah Valley, a critical region of Confederate supply and its preferred strategic corridor northward. Davis must needs defend it but could only scrape up half that number to occupy it, and some of these were teenage cadets from the Virginia Military Institute in Lexington. Surprisingly, that cheeky force achieved a limited Confederate success in May and even secured the spring harvest. Yet Union pressure was too forbidding to hold the Valley indefinitely. By early June another Union force had been constituted and given over to the command of David Hunter, and this was a dastardly omen. In keeping with the proclivity to name as *black* anything or anyone darkly threatening to racial order, Hunter's enemies called him "Black Dave" – he was among the earliest advocates of emancipation and the enlistment of black soldiers. Subsequently Hunter would be infamous in the Shenandoah for the baseness of his treachery (there were abiding family connections in the Valley) and his tactics. He advanced entirely through it to Lexington, where he preempted further adolescent cheekiness by burning the Virginia Military Institute. For good measure he ashened the combativeness of their elders by torching the home of the governor who had led Virginia out of the Union in 1861.

The Valley was vital, the most crucial of all secondary operations east of the Mississippi River, but not the only. Grant was also sending grasping armies into western Virginia, into coastal Alabama, and, even prior to going there himself with the entire Army of the Potomac at the end of the Overland Campaign, toward Petersburg. A small army, including a contingent of black troops, had been gathered to threaten the all-important city of supply under the now-infamous Benjamin Butler (his birth-given name; his Confederate-given one was the Beast, an apocalyptic variation suited to blackened figures of the abolitionist mien). Still, these were skinning places. Grant threatened them as means to his larger end. From Davis's vantage, Richmond must absolutely be held at all costs. The other absolute was Atlanta. After the rolling collapse of the Confederacy's continental aspirations following Vicksburg and Chattanooga, Atlanta was all that remained of the nation's kicking power at the hind.

Defending it, as ever, was the Army of Tennessee. By 1864 Braxton Bragg's tenure in command of it had become untenable. The second of the two great rebel armies had little to show for its valor, and its disappointments were all the more lowering for its tantalizing near breakthroughs. To old complaints about Bragg's cantankerous, imbecilic authoritarianism (only the second adjective seemed debatable) were added failure's indisputable reality. Whatever the merits of the legend that Bragg savored a good argument, even with himself, the tale seems as if it would have been invented even were it not true. It was a ready-made allegory for the Army's pathology of bickering, and unpalatably tangible in its sad-sack mien. Much of the quarreling involved matters of rank and status and power, the baneful vanities familiar to human organizations everywhere. At least one disagreement, though, went right to the great triumvirate's essential core in the Confederate cause.

In January 1864, a year's anniversary of the Emancipation Proclamation, one of the army's generals quietly circulated an explosive prescription among several officers: the Confederacy should emancipate its slaves, arm them, and enlist their aid as Confederate soldiers. This was from the pen of Patrick Cleburne, an Irish immigrant turned Arkansas apothecary. Matters had come to the point where the Confederate revolution could only be sustained by actuating an internal revolution. Nowhere else was there manpower for the cause, aside from cadet boys or the old men of the state militias whose efficacies might be trolled from A. J. P. Taylor's devious appraisal of the British home guard in the Second World War – its membership contributed petty harassments and archeological curiosities to the war effort but "would have been massacred if they had managed to assemble at all." More vitally, Cleburne did not deny what everyone could see, and knew for themselves, whether or not they had courage to acknowledge their self-awareness. Black soldiers already were fighting for the Union, and "the experience of this war has been so far that half-trained Negroes have fought as bravely as many other half-trained Yankees." Experience and courage, then, were Cleburne's operative words. The theory by which slaves were held as slaves, and the ideology that had exalted the rank and status and power of white men, had been swept away. The Confederacy was on the precipice of joining its theories in oblivion. Men to prevent it – black men – could only be found on home ground.

Some likened Cleburne's relentless battlefield instincts to those of the incomparable Stonewall Jackson, but, aggressive as this vision was, the proposal went as far as Cleburne was willing. Slaves would be freed from slavery, that was all. He proffered no path to citizenship and made no advocacy for equality. The Confederate polity would somehow see to it that emancipation ended at emancipation, for emancipation was not freedom. The former slaves would fight out of loyalty, for their former masters, for their homes. Yet those in the army to whom Cleburne offered his recommendation received it in silence, because they knew what it meant. The same republican impulse that channeled citizenship and equality through military service, and which already was revolutionizing the Union, would do the same in the Confederacy, only to cut darker pathways. If it enlisted a black soldiery, the Confederate nation would need a new organizing idea directly at odds with the overwhelming sacrifices made in service to the old one. "You cannot make slaves of soldiers, nor soldiers of slaves," one Confederate leader eventually argued, less in reply to plentiful contrary evidence than in fealty to ideological purity. "The day you make a soldier of them is the beginning of the end of the Revolution." Soon the contents of Cleburne's proposal were known more widely, and the dissension among Bragg's officers threatened even more demoralization, because this was precisely what Lincoln had argued in 1862. We must free the slaves, Cleburne maintained, or be ourselves subdued. Davis ordered the proposal and all discussion of its contents suppressed.[12]

But the president could do nothing to tame the feuding focalized around Bragg. By 1864 Davis had plucked from himself so many slings and arrows to know their sting owed something to simple, ungenerous antagonism. Bragg's record was not disastrous – if he had not won the War in the west he had not *lost* it, either – but no other course could assuage the Army of Tennessee's incurable ill feelings than Bragg's removal from it. In February, after Cleburne's shocking proposal had been stuffed inside a cubbyhole, Bragg was called to Richmond to sit in the same bureaucratic nook occupied by a similarly star-fallen Lee two years before. Reluctantly, Davis turned the western army over to Joseph E. Johnston, whose wounding in Virginia in 1862 had been the unwitting shot that freed Lee and his vision. Davis could not have been looking for a similar stroke of fortune, not when miseries abounded or when they were shortly to be multiplied into torment by the accidental playtime death of his 5-year-old son. For here, as he knew, was merely resolving one set of contentions by replacing them with another.

Johnston's conviction that Davis had wronged him from the very start of the War had never abated. He had certainly been employed since returning to service, but to his salted mind ill-used. It had been Johnston in nominal authority over the improvised force that Grant swept aside like a horde of summer flies at Jackson, during the Vicksburg campaign. By then Johnston had also become associated with a power bloc of striving politicians and officers (itself riven by envy, rivalry, and competition) clamorous for a concentration of Confederate efforts and resources in the Western theater. Davis suspected these men as seekers of smooth things – while Johnston, for his part, was aggrieved to be put in the awful, impossible position of commanding an army of summer flies in Mississippi. More substantively, Johnston never felt that Davis trusted him. This was for the very good reason that Davis didn't. He didn't fancy the likeness of his own faults mirrored in Johnston's prickled sense of honor and Johnston's unfortunate habit of self-justification.

Figure 29: Joseph E. Johnston (1807–1891), Public Domain.

Johnston was not Lee nor even Bragg. His Fabian mode of warfare, as in his campaign outside Richmond in 1862, traded territory for conservation and timely advantage. Yet much like Lincoln had once felt a necessary evil in relying on McClellan, going as far as to say that he would hold McClellan's horse if it meant victory, Davis felt the imperative of no other choice. Johnston commanded the admiration of his soldiers. Their morale would (and did) brighten. And, at least for the time being – or better said: especially in this, the time being, with Lincoln's reelection on the horizon – Johnston's strategic strengths might be useful. The provisos, of course, were that his decisions be neither too defensive nor too Fabian. Here was an intricate balance, and an impossible one if Davis suspected that Johnston already believed the cause too desperate to win, or that Johnston projected a personal mystique that, like McClellan's, was very much screened by the things he could have done *if only* rather than the general he was when he did them. No Fabian decision could be trusted if either were the case.

Ultimately mistrust won out. At the beginning of May, Sherman, Grant's most gifted subordinate, left Chattanooga with 100,000 men divided into three operational armies and opened the campaign for Atlanta. There was no immediate devastating Confederate counterpunch, as Lee had launched in the Wilderness. Instead, Johnston sought advantage in maneuver and position, using the 50,000 men with him and the hilly, clay-red terrain of northern Georgia to lengthen his opponent's supply lines, bleed his forces, and deny him a breakthrough. Where Lee and Grant clawed at one another like backwoods wrestlers, Sherman and Johnston whirled like swordsmen, Johnston falling back from one prepared defensive position to the next, Sherman avoiding the futility of frontal assaults, each awaiting, patiently, an opportunity to cut. Sherman moved almost always to his right: Resaca, New Hope Church, Dallas, Marietta – only at Kennesaw Mountain, on June 27, did impatience best him. He launched a frontal attack there and wasted 3,000 casualties in two hours. Although not the equivalent of Grant's homicidal mistake at Cold Harbor, Kennesaw was horrid enough. He never repeated it. Johnston's loss in killed and wounded had been fewer than 1,000.

Had there been more of these efficient bloodlettings, and less the elegance of maneuver that one latter-day novelist imagined as a red-clay minuet, Johnston might have been vindicated. As it happened he became for Sherman what he already was for Grant – the most respected of opposing generals. He had kept the Army of Tennessee intact, had managed to keep Sherman out of Atlanta, and had rather significantly reduced the disparity of force between them. Even the quarreling among his army's leadership had diminished. (Most certainly, sniping had not ceased, not even after the cessation of one its most self-satisfied generals, Leonidas Polk, the Episcopal bishop who had taken it on himself to seize neutral Kentucky back in 1861. Beloved by his men, not so revered by peers doubting him as a messianic martinet, Polk was torn into strips by an artillery shell in June. "We killed Bishop Polk yesterday," Sherman reported, "and made good progress today.") Within ten days of Kennesaw Mountain, Sherman was as close to Atlanta as McClellan had once been to Richmond. In Virginia, Grant had lunged across the James River and was threatening Petersburg. On July 17, after Johnston moved the Army of Tennessee behind the

Chattahoochee River, the last significant natural barrier between Sherman and Atlanta, Davis sacked him.[13]

****

The spirits of the republic's founders had never been far off, warning as they had, within the lifetimes of some of those now grandmother and grandfather to the dead, that "when a people or a family so divide, it never fails to be against themselves." Those were now voices hearkening across a wilderness mutilated by their filiopietistic sons, Cain slaying Cain, in rivalry. Yet it seemed by the summer of 1864 that there were other silhouetted presences revisiting the landscapes of war and memory. One was George B. McClellan, whose Janus apparition, like July's haze, hung over the summer campaigns in north Georgia and Virginia, one face the foil for Johnston in his familiar defense of Atlanta, the other wisping with Grant outside of Richmond, not for anything Grant had done like him but for what Grant promised to do in gory contrast. After two years' absence McClellan was still admired by thousands of tattered, war-grim veterans in the camps of the Army of the Potomac. They had followed him out of empowering affection. The resolve they gave to Grant was genuine yet brokered, Grant the middleman in a consensus transaction of making their arithmetic work for the cause. His enumerating competence tended not to make McClellan a forgotten man but rather to keep kindled a fondness for him as a kind of soldier-prince in exile.[14]

McClellan might have been at home in New Jersey, yet in the summer of 1864 he was still very much in the War *as is*. He remained the leading apologist and symbol of the conservative war, and remained, as always had he been, even while commanding the Army of the Potomac, a leading visage in Democratic Party politics. Surely he knew he would never be summoned again to take the field as long as Lincoln was president and the Republicans in power. Just as surely, in a divided North, and predictably too, there were steady calls for his reinstatement. For significant numbers of Northerners, the principles of his Harrison's Landing Letter had been vindicated by carnal violence and revolutionary whorl.

Far from benumbing, death and suffering had become disembodied and created a liminality across which all sorts of spirits might move. To the unfathomable gogools of the dead had been added the many thousands gone of the spring and summer campaigns. For loved ones in greater and greater sums, desperate in grief, visitations from the afterlife were longed for: spiritualists, mediums, clairvoyants, and other masters of the occult answered for the yawning chasm between the Good Death's ritual and its failure to comprehend yearning. The disappeared by now included more than 50,000 held in the swollen, overcrowded prison camps on either side. They withered away in these places, diseased, emaciated, as skeletal flesh-forms discomposing into graves. Before 1863 many of them could have hoped to be exchanged. The hard war of 1864 had collapsed those protocols. Grant's refusal to exchange was partly a retaliation for Confederate policy toward black Union prisoners but manifestly strategic. A greater inhumanity – the usurping gods of war adjudicate morality for themselves – was prevented thereby, averted therefrom: Union soldiers would constantly be killed by a replenishing enemy. The requirement of vanquishing the enemy would, in turn, require the enemy's utter extermination. The resulting breakdown bloated prison populations and multiplied prisons, even where, as at Andersonville, prisons were not much more than fence-piles and girdling stockades.

Somehow the notion of swollen prisons feeding on war's girth seemed an existential absurdity too massive to contemplate when set against the vanishing size of the individuals in them. Almost no abstraction or metaphor worked to interpret the experience without confronting its own collapse. Domestic images of a family or a people or a house divided embossed sentiment upon enfeebled convention, for a hardened ruthlessness had darkened even the indwelling places. In neighborhoods across the South, irregular warfare had long since lost any semblance of coherence. From their earliest incarnations, many Confederate guerrillas had severed themselves from any practical relationship to the war effort and become indistinguishable from vigilantes, deserters, marauders, and bootlegging outlaws who as often as not terrorized the local populations they were supposed to protect. Wherever these vacuums of power appeared the so-called brothers conflict was hardly metaphorical but substantiated in intimate factional conflicts between Unionists and Confederates spun loose from the conventional war and so callous as to devolve into the basest inhumanities.

By 1864 the Confederacy abandoned the electric hopes that had greeted its sanction of local defense two years earlier in the Partisan Ranger Act and repealed it. That was a paper decision. Called by whatever name – guerrilla insurgency, partisan war, irregular operations – local violence between mutated adjuncts was anything but divorced from a conventional war of increasing vindictiveness. Their savage descent *was* the War. Mass hangings, lynchings, back-against-the-wall executions – in Gainesville, Texas, in 1862; at Shelton Laurel, in the mountains of North Carolina in 1863, as in these places of infamy so in Virginia, in Tennessee, in South Carolina or Florida or Georgia, so everywhere where terrified neighbors and kin, sympathetic Unionists or die-hard Confederates, sought security, advantage, the first strike, or reprisal. The war in Missouri became a dystopian birthing ground for exploitation and manhood-as-murder on both sides, its stakes measured in its humiliations and its Manichean all-or-nothingness. Even today its malice remains translucent in the figures of those who were called ghosts or phantoms or demons, not to liken them unto surreal figments but to objectify their fear. They materialized suddenly as both merciless tactic and heinous affect, and they were only the most vicious in the ranks of known and unknown vigilantes: Jesse James, Bloody Bill Anderson, James H. Lane, William Quantrill – the first became America's most famous outlaw, the lattermost was already infamous for a criminal massacre in 1863 in which his guerrillas rode into Lawrence, Kansas, and killed or executed outright 150 men and boys. To this act of mayhem a Union general responded by ordering the depopulation of several Missouri counties, which he then wasted by fire of fodder and forage.

Local vacuums were increasingly widespread in 1864 as the Confederacy contracted. Incidents such as these may neither surprise nor tell in an era habituated to vile cruelty and genocide. For Americans who had prided themselves on their civilization's triumph above barbarism, they were hideous self-portraits. One of the few effective Confederate partisans, John S. Mosby, operated in northern Virginia and the Shenandoah Valley, and understood his role as complementary to Lee's Army of Northern Virginia. Yet for every Mosby was an anonymous renegade, such as John W. Mobberly, disconnected or disaffected from the cause, killing for fun, local reputation, profit, or the *lex talionis*. Mobberly's death,

Figure 30: Turner Ashby, 1862, Public Domain.

Figure 31: William T. ("Bloody Bill") Anderson, by Robert B. Kice, October 27, 1864, Public Domain.

surely at the hands of men he knew and as eye-for-an-eye sudden as his rise, remains a blood meridian of the War's brutally familiar, equally consanguine American brutality. Lured to a Virginia farm in the spring of 1865, Mobberly cantered up into the barnyard only to hear a cock of his killers' guns. He could only mutter his sudden awareness – "Oh Lord, I'm gone" – just before, in the blast of murderous fact, he was. Hardly more loquacious is his tombstone. It is visible even now as the epigraph of a liminal brutishness: "was born, was assassinated."[15]

Of all harrows, it was this, the twitching echo of John Brown's prophecy of blood-purging, which seemed a harp-song hanging in the blasted trees of the land. And it was Brown, verily, whose presence stalked far and near in 1864, north and south, very much himself still in the War as is. He was marching in Union legions multiplied many times over his original band, and the cause for which he was executed was now the national one. He had appeared to Confederates, too, earlier in 1864, as a palimpsest in Cleburne's proposal: victory *depended* on black men as the difference between independence and subjugation. This was the shattering fact of the War, its *logos*. Emancipation was the only available path to victory. Looming in the shadow of that truth was the question of taking it or leaving it, the proverbial Hobson's choice that both would-be nations had been brought to face. Confederates had suppressed their choice under a psychological and ideological mandate, abstracted from democracy because Davis quashed it by fiat. But in fact they chose leaving it. For Lincoln and the Republicans in 1864, the choice was democracy's essential looming decision.

Time was not necessarily Lincoln's ally. Stalemate was failure – it was tied to the capability of Confederates to force the issue in front of the Union before it rose to confront their own cause. Under stalemate's pressure ("you must *act*," he said) Lincoln had sent McClellan home as early as 1862. Still, all summer, all along the line, more pits – digging for entrenchments, digging for graves – and no closer to bottom. Sherman had advanced on Atlanta, so had Grant on Richmond, and while both were within sight of Confederate strongholds, neither seemed immediately closer to victory. McClellan, after all, had been there before. The worst of all catastrophes occurred outside Petersburg in July. After six weeks of siege war, Grant's Union miners secretly tunneled under the Confederate works and packed the shaft with 3,600 kilograms of gunpowder. On the morning of July 30, they blew it all to smithereens, only to see hope extinguished in a botch. The shock troops selected to pour through the gaping hole in Confederate lines instead stormed into the massive crater created by the explosion. They were murdered there like rats scurrying for lees in an earth-turned cellar. Grant was utterly saddened (the depressions of the Crater are still visible today) and took solace only strangely, that is, in his own mistake, which had been to replace the black troops specially trained for the mission with unprepared white ones.

He had done this bit of shifting, he said, so that if the attack failed the cause could not be accused of butchering its own black troops. It says much about the state of things that Grant must worry about such cynical voices gaining audience. For on the heels of the Crater fiasco the face of conservatism seemed to rise from it, in the flesh. In August, meeting in Chicago, the Democratic Party convention nominated McClellan as its candidate for president. A cacophony of convention voices howled above the deadened military doldrums, yet as one decried the wicked bastardization of the War: a Union requiring emancipation to save was not worth the costs of securing it. Unimaginable casualties were the supreme first of all tolls. The levies were laded also in the stacks of treasurer's bills, extorted in the unholy tributes taken by war profiteers, exacted by the evils of conscription, wrung from the Constitution by gagging civil liberties. They were measured, all of them, in the corruptions of emancipation and a miscegenated republic. Even Clement L. Vallandigham, the symbol of ultra-resistance to the Republicans and to Lincoln, who had been banished to Confederate lines and then to Canada in 1863 only to run (and be defeated) for governor of Ohio *in absentia*, had returned and made his way to Chicago unmolested.

Peace was the party's central plank. Upon a Democratic victory the War was to be stopped and reunion sought by negotiation and compromise. Only the truest disciples actually thought the plank plausible – not because emancipation couldn't be reneged but because halting the War was tantamount to acknowledging Confederate independence. McClellan himself favored continuing the War, though weighing on his stance was the plank's inherent revocation of the sacrifices tendered by soldiers he once commanded.

He might also have considered the heavier burden of history, which then as now suggests the difficulty of any American political party sustaining an oppositional position in wartime. Thus did McClellan accept the nomination but repudiate the peace plank. On this matter, and the uncertain prospects Democratic divisions offered for McClellan's victory in November, the chroniclers of the War have scuttled and scrawled in disagreement. Their arguments can be reduced to the proposition that the Democratic party was too riven by its own dysfunctional conflicts to win the 1864 election.

Yet those considerations presume clarity elsewhere when conflation was everywhere. There had been progress – but over four punishing years. To Lincoln belonged ownership and burden of unprecedented weights and pressures, convulsions, unprecedented costs, all of which seemed hollowed in the skeletal gauntness of his face and frame and gave to him the semblance of nothing so much as a prisoner of the War. His burdens were cumbered in an unreachable heaviness of spirit that he called, simply, "the tired spot." The discordant voices of his own party, for example, are not to be dismissed. Republican factions battered Lincoln on the right, while powerful but dissatisfied influences on the left sought to deny him renomination. Among them were Salmon P. Chase, a cabinet secretary and conscience of the radicals, whose backroom machinations – one might call them ongoing contributions to the tired spot – Lincoln had deftly handled before. In June Lincoln removed Chase from his cabinet, and from his path to renomination, by subtly exchanging Chase's resignation for an assurance of appointing him chief justice of the Supreme Court. In this did Lincoln satisfy elements on his right for whom Chase was threat and torment, yet also transpose disquiets on the dead: for surely did Roger A. Taney, whose death in October opened the vacancy for Chase, the Taney who in 1857 authored the doctrine that black men had no rights bound to a white man's respect, quiver in his tomb. Concurrently, Lincoln accepted the resignation of another secretary, the conservative Montgomery Blair, long the bane of the left wing. Neither appeasement nor egg-and-spoon balancing prevented a radical faction from breaking anyway and nominating as its own candidate John C. Frémont, the standard-bearer of 1856. His generalship may have been tinctured, but his abolitionism was not.

Meanwhile the party must maintain and attract as much of the nationalist element as it might, consistent with emancipation. Very much wanted and needed was the support of War Democrats and other conservative nationalists who might first flinch at emancipation but could not countenance McClellan and the Peace Democrats. But to these the mark of the Republican Party might carry the tinge of revolutionary "black Republicanism." By a nifty bit of trimming did tipsy Republicans begin to call themselves the National Union Party, and they nominated Lincoln for a second term in July at a convention in Baltimore. Pragmatically, as another shill to national unity and conservatism, the vice-presidency was tendered to Andrew Johnson. Johnson was a hard-crusted Unionist and former Democrat born in North Carolina in direst poverty, the son of a washerwoman. He had since moved to the mountains of eastern Tennessee, where he hung a tailor's shingle and by the special help of a wife who taught him his letters had also become a politician of means. His home region was one of the areas turned upside-over by local violence. Johnson's selection was further evidence of the dilemma of Union and emancipation, always fraught even in the best times of military progress, and it became a choice the Republicans would rue. His support of emancipation was conditional. It was also rather typical of a conservative position diffused in the fog of hard war. To Johnson, emancipation was punishment for rebellious slaveholders, not freedom for slaves, a retribution on the arrogant exacted as the impost of their conceit.

All by 1864 was cruelly different, altered and expanded, the vestigial and liminal compounded. War was also more of the same. Its unfolding could seem less like progression than mere crumbling, sliding, bottoming. The bloodier the combat, the harder and more violent yet more grounded and stalled, the more persuasive the Democratic case might become that the Union had been the cynical leverage by which emancipation was to be grinded out from the fighting and radicalism accomplished. In that vision the Union dead became the nightmare spirits of those sacrificed in an unholy tribulation, and the election a choice between emancipation or not emancipation – that Hobson's choice – revealed to voters in abiding stalemate. For if the Confederacy were forever separate, so too were all the hazards that had long plagued the conundrum of slavery and Union. Most presently, so were the potential dilemmas

Figure 32: The Crater at Petersburg, Public Domain.

of a victorious aftermath, bound up as they now were in Union and emancipation. The choice was before the people with a clarity and vitality as never before, not even in the 1850s, when the questions were abstruse, not in the election of 1860, when they were obscured by secession and the *rage militaire*, not in 1861 and 1862, when they were attenuated in conservative war.

The difficulties were akin to staring up from the Crater and could be spanned by no meaningful metaphor other than the hole's own inexhaustible darkness. Almost rhythmically, then, in late August, in a despondency that seemed to sound the depths of the tired spot, Lincoln took up a piece of paper and wrote something on it. Two years had passed since his newspaper letter to Horace Greeley in which he had first, tentatively, publically, broached emancipation. A year ago he had been hard at work on the Springfield letter. Folding the paper he now passed it around for his cabinet to sign unseen as a blind pledge. It read: "This morning, as for some days past, it seems exceedingly probable that this Administration will not be re-elected. Then it will be my duty to so co-operate with the President elect, as to save the Union between the election and the inauguration; as he will have secured his election on such ground that he cannot possibly save it afterwards."[16]

****

Confederates were no better guided in their own fog of war, of course, and saw no certain way through its obfuscations. Jefferson

Davis's removal of Johnston outside of Atlanta in July was trusting in the return of boldness as a clarifying agent. The Confederate president's impassioned nationalism for his cause and his brooding skepticism that Northern politics would deliver it comfort and aid were together the ground for his belief that independence could be achieved only by force of arms. The Army of Tennessee's new commander, the fiercely leonine John Bell Hood, considered himself the master pupil of the Lee-Jackson school – of aggressive warfare that "elevates and inspirits." He had paid for his tutelage with paresis of an arm, his left, at Gettysburg, the loss of a leg, his right, at Chickamauga, and the loss of Confederate society's most bewitching belle, whose gaggle of suitors was choicest but also presumably whole (the "hardest battle I [have] ever fought," he said, after she broke off their courtship with the crushing finality of telling him "there was *no hope*"). Fortunately for Hood he had not lost his right hand and so was able to advertise Johnston's strategic frailties in letters to Richmond consistent with the western army's penchant for politics and self-peddling. He remained heavily engaged in that enterprise for the years to come as a combatant in the interminable penstrife of the Lost Cause. The "Joe Johnston mode of warfare," Hood wrote in his memoirs, in response to Johnston's memoirs, which Johnston wrought in response to the emergent Lee-Jackson style in the earliest memoirs, "depresses, paralyzes, and, in time, brings destruction."[17]

The choice of Hood was fraught, doubtful because the headmaster himself was supposedly not convinced of the pupil's first-class honors. "All lion, and none of the fox," Lee was reported to have observed, on learning of the appointment. The comment may very well be falsified, as it fits the postwar's favored offensive tactic of ventriloquizing from the dead Lee any needful testimonial. But the fox's game was exactly what Lee himself had tried, outside Petersburg, at just about the same time Johnston was falling back, and further into Davis's distrust, outside Atlanta. In mid-June, Lee sent a small corps northward through the Shenandoah Valley. Its commander was Jubal Early, yet another of the bold-talking (and later loud-writing) Confederate generals seeking the laurels of the old school. Time and circumstance seemed propitious. A reprise of Jackson's legendary campaign of 1862, undertaken opportunely by Jackson's old corps in its featured locale, was possible once Early's

Figure 33: John Bell Hood (1831–1879), Public Domain.

veterans confronted and handily pushed aside the diabolical force commanded by "Black Dave" Hunter.

By vacating the Valley altogether, Hunter's retreat abetted the game. Early marched through the Valley all the way to Washington, where Jackson himself could not go. In early July he arrived at the very gates of the city. By now the Union capital was surrounded by an inhospitable ring of forts and earthworks, and when a part of Grant's army from the Petersburg front arrived more or less at the same time, Early chose discretion over a Cold Harbor valor. On the way back to Virginia (on the very same day of Grant's ghastly error at the Crater), Early laid fire to Chambersburg, Pennsylvania, leaving it smoking dross in retaliation for Hunter's pillaging. When he returned to the Shenandoah he remained there, at the northern end of the Valley, threat but also feign. Early had not meant to take Washington so much as to "scare Abe Lincoln like hell." His diversion had been to relieve pressure on Petersburg, a gambit to buy time. As always when Lee moved north – all the more so given the November stakes – part of the scare was designed to tilt the enemy's roiling politics.

Not quite so with this new commander, this Hood, facing Sherman's legions outside Atlanta. If the game in Virginia was deceit, Hood was perhaps too devoted to the old school's aggressiveness as a kind of conceit. Davis's initial decision may have leaned on an ever-strong faith in Bragg, a mutual regard that seemed to grow from the antipathy seeding their relationships with many others. Bragg had abetted Davis's doubts in poisoned counsel against Johnston and recommended Hood as a worthy replacement. Yet there is the salience of this fact: once Davis chose Hood, he kept him in command of the Army of Tennessee until Hood's tenure ended in magnificent disaster and there was virtually no longer an Army of Tennessee to command. Some other element, then, might have come wending. The one-legged, one-armed man to whom Davis gave the defense of Atlanta also had something of the last romantic in him – a bit of Sidney Johnston, something too of the courtly-wedded John Pemberton, though Hood's pursuit of the highest of society marriages ended desperately, and, at last, a touch of Bragg himself. Hood believed in Davis (Hood flattered Davis, too) and Davis believed back. In this complex was a certain affect, inarticulate but finessed, an attendant, discernible frisson joining war, masculinity, and romanticism. Something, perhaps, was needed to restore not merely belief in the cause but a belief in war and belief in manhood. Aggressive war elevated and inspirited even the finer feelings, and the finer feelings lifted man.[18]

Salience of fact, sheerness of speculation – whatever the measure of insight – Hood's aggressiveness was feral. Two days after taking command Hood launched an attack at Peachtree Creek. He launched another two days after that. Both were costly to no avail. Sherman's army had hardened into a force of matchless prowess, and it maneuvered in three wings to either side of Atlanta and then south of it, coiling around the city's supplying railroads. By now his operation was a siege in all but name, as with Grant's in Virginia, warfare with a place as prize. Hood either must abandon Atlanta

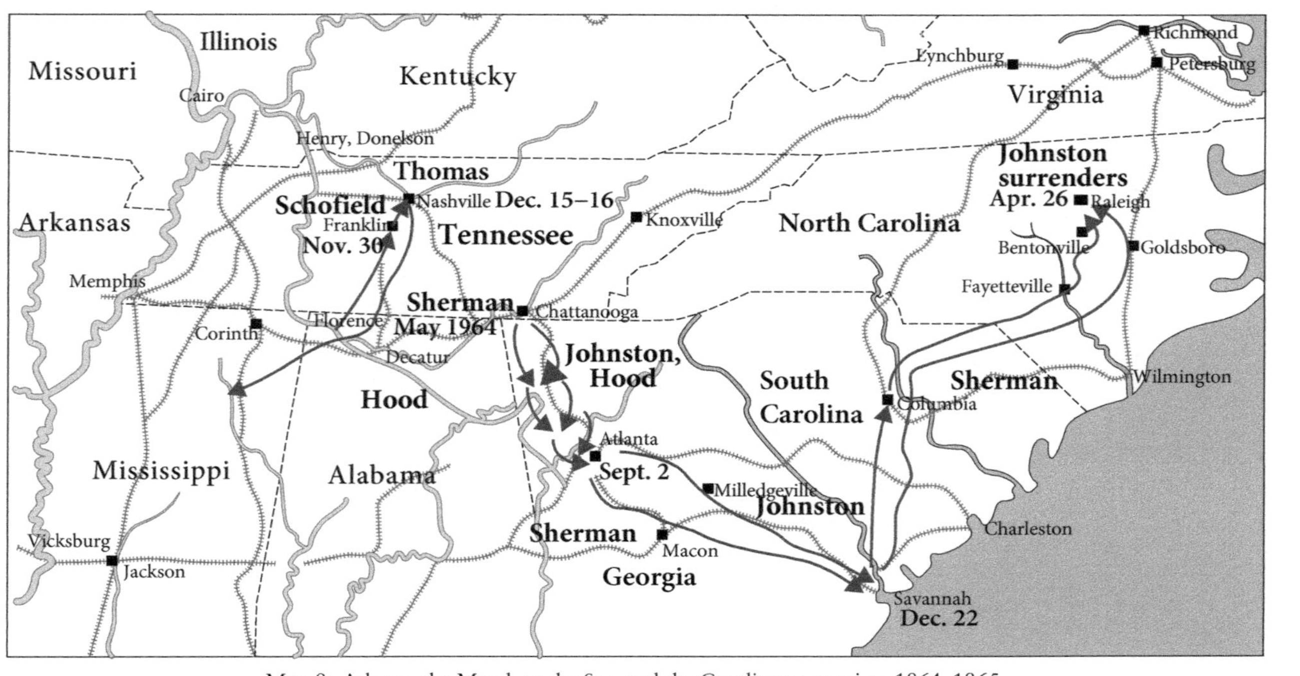

Map 9: Atlanta, the March to the Sea, and the Carolinas campaign, 1864–1865.

or attack even more desperately (and futilely) if he could not protect the railroads that were his vitals. To recommend the former course on his enemy, Sherman began a shelling that lasted the better part of August and occasionally threw 5,000 daily rounds into the city. Hood could do as much about that as he could suspend the endless boom-and-rumble of traffic reverberating off the concrete interstates and overpasses ringing the modern metropolis. Nor could he prevent Sherman's conclusive assault near the artery at Jonesborough. On September 1, Hood blew up all the munitions he could not evacuate – some eighty boxcars full of ordnance – and left. Against that inferno-opening detonation the fury of the Crater might well have been a bonfire lit in a ditch. Atlanta was rubble and ember, but it was Sherman's. Hood slid westward, carried by a dark emotion. "According to all human calculations," he wrote to Richmond ominously, "we should have saved Atlanta had the officers and men of the army done what was expected of them."[19]

Traditionally, Sherman's capture of Atlanta is regarded as a clarifying September moment for the Union cause, and key to Lincoln's electoral victory over McClellan two months later. Some dividends payable upon war-stasis and death-weariness were cashed out immediately. The Republican left, for instance, abandoned Frémont and reunited under Lincoln. The fall of Atlanta discredited Peace Democrats, and disabled McClellan too, since peace had been augured with just the kind of victory that McClellan, whatever his stance in favor of prosecuting war, had been unable to deliver when he was in charge of it. And in some sense Lincoln's reelection was decisive, at least according to the idiosyncrasies of the American system. He polled 55 percent of the popular vote and collected 212 of the 233 contested electoral votes, enough to win handily even in 1860. Had the election been held in 1862, the outcome would surely have been closer, or perhaps a not particularly controversial McClellan victory. As it was, McClellan still drew more than 1.8 million votes, the difference of 400,000 in Lincoln's favor perhaps substantial but also indicative of powerful, persistent conservatism. The decisiveness was in the mandate given by Union soldiers. These were Lincoln men now. Almost 80 percent of all ballots cast in the ranks went for Lincoln, a deluge that would have been biblical had black Union soldiers, barred by race, been allowed to vote.

Figure 34: Democratic Flyer from 1864, Public Domain.

Their choice was four more years of war, if four more were needed. Probably most thought not after Atlanta, and undoubtedly that was the election's motive understanding. But something else had been gathering, and this dynamism seems clearest in the surging plebiscite of the soldiers' vote. To achieve Union and emancipation, the War's character itself must come to embody the *momentum* of Union and emancipation. Setting aside Lincoln's very real fear (no light matter) that he would lose the election, it is certainly possible that the Union might have eventually overpowered the Confederacy by its girth, even sooner rather than later. Many fine military writers, not one of them Lost Cause apologists, have said that is precisely what happened. Yet such a view supposes no necessary connection between those vast advantages and the War's vastly different character since 1861. Quite clearly, Union resources had not been deemed advantageous enough to forego augmenting them (and consequently diminishing them for the Confederacy) under the Emancipation Proclamation. The bleak, pallid mood of 1864 suggests that war by numbers was not enough to achieve transformational purpose: feeling its drear and inertia took Lincoln to the very depth of woe in pledging to save the Union by cooperating with McClellan – meaning: a soul-leaving retreat on emancipation – in the event of the latter's probable election. Girth might secure the Union, but it could not have attained the momentum of or aspired to the war aim of emancipation.

With the armies, the attitudes of Union soldiers embracing hard war were long since advanced. Indeed some 235,000 of them had completed their three-year terms of service earlier in 1864 and were eligible to retire. Almost 100,000 of them did so. But the adoption of destruction to achieve a punitive, permanent change – who wanted to fight this war again? – had perhaps been suggested in the 136,000 who reenlisted. Presumably these voted for Lincoln by huge majorities and carried their purpose through in their war-making. For those who experienced the War at home, among them Lincoln in dismay, the relationship was less tactile. Like so much of importance in a democratic war, the affinity between the War's character and the nation's character was a matter of the resonances of physical power, not the mere confidence in it. Carrying public opinion over the threshold of its ambivalence and conservatism would require the character of the War to embody fluidity and dynamism. The Union war must be war-making as the mighty, ageless Mississippi River, irresistible, imponderable, enduring, its power the potency of earthshaking physical force but always flowing with the lithe, liberating imagination of the future-possible. What was needed to achieve victory at the polls, and through that synergy in the field, was a war *freed by and from* its girth.

This, too, was both catalyst and motive assumption in the election's outcome. Indeterminate as perseveration, paralyzing as stasis, in the fall of 1864 the Union war gathered unto itself the dynamic potency and the character of that which it would create. First was the consuming devastation loosed upon the Shenandoah Valley – in the antebellum era the arcadian setting for the nebbish pastoral novels of the plantation South, now the coda to scenes more darkly foretokened in *The Partisan Leader,* an apocalyptic tale of secession that appeared in 1837. There Grant had resolved to murder the last-born of Lee's creation and leave his corridor northward forever fallow. Grant gathered 30,000 soldiers under Philip H. Sheridan, another of his trusted firebrands of the west, withal a booming squatter of man, wiry-limbed, heavy-headed, heavy-trunked, ungainly gaited, whose bellowing preference for bulldozer war seemed as if it could be the subject heading of Grant's orders. These were given with all the nuance of a Monday morning memorandum. Sheridan was to follow Early's daring Confederates "to the death" and to desolate the Valley so completely that even the crows "flying over it for the balance of this season will have to carry their provender with them."[20]

In late September Sheridan drove Early from Winchester and nearly crushed him at a place called Fisher's Hill, a defeat that sent Early tumbling almost 150 kilometers in retreat. The crows flew now as omens, and Sheridan's army marched as land-wasters, doing their work less thoroughly than his reports later suggested, somewhat less than totally, but ruthlessly enough that the heavily Germanic population of the Valley reckoned with it as a kind of visitation from lost time and de Melac's Burning of the Palatinate two hundred years before. Even today Sheridan's violence is known locally in a kind of palimpsest form, as the Burning. With no force to oppose him or to protect fall harvest, Sheridan's men torched a blackened blister more than 100 kilometers long and half as wide in the fertile heart of the Valley, and from the ground up: crops, corncribs, haylofts, barns. They slaughtered sheep and hogs and cattle as if these, too, were burnt offerings. Partisans and guerrillas were hanged (and captured Union soldiers hanged back). Lootings and harassments proceeded despite orders. When Confederate scouts shot John Rodgers Meigs, the son of the Union army's chief quartermaster (incidentally, just then planting a national cemetery in the gardens at Arlington, Robert E. Lee's confiscated mansion house), Sheridan burned part of the town nearest the incident and all of the homes and farms immediately surrounding it, convinced the assailants were local bushwhackers.

An ashen rime descended on the land, the conventional war's scabrous brutality come to overspread the local violence long pulling up the Valley, as elsewhere, at the grassroots. Early sought one last surprise, mobilizing quickly and secretly, appearing suddenly, in a mist-shrouded dawn on October 19, near Cedar Creek. He very nearly pulled off a stunning victory by rolling up a waylaid foe. Sheridan, who had been in Winchester, twenty-five kilometers away, raced to the field, bellowing and bullying his men as he went and cuffing and collaring them as he arrived. They turned from panic and torpor and smashed Early so completely that his force was not just knocked backward but knocked out of the war, only to have left behind at Cedar Creek the last might-have-been of the Lost Cause.

Together with Sherman's capture of Atlanta, Sheridan's devastation and freedom of movement in the Shenandoah Valley was a vitally new momentum. The felt energy of re-creation through destruction gave all stakes a dynamism – the stakes of war-making charging and charged reciprocally by what was at stake at the polls at home – needful to Union victory. Design and instrument were one and inscrutable with a War to punish and preserve, to renew and revitalize. In War was Union and national sovereignty. In War was the forward meaning and democratic purpose of Union and emancipation by the destructive abolition of what had been there before.

The living force of that synergy catalyzed and became reified in the campaign that more than any other is the essence of the American Civil War, and gave to its author, William Tecumseh Sherman, a legacy as its primal warrior. Sherman's enduring reputation for ferocity owes much to the blunting physicality of his language and the legends wrought by his March to the Sea. It also obscures his visionary genius, which was a kind of fulfillment that war brought to him after his first few manic months in it, in 1861, when he had been packed off on leave trailed by whispers of insanity. Red-haired, caffeine-volatile, and bursting with wit, quip, idea, and deed, Sherman was one with a libidinous energy, as his postwar tomcatting attests. Even his sanity, when affirmed, was intense. He had served under Grant in mutual trust since his recuperation (both had been slaughtered by the newspaper rumor-writers whom Sherman wanted God-damned in literal and figurative senses), first at Shiloh then at Vicksburg, and most recently prior to Atlanta, in a minor campaign in February of 1864 that ended in the leveling of Meridian, Mississippi. The army that Grant gave over to his independent command in May, and which had seized the bombed-out remains of Atlanta, was now the most fearsome on either side.

Sherman would now leave Hood to do as Hood liked – the latter had moved off to the west, hoping to threaten Sherman's supply lines, and might even move from there northward, into Tennessee. To Sherman the offensive move was a pointless diversion. Hood's defensive positioning on his communications was irrelevant, too, because Sherman had no intention of needing or keeping a supply line. On November 15, he set out for Savannah, on the Atlantic seaboard. It was a distance of almost 400 kilometers to the coast, served by no line of supply at all. Even Savannah itself offered nothing but destination. Grant didn't quite see the design (he worried also about Hood's thrust into Tennessee) and Lincoln, feeling an anxiety to wrap up the war without yet seeing Sherman's object, fretted it. Sherman nevertheless knew he could make the march, as he said to Grant, "and make Georgia howl." Before the war he had lived in the South and was aware generally of its agricultural produce – but he had also studied the census charts of 1860 and knew more particularly, county-by-county, the bounty immediately before him. He could subsist his army on it and, in destroying the vastness of what his army did not need for itself, just as Sheridan had done in the Valley, waste the richness of the Confederacy. His was a physical but also powerfully psychological act of imposition. "I propose to demonstrate," he said, unwittingly freeing himself of the stasis implied in Grant's earlier proposition to fight it out all summer, "the vulnerability of the South and make its inhabitants feel that war and individual ruin are synonymous terms."[21]

Like the spiritualists and master mediums now everywhere seeking communion with the dead, Sherman was a clairvoyant. No figure of the war better perceived the relationship of war and democracy and none saw farther into it. The journey to Savannah, not the destination, would be the channel of Sherman's profound insight: he envisioned his army embodied as the unfolding, rolling power of a legitimate democracy. In peace that power was triumphantly civil in the political mechanisms of liberty, of equality, of freedom. In war the power was irresistibly, ineluctably martial. War was both absolute and absolution; war in its fullness was the uninhibited capacity to clarify and authenticate the confused, contested terms of democracy. Much as it had been the irresistible force of persuasion that autumn for Northern public opinion, the sheer movement and relentlessness of a war on resources was warfare on felt things, war waged on the very territory of the Confederacy as it existed in hearts and minds, on the liminal, numinous places where the Confederate nation bound its people to itself. The might embodied in the March to the Sea was as pointless to resist as a geological force, as futile to withstand as the pommel and tide of the Atlantic Ocean to which Sherman's army coursed unbound, a 62,000-man natural wonder.

His columns cast a tempestuous swath widening out to 100 kilometers, his soldiers "raising hell generally," as one of them described the experience. They burned crops and mills and foundries, occasionally torched a home or manse, destroyed railroads and warehouses and cotton gins. To feed themselves they foraged in compliance with orders or "bummed" without them, the latter term a slanging vernacular of the campaign that came to be used indiscrimately for soldiers and stragglers alike who swung out here, then there, to raid farms and plantations, to loot

Figure 35: General William Tecumseh Sherman, 1865, Public Domain.

grain houses, spoil smoke houses, and even sack a few dwelling houses. What stock they could not eat themselves they killed or confiscated (the sporting marchers said "liberated") so that 13,000 head of cattle and another 6 million rations of bread and beef were either consumed, driven, or destroyed. The army flounced virtually unchallenged. Behind it were shafts of smoke and fire, while as Sherman predicted the cries of anguish echoed before and after. Georgia howled, but there was no Confederacy to hear or respond. On December 21, Sherman showed up at Savannah, abandoned the day before along with 25,000 bales of cotton by Confederates with no hope of resisting him, and presented the city and his cotton booty to Lincoln as a gift for the holidays.

The March was the war's telling blow, its quietus in form if not in fact. The depth of its resonance as the war itself presaged the completeness of total war. Sherman did not target Southern civilians for death or bodily mayhem, though certainly some – an indeterminate number – were killed, both black and white, and harassments and intimidations not exclusive of rape (many on black women) were not unusual and even condoned. The worst of these incidents not only lacked frequency but were without design or intent in the sense of what total war has come to signify since the twentieth century. Sherman's way was not the way of the mutual bombing campaigns of the Second World War nor the way of atomic holocaust that ended it. The March's totality was in recognizing that both the strength and the weakness of Confederate nationalism existed materially because its home ground existed spiritually. The territory Sherman sought to ravage was psychological, and the resources he destroyed were not only physical but emotional. A successful campaign might not return those hearts and minds to the Union, but it would withdraw them from physical connections and commitments to the Confederacy.

The March's *restraint* was precisely its point: to demonstrate the legitimacy of the Union by its power to reveal the vacuity and feebleness of the Confederacy. The only power capable of defending white Southerners from Sherman was, in fact, the Union and its army under Sherman. Fashioned another way, placed in the light of Sherman's proposal that war and individual ruination were indivisible, the only power capable of making peace was the one just now making war. As a matter of philosophy Sherman did not believe in War circumscribed by restraints – as a matter of experience, indeed, that kind of boundless war existed in this one, elsewhere. "Many, many peoples with less pertinacity," as he said to a Southern civilian earlier in 1864, explaining essentially that it could be worse, "have been wiped out of national existence." That Sherman's March has nevertheless maintained a particularly harrowing, encompassing presence in white Southern memory is evidence of a different totality and completeness. The swath left a powerful folklore, a vividness of experience in memory that remains one of its lasting endowments. When still-told family stories echo ancestral cries of helplessness, when legends and myths of the March frame the threats and curses of the vengeful people in Sherman's path who delivered them, the response comes from a mystic chord touched as the South, identity and nationality as a felt thing, in the total absence of – because there could not be – a Confederacy.[22]

The March was total in one other way. Only in it, as War, did Americans finally and utterly find the scale to confront an experience that in all other respects confounded them. War reached beyond the inadequacy of modifiers such as conservative, beyond even the limits of a conception such as destructive, to come to transcendent the place its ghosts visited from. For the people of defeat, transcendence would come by way of an enduring distinctiveness apart from the political form of the state, one perhaps that could only be begotten in suffering and war. For the people of victory, transcendence was in the synchronicity of a national state, the Union, in consonance with its promise and visionary hope at creation. Lincoln had tried to embody this force with words. Yet to be irresistible as persuasion the force could only be embodied as its instrument, onomatopoeic as war itself.

There was, of course, another March, and its seekers also understood war and sought transcendence in it. Following Sherman was an exodus. Thousands of former slaves had thrown their lot behind his soldiers and joined the columns on the way to the sea. They experienced the March just as Sherman and his men experienced it, and as Northerners and white Southerners experienced it – both vicariously and immediately, as the embodiment of the American nation under their feet. By the time Sherman reached Savannah the March had emancipated tens of thousands more in the Georgia and Carolina Lowcountry. More than 40,000 men and women and children were now, as 1865 opened, not slaves.

But emancipation was not freedom. Emancipation was an act mandated and effected by war, and freedom a condition possible only in the absence of war. Verily, Americans might be indifferent to that dynamic when war left the nation. During the March, at a place called Ebenezer Creek, one of Sherman's generals had pulled up his pontoons to keep the freedmen from following his men across. Hundreds of African Americans drowned in desperation, sinking like stones as they tried without help to make the swim. Hundreds more fell back to an uncertain fate in the hands of Confederate patrols or pursuing local vigilantes. A saving affinity – a recognition of the implied promise of Union and emancipation, which together might be freedom – might be, perhaps, in the strident outcry of a Northern public opinion outraged at news of it. All would depend on aftermath. In the coming absence of war, words only could accomplish it: to be one with democracy, transcendent, the promise of emancipation must be in the hearts and minds of Americans as freedom. Having come before the waters tithed to a vision of themselves as the first-born citizens of a new nation outspreading to meet its promise, the emancipated might wonder whether words would endure against the crashing tides, the antediluvian disquiet, of the sea.

EPILOGUE
UNITED, OR UNTIED?
1865 ...

To be asked about the events in America between 1860 and 1865 is one thing, and to tell about the American Civil War another. For stories require endings, but wars do not. The methods by which the Confederacy was extinguished in the spring of 1865 were swift, the moments dramatic, but its life was exhausted probably months before, in the winter, when the bleak realities of defeat and January cold presaged a vigil. Thousands of Confederate soldiers, many of them proud veterans of long campaigns and glorious victories, began leaving the ranks in twos, then threes, then in epidemics of fives and tens and hundreds. The Confederacy sufficed no longer as a national proxy for the pleas coming from their homes and farms. Patriotism could no longer encourage them – the bucking up, for the cause – as in the days of glory. Many did return home, but some joined much-feared marauder bands that plagued virtually every region of the immediate postwar South and called to mind nothing so much as the banditti ranging wide in the days of the old Revolution or, even earlier, in colonial America, the militant maroon communities of slave runaways. Thousands did remain in the ranks, the stalwart or the stubborn, "Lee's miserables" as the grim of humor called themselves in the Army of Northern Virginia. More and more their decisions began to look like musket-gripping, teeth-clenched reconciliation with a bitter end.[1]

What remained of the Confederacy was not so much a state as a state of desperation. Disorder and even anarchy threatened.

Shortages on all things were everywhere. John Bell Hood, perhaps swirling with a dark desire to school his own men in aggressive manhood, took 40,000 of them to Tennessee – the fantastical dream offensive that opened for Sherman his way to the Sea. Hood was met first at Franklin, on November 30, 1864, and then again at Nashville two weeks later, by a Union army under the overall command of George H. Thomas. At Franklin, Hood launched a series of punishing frontal assaults that cost him almost a third of his force and in hindsight look not like one Pickett's Charge so much as several. Among the dead – one of twelve generals lost as casualties, but just a fraction of the scores of officers killed and wounded – was Patrick Cleburne. Hood's decision to go on to Nashville went beyond the punitively suicidal to the calamitous. Thomas, a Virginian and a career military officer who remained rocklike right where he was in the old army after secession, and who had distinguished himself in rearguard if not day-saving fighting at Chickamauga, delivered unto Hood a palpitating *coup de grâce*. In recalling the Confederate lion's remarks about inspiriting war in general and his supposedly passive army in particular, it is hard to imagine Hood's men had done else but what was expected of them. In any case, they were dead on the field.

The War closed quickly in 1865, in all corners. Desperation at the table: At Hampton Roads in February, Lincoln met with Confederate representatives in a peace conference that in reality reprised the Southern tactics of 1860–1861. Then Southerners had attempted to extort concessions on slavery that would have forced Lincoln to give back the terms of his election. Their peace terms, a recognition of Confederate independence, would have him hand back the War. No agreement was forthcoming nor could have been expected. Desperation in the streets: Black Confederates were now drilling in the Richmond thoroughfares – less as evidence that the Confederacy sacrificed ideology to the goal of independence, more as prime recognition of the coming end. There were merely three companies of them. These were emancipated not by the legislative action of the Confederate Congress, as the slain Cleburne had proposed, but by the same executive fiat that Davis employed when squashing Cleburne's initial proposal because the nation's representative body to the end stubbornly refused it. Desperation in the field: Sherman had not contented to winter in Savannah.

With an urgency born of his supreme confidence in war-making, he marched his 60,000 men right through sop and bog into South Carolina, where they capered in the punishment given the cradlers of secession. Their wreckage was especially fearful, and their glee in it extravagant, and it included in February the burning of Columbia during a wind-driven, alcohol-fueled conflagration even now roaring in heat and controversy. To this day it howls in folklore so that some Carolinians hear on the wind the city's stray dogs crying havoc.

Unstoppably, relentlessly, Sherman kept going, into North Carolina, intent on joining Grant's siege of Petersburg. In March he was finally and futilely challenged by a last remnant of Confederates, an army of some 20,000 men, near a place called Bentonville. The measure of Confederate desperation was in the evidence of this force's commander, Joe Johnston, who by now was quite literally fighting for defeat. He hoped not to win – and didn't – but to affect peace terms that shortly would be forthcoming.[2] For at the beginning of April Grant finally broke the ever-thinning Confederate lines at Petersburg and forced a crisis. Lee sent word to Davis that the Army, now leaner by death

Figure 36: Burned-out remains of Atlanta, Public Domain.

Figure 37: Burned-out remains of Richmond, Public Domain.

and desertion, gaunter by hunger, and constituted of only 49,000 effectives, could no longer defend Richmond and began racing them westward. Davis soon fled, too, with the government nearly in his person and the treasury in his baggage. In due course Richmond fell, and Lincoln was among its freed people and in Davis's vacant chair. The ruination along the city's seven hills was as amazing in its grime as the capital had once been in classical splendor – retreating Confederates detonated a spectacular inferno soon fanned to babel by looting perhaps made more riotous because two years deferred.

A week later Grant cut Lee off near Appomattox Court House. With "nothing left to do" other than wish for a thousand deaths, Lee sued for a conference. The rest has become something of an American drama set on April 9, 1865. Lee's proud host of swaggerers – the "survivors of so many hard-fought battles, who have remained steadfast to the last," as he fondly called them in farewell – were a figment only memory might recall: a wretched 28,000 remained. They were surrendered when Lee and Grant met in the parlor of a house whose owner, who did not wish the fate of the poor widow Henry four years before, had exchanged his former residence on the old Bull Run battlefield for this one, far

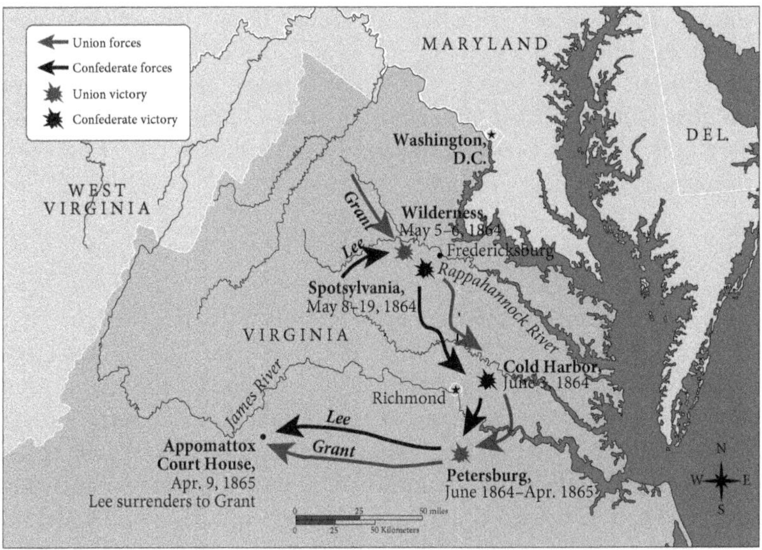

Map 10: The Campaign in Virginia, 1864–1865.

from the War that followed him anyway, to the last. The terms of the surrender of the Army of Northern Virginia were technicalities synonymous with the end. Lee's men were sent home until paroled. They could keep their horses and their mules if they owned them, and officers their side-arms – farms needed tending, and the banditti and horse thieves marauding as ghosts in the fog of the postwar might need trespasser's warning. By the measures of failed rebellions, this was leniency. Lee himself returned to Richmond, where a photographer captured him in a haunting portrait of a ruin impersonated, the defeated in desolation, already marbled in black and white. He was dead five years later.

There had been one other option – there was nothing else to do, Lee had said, but only after rejecting an electric proposal to allow his army to disband and by dispersion make their way home to fight as partisans in an ongoing, large-scale guerrilla war. Whatever else may be made of Lee and resistance at Appomattox and beyond, he wanted nothing to do with the horrors of an American dystopia. His desire for national healing and reconciliation, if only on something like terms he deemed honorable, was sincere. But many of the men in his army were already gone anyway. Thousands upon thousands of them had disappeared into the woods and deserted while on the march. "My God," Lee exclaimed on seeing his army on the move, not the 90,000 strong of the greater days but almost a third of it, and these so starved and bedraggled they were half the men they used to be: "My God: has the army been dissolved?"[3]

****

Lee's surrender of the Army of Northern Virginia was the first of Confederate surrenders and the one that most mattered. There was little left to capitulate of the second of the great rebel armies. The body of the Army of Tennessee was like unto its last leader, John Bell Hood, and what remained of it, not just those who had been killed or wounded at Franklin and Nashville but those who had deserted and gone home, was dismembered and scattered. Some were with Johnston when he formally surrendered to Sherman in North Carolina three weeks after Appomattox. (Johnston eventually lost his life – depending on one's view – either to disease, the war-era killer more relentless than even Sherman, or to his own stubborn honor. The old Confederate, honorary pallbearer at Sherman's funeral in 1891, a day of bone-locking, bitter February cold, refused to wear a hat. Sherman would do the same for me, Johnston insisted. He caught pneumonia and died four weeks later.) Other Confederate forces, some by unit, some by army, including those over the long-closed Mississippi in the distant west, gave up in due course. The last Confederates typically to know were among its ocean-borne navy. But the final abdication of importance was Jefferson Davis's. He had fled south after Lee announced Richmond's doom, fire-breathing as he went a nationalist's fealty to his cause. On the morning of May 10, Union cavalry cantered into his campsite in Georgia and snared him unawares. It was messy – Davis was taken prisoner wearing his wife's clothing (actually, it was soon claimed, her dress; and allowing for the occasionally bawdy indignities thought up to disempower the defeated, in the language of honor this was not a smallish humiliation) or at the very least a lady's coat or shawl. In prison, he in effect was the shriveled Confederacy, and it was only there, captive for two years in often the dankest of circumstances, that he began the apotheosis of the Lost Cause.

The Union lived. It was perhaps to greater purpose, perhaps to greater harm, that Lincoln was shot by an assassin on Good Friday. For the deep sadness and momentary bloodlust occasioned by Lincoln's murder was accompanied also by elements sublime enough to live beyond those immediate emotions. Many at the time ascribed to Lincoln's death an abounding divine purpose meant to confirm among a victorious Northern people that God had been with them all along. The Almighty would and ultimately did act unmistakably to be comprehended and understood. After four years of the most profound horror and suffering and darkness and uncertainty – some had said silence – He had finally and fully revealed Lincoln as His instrument, a savior of the Union, in the War's ending days. The sense of providential mission and special favor in America is still lucent in a sacred triumphalism that remains with the people of victory.

Its most tragic provenance is that such national satisfaction is precisely what Lincoln had warned against, urgently, with his last and most meaningful words.

"Fondly do we hope," Lincoln had said in the climactic moment of his Second Inaugural, given on an overcast March morning in 1865 that dawned in the same cold drizzle greeting his first, "fervently do we pray, that this mighty scourge of war may speedily pass away." Four years ago the War had not yet begun. It yet continued, and still he remained unwilling to predict an end or outcome.

None could be certain, he said. "All knew," after all, that slavery was "somehow the cause of the war," but neither side had "anticipated that the *cause* of the conflict might cease with or even before the conflict itself should cease." Neither side anticipated anything that had befallen, least of all the War's unthinkable suffering. All that could be known about what happened and why and why it continued was something akin to a felt thing. Both sides had called on God for comprehension, for answers, for aid and succor, for victory, and yet His will was only to be grasped as He willed it to be found. Beware righteousness, then: "It may seem strange," Lincoln said by way of representing Confederate supplications to the Almighty, "that any men should dare to ask a just God's assistance in wringing their bread from the sweat of other men's faces, but let us judge not, that we be not judged. The prayers of both could not be answered. The prayers of neither have been answered fully." Beware pride, then: for a hard teaching had wizened the nation to a harder truth in its crisis: "The Almighty has his own purposes."

The Second Inaugural was Lincoln's last major speech, the greatest ever given by any American. Its stunning vision and affect was a wisdom in the cadences of an ancient idiom, a vast, surpassing humility before a power beyond comprehension, an Almighty whose own cadences were the reverberations of time in abyss. Lincoln did not claim himself as a demigod. He did not claim to have saved the Union by himself nor to have fixed anything alone, for he knew the foolishness of those claims and all too well the fools who exalted themselves making them, men like Buchanan, palsied by crisis but insisting on infallibility, or generals of pomp lacking circumstance such as John Pope or Joseph Hooker, or even McClellan, or Andrew Johnson in the presidency to come. Such empty vanity had been among the very reasons for this, the American carnage on which did all else chiefly depend. The purpose in a war so terrible could only be in a totality beyond the shrill sureties of Manifest Destiny and beyond the feeble powers of man. And so did Lincoln come to his apprehension of it – the tug of it, as he had once used the expression – in the gospel of Matthew: "'Woe unto the world because of offenses; for it must needs be that offenses come, but woe to that man by whom the offense cometh.' If we suppose that American slavery" – not Southern slavery, he said, but *American* slavery – "is one of those offenses which, in the providence of God, must needs come, but which, having continued through His appointed time, He now wills to remove, and that he gives to both North and South this terrible war as the woe due unto those by whom the offense came, shall we discern therein any departure from those divine attributes which the believers in a living God always ascribe to Him?"

Lincoln had said after Gettysburg that he feared his address there, now his most celebrated, would not "*scour.*" In that he was correct, for the Gettysburg Address did not achieve its place in American literature until generations had passed, when tragically the fullest reach of its "new birth of freedom" was shielded and insulated by a comfortable forgetfulness of its meaning. He was immediately aware of the force of the Second Inaugural. "Lots of wisdom in that document, I suspect," he said to one of his secretaries. It was a speech in the prophetic mode or even a kind of Shakespearean soliloquy – its design was not persuasion – and so his words might scour without requiring democracy to ratify them. The War (as God had given men to see the right in it) was about Union and emancipation. And yet, while slavery had been removed, the War went on. Perhaps, then, war was atonement for the darkness of the Union's original sin in slavery:

> Yet if God wills that it continue until all the wealth piled by the bondsman's two hundred and fifty years of unrequited toil shall be sunk and until every drop of blood drawn by the lash shall be paid by another drawn with the sword, as was said three thousand years ago, so still it must be said, the judgments of the Lord are true and righteous altogether.[4]

Figure 38: Lincoln's Second Inaugural (March 4, 1865), Public Domain.

But perhaps the War continued because the offense was not confined to slavery and had not yet been fully removed, in which case not even the Union might outlast the expiation. And if that were so, it may be that in the judgment of the Lord only *one* of the missions of Union and emancipation was worth, and was the purpose, of a pitiless American suffering. These were the professions of abolition, not mere antislavery sentiment. Only the abolitionists had said slavery was wrong because slavery was a sin. Only John Brown had talked as prophetically of purgation. And only the abolitionists had said emancipation and freedom were as one, that emancipation must lead to freedom from slavery *as well as* freedom from racism, in the security and fullness of American citizenship. In our time, this understanding has been lost in a myth-mist of triumphalism, and its essential apprehension, which brooked nothing of the surety victory soon ascribed to it, has been convoluted in an ongoing conflation of God's kingdom with the exceptional American nation. But it has also been withered by Lincoln's fiercest liberal critics, whose attacks often deform his ongoing, radical movement on the spectrum of antislavery by attempting to fix him in the places he grew *from*. There can be no mistaking it. Indeed Frederick Douglass – to Lincoln's great pleasure – called the speech "a sacred effort." The sin he confessed was national, not sectional. Slavery alone did not embrace its vastness. The Lincoln who had presided over an unfathomable blood-spilling for the nation could not go quite as far as to place emancipation above even Union. He was also too exacting a logician to deny that the logic might indeed go so far and too sorrowed to believe that saving the Union was a political or martial act within his or the ken of any human being.

Perhaps, then, only the consummation of emancipation, in freedom, might remove the scourge. Whatever might be made of it now, Lincoln's allusion to emancipation's fulfillment in freedom was ultimately why he was murdered. On April 11, two days after Lee's surrender, Lincoln gave a short address from a balcony overlooking the White House grounds. Gathered on the lawn below was an exultant crowd anticipating his remarks on the momentous moment of their victory. Lincoln's thoughts quickly turned to the postwar and the course of Reconstruction in the Southern states. His posture was generally already well understood – in the peroration of the Second Inaugural he had declaimed in favor of a just peace and a full reintegration of the Union "with malice toward none, with charity for all." From the balcony, it was clear he had meant none and all in the fullness of North and South, but also black and white. His foray was limited, yet its import was total when set within the momentum of war, emancipation, and the difficult philosophy of the Second Inaugural. Speaking specifically of Louisiana, he proposed that the right to vote "be conferred on the very intelligent" among the former slaves as well as "those who served our cause as soldiers." (Some of these Louisianans had in fact been engaged in one of the War's bloodiest days, at Milliken's Bend in 1863.) At least one of the audience understood the force of Lincoln's vision straightaway. "That means nigger citizenship," John Wilkes Booth mumbled to a companion. "That will be the last speech he will ever make."[5]

Booth was already listening as a conspirator, not an auditor. He had been plotting for weeks, and he was not alone. Lincoln had been in danger from "insurgent agents in the city" long in advance of Booth, some real and some figments. As early as 1861 he had been slipped through Baltimore in the night (disguised, some said, in a lady's shawl) to avoid a reported threat on the way to his first inauguration. Nor were plots against him limited to assassination. Booth – a stage actor of some notoriety as a Shakespearian dramatist – was a Southern sympathizer implicated in the networks of Confederate espionage. He and several conspirators originally intended to capture Lincoln, perhaps to ransom him for Confederate independence. Yet at some moment between the Second Inaugural and this night, if not on this night, Booth unilaterally decided instead on murder. The issue he put before his cabal of associates was no longer solely about the end, or about preventing or avenging Confederate defeat. Killing Lincoln was about a beginning and the new Union in the ongoing war of the aftermath.

The design was comprehensive. Booth, casting himself as Brutus, Shakespeare's "noblest Roman of them all," would shoot Lincoln. Another assassin would dispatch Andrew Johnson, the newly elected vice-president. Another was to murder William Seward, the secretary of state. Thus now to tyrants, for the government would be decapitated. On the night of April 14, a Friday, Lincoln went to watch the players at Ford's Theater perform a popular comedy called *Our American Cousin*. Booth slipped into the president's box overlooking the stage and shot Lincoln in the back of the head – he died the next morning. (The plotters also intended to murder Grant, whom Lincoln invited to the theater but who declined under a polite artifice designed to mask his wife's contempt for the company of Mrs. Lincoln.) Booth hurtled below and landed thumpingly onstage with a grandiloquent oath subject to many ears and interpretations – most often rendered: "Sic semper tyrannus!" – and hobbled out a backdoor on a broken leg. Two weeks later he was caught in Virginia by Union cavalry and surrounded in a burning tobacco barn. One shot from a revolver went clean through his neck and paralyzed him from the shoulders down. Death would come momentarily, but Booth seized aplomb even in that. He recited his last lines as the tragic hero, the Great Man of History, the stoic son of the Good Death. "Tell Mother," he said, "I die for my country." The other collaborators were rounded up quickly after a sweeping investigation that netted scores of arrests but ultimately implicated eight people. Four of these were imprisoned and four, including the widow who owned the boarding house where the conspirators schemed, were executed on a hangman's noose.

Booth's plot was a kind of epilogue, a closing-act conspiracy of resistance to John Brown's opening conspiracy of liberation, right down to the dramaturgy of the words and deeds of the actors. It was prologue too – for reasons Booth did not anticipate. Seward was stabbed five times in the face but survived. The assassin sent to kill Johnson lost his nerve in whiskey and stupored instead in a hotel barroom. His sensible drunkenness may have altered the course of the postwar decisively. Booth had not known it, his caballists could not have known it, but Andrew Johnson proved far more estimable to a white Southern resistance above ground and alive than he possibly could be, as a last or first casualty, six feet under.[6]

****

Or perhaps it is wars that end, and stories that do not.

In the months of the aftermath to come, in years to come, an intense period of ferment and political change shaped the postwar. A full account of that era, called Reconstruction, must be given

Figure 39: John Wilkes Booth (1838–1865), Public Domain.

elsewhere.[7] It may not be enough to know (but is crucial to know) that the events of Reconstruction were simultaneously revolutionary and reactionary, and that for a brief period the momentum of war's transformations sought a reach in the nation's fundamental politics. The achievement of the so-called radical impulse fell short of its most visionary, idealistic scope. The economic reconstruction the radicals desired would have granted land and property to former slaves, a so-called competency in the Jeffersonian tradition of tying personal and political independence to economic security. For many freedmen, that hope and ambition was bound up in the slogan "40 Acres and a Mule." But it did not happen. The impulse abided instead in revisions to the US Constitution. Between 1865 and 1870, the Reconstruction Amendments – the Thirteenth, Fourteenth, and Fifteenth – formally abolished slavery, a necessity given that emancipation had been an executive act of war, and finally turned the shovel over Roger A.

Taney by establishing citizenship and civil and political rights for the black men whom the old judge had said, in 1857, possessed none such in America.

Yet if the murder of Lincoln was the first deed of political violence designed to kill "nigger equality," as Booth had menacingly vowed, it was also the model act in the white South for the terror unleashed against former slaves almost immediately after the War and continuing, in gradually consolidating tiers, for a long time thereafter. Initially against the firm checks given by their former enemies in the North, then with their tacit toleration, then with their collaboration and affirmation, Southern whites instituted a system of white supremacy arguably as savagely oppressive as slavery, and inarguably awful, well into the next century. By the eve of the Great War the Reconstruction Amendments had been all but eviscerated, and the screws of race refastened, in an embracing apartheid known colloquially as "Jim Crow" and more genteelly and hospitably as "the Southern way of life." The language had merely been displaced to fit new structures of power: the antebellum era's lexicon of slavery, race, and civilization rang through with a clarion continuity. Formal segregation and disfranchisement, like slavery, was sectional, but white supremacy was national. The acquisitiveness of a Western imperialism underpinned by the smug assurances of Western science were the new answers of democratic civilization to its vexing antebellum questions. These were hailed as modern solutions to racial facts fixed naturally. As ever, they were regressive compulsions to facts fixed socially and culturally and economically.

The counter-revolution launched by Southern whites did not merely *happen*, as it were, or *develop*. It was stratagem and aim, the vision and goal of the long resistance that began virtually at once after Appomattox. The story of unmaking and remaking is, also, a story to be recounted elsewhere. It may not be enough to know (but is crucial to know) that a facsimile of the fanatical guerrilla war Lee disdained at Appomattox, the local and neighborhood war of lasting brutality he had hoped to prevent by an honorable surrender, took place anyway. In a very real sense it always *was* the War. The most immediate phase of resistance, during Reconstruction proper between 1865 and 1877, dismantled and overthrew what white Southerners considered "Negro rule" and occupation under venal, corrupt state and local governments. Its victims were assassinated, mobbed, jailed, whipped, and in the case of infamous examples at Colfax, Louisiana, in 1873 and Hamburg, South Carolina, in 1876, massacred collectively according to what euphemisms termed "The Mississippi Plan" or "The Shotgun Policy."

The terror of paramilitary and instrumental violence in Reconstruction's first stage remained ever-present, always, long after, a shadow following a multigenerational pattern of enforcing that which had been won back. The scores of blacks murdered in the streets of Wilmington, North Carolina, in 1898 were victims of it, just as Willie Earle and Emmitt Till and Addie Mae Collins and Louis Allen in the 1950s and 1960s were casualties of it; the lynched and the knifed and the shot-gunned of the next century were all victims of it just as the black leader Benjamin Franklin Randolph, assassinated on a train platform in South Carolina in 1868, was but one of scores of the bullet-riddled corpses littering Reconstruction. The answer to Lee's pained rhetorical question at the end, just before his wished-for one thousand deaths at Appomattox – "My God, has the army been dissolved?" – became, emphatically, indomitably, yes. The army had gone home to fight in other guises.[8]

Yet the devices of Reconstruction were also archaically ancient, in epic-making, as Americans tried to make sense of their war and find meaning in it. The dual reconstructions of state-creation and story-creation were mutually intensifying and galvanizing between 1865 and 1900, and mutually dependent. There can be no illusion about the cynical motives at work in the mythologies of victory and defeat – ultimately, they were stories used to secure white supremacy, the reaction of the postwar, and the final reconciliation of American adversaries. Yet neither can there be misunderstanding of how painfully both sides yearned to heal the massive physical and psychological wounds of the War, apart from its causes, or to relieve their dread of the postwar. As Confederates, after all, white Southerners had insisted that defeat was unimaginable, because, as they had told themselves (and others listening), no people worthy of freedom ever lost it. Here was the precise ground on which they justified enslavement of African Americans. Encountering their dissonance – to sense the sheer violence of its immediacy in defeat – is to realize the Lost Cause as a story accompanying their furious,

Figure 40: Early Ku Klux Klan, *c.* 1871, Public Domain.

here-and-now resistance to what they considered the humiliating degradations and subjugations of Reconstruction. It is also to recognize how and why the grandiose scale of their mythology was to need. They had struggled colossally to *Götterdämmerung* – otherwise was the inexorable working out of their belief that slaves were those who deserved to be. Their epic allowed them to hide, from their adversaries but perhaps also from themselves, that they had merely surrendered one worldly interest and cause in slavery to pursue another in white supremacy.

Over time they need not hide even that, for the people of victory joined them in affirming white supremacy. By the 1880s and 1890s, the victors – always divided on race – had become fatigued and willfully forgetful of the gritty, everyday commitments of ensuring the legacy of emancipation. Against fierce white Southern intransigence, against a longer-standing national prejudice that had nearly been too much to overcome even in war, the burdens had proven too much. A generation after the armies disbanded, it was, then, the North that finally surrendered. The people of victory gave in not merely to Southern resistance as it was carried out in violence and political struggle but to the defiance of their former enemies as it was carried out in story. The resonances of the Lost Cause's heroic pattern, after all, were in the supreme values of honor, virtue, courage, and sacrifice. These met powerfully with a culture of remembrance in the North just now needful of a release to faerie land – from a postwar depression, from suffering with the torments of the great upheaval just passed, from ennui, perhaps, in the heedlessly capitalistic, industrial, Darwinist displacement of the new American era careening headlong. The strangest career of the Lost Cause was the one that intertwined it in the skein of the mythology of victory. There it wove discursively, in contrast, but also functioned essentially, as contour and theme in a heroic national epic that ultimately expunged trauma for triumphalism and mystified war-glory into a nation's creed.

The people of victory and the people of defeat could agree, and did, that they had fought a magnificent war on battlefields that were proving grounds of known things. Those fields were the earth of their mutual honor and their mutual virtue and courage and fame. They could agree, again, that the War and its spoils of prestige belonged to white men – and that their white supremacy was as authoritative as black degeneracy. When race became settled again, when white men North and South could agree again on race as fact again, the Union victory that had been perilously contingent, and that birthed emancipation in the direst need of that contingency, became also, silently, a fixed fact. Blacks were no cause for argument or lingering friction between brothers-in-arms, North and South, who, with no outcome in doubt, had nothing more at stake in the War than the trial of their mettle. The War was no tenuous cataclysm, no transformative crucible by which the Union had been blood-purged of its offenses, but a war to refine the highest values of American civilization: war not terrible, but war sublime. In memory, in remembrance, the American Civil War had again become the conservative war of preservation.[9]

So freely did the peoples of victory and defeat thus comfort themselves that their contented fabrications about those they re-reduced to subjugation should not be surprising. Emancipation as both economic security and fundamental civil and political rights – the possibilities so crucial to a black future in America, so crucial to Reconstruction in its earliest stages – were by the turn of the twentieth century seemingly placed out of reach in the state reconstructed and in the story told. In 1915 roaring, roistering audiences of whites packed cinema houses across the country to see America's first epic film, *Birth of a Nation*, and the black soldiers who had made the difference of Union victory portrayed in it (by white actors in blackface) as rape-crazed, shiftless degenerates. Two years later in the shadow of the Great War, half a century after they had been exploded, old arguments reappeared about the ability, effectiveness, and courage of black soldiers, as if they or the Union they helped to save had never been put to proof, as if they had never been Lincoln's truest soldiers of clenched teeth and steady eye, as if black people were not again made and kept unfree, white Americans north and south would be themselves subdued.

****

The lastingness of the American Civil War, its ongoingness, is here, in the union of two peoples – no longer merely "Northern" or "Southern": but a people of defeat, and a people of victory – joined in their epic, at the weakest points of both. The Lost Cause came to the tenet that slavery was not the foundational issue of the War, but it was. The mythology of victory embraced emancipation, with Union, as the War's higher, sacred purpose, but it wasn't – its higher purpose was betrayed soon after the fighting stopped, and even the forgetting of the betrayal was soon forgotten. As it was in the beginning, so it can be among Americans now, though seldom manifested outwardly in the same ways over time, and with many fewer direct adherents to formal creeds. For if the mythology of victory is quickened by its forgetfulness, the Lost Cause moves by remembrance – not of Confederate defeat one time but defeat over and over and over again, because its cosmos was created in a modern war and remains always in tension within the dislocations of an ever-pulsing modernity. The finesse of it seems profoundly in keeping with contemporary currents of cynicism toward authenticity and authority. It has become an awareness inwardly *knowing of itself* that comprehends the claims of victory, also, as a posture cynically not yet at terms with its meaning and decided on its version of untruth as equally worthy of belief.

The mythologies whirl together inseparably, unresolved in America as long as the legacy of emancipation is unresolved, destined to continue together so long as race is the unfinished work of America. The American Civil War settled the question of nation-building. It remains unsettled as the question of the national design and its inclusiveness: America has always promised that its substance is fulfilled through its founding idea. The mythology of defeat cannot and dare not confront race without turning a lost cause into a guilty one. The mythology of victory has never fully confronted race and more often retreated from it, time and time again, and from the implications of emancipation purchased at unimaginable, almost irredeemable costs, a suffering so enormously hideous that today, perhaps, the War's costs would not be borne for any reason or cause whatsoever.

The American Civil War gave an experience in shared pain, suffering, struggle, and division to a people whose founding Revolution could not bestow these things, because its vision purported ever-renewing, everlasting life. It must be that death and not birth, the American Civil War and not the American Revolution, fulfilled America. Only death can make a people and a history. "We still have not had a death," says the grand patriarch about his utopia in *One Hundred Years of Solitude*. "A person does not belong to a place until there is someone dead under the ground." The many hundreds of thousands lying underground by 1865 were black, and were white. Those left above were free only to fuddle in the fog of the postwar, in the lastingness of a war-story enthralling all of them. That epic could not embrace the scale of a war that destroyed all other scales of meaning and experience, except the absolute of War itself, because ultimately it could not face the magnitude of Emancipation. And yet because Americans must be a story they must have one. For while the American Civil War created a United States, its words *is* the nation, and its people's valor and courage abound in the honor of the very words that make America aspirational, in liberty, in freedom, in equality. We do not even yet feel clearly our way.[10]

Notes

INTRODUCTION

1 The Oxford History of the United States is the best place to begin. Especially useful are James M. McPherson, *Battle Cry of Freedom* (New York: 1988); Gordon S. Wood, *Empire of Liberty* (New York: 2009); and Daniel Walker Howe, *What Hath God Wrought?* (New York: 2007). But see also Sean Wilentz, *The Rise of American Democracy* (2005) and Orville Vernon Burton, *The Age of Lincoln* (New York: 2008). A reader should also note how the emphasis on "civilization and progress" ultimately became an ideology intimately associated with race and democracy. See Steven Hahn, *A Nation Under our Feet: Black Political Struggles in the Rural South from Slavery to the Great Migration* (Cambridge, MA: 2003).

2 See Elizabeth R. Varon, *Disunion! The Coming of the American Civil War* (Chapel Hill, NC: 2008).

3 The editor is quoted in McPherson, *Battle Cry of Freedom*, 151. See also Leonard L. Richards, *The Slave Power* (Baton Rouge, LA: 2000) – but note the author's omission of "conspiracy." An older school is reflected in David M. Potter's still vital *The Impending Crisis* (New York: 1976).

4 Tellingly, the literature on slavery and race in America has its own vastness to rival the War era. Equally telling – for reasons I hope will become clear – that literature's explosion has come only in the last fifty years. The recent historian emphasizing force and violence as the factors of increased production is Edward E. Baptist, *The Half Has Never Been Told* (New York: 2014).

5 David Brion Davis, *The Problem of Slavery in the Age of Emancipation* (New York: 2014), is the place to begin.

6 Varon, *Disunion!*, 133–135. Abolitionism was not monolithic, and it changed over time. The most accessible overview is James Brewer Stewart, *Holy Warriors: The Abolitionists and American Slavery* (New York: 1997). But see also John Stauffer, *The Black Hearts of Men* (Cambridge, MA: 2004).
7 *A Declaration of the Immediate Causes Which Induce and Justify the Secession of South Carolina* (Charleston, SC: 1860).

CHAPTER 1

1 See Stephen B. Oates, *To Purge This Land with Blood* (New York: 1970), 352, 351. See also Evan Carton, *Patriotic Treason* (New York: 2006).
2 See Edward L. Ayers, *In the Presence of Mine Enemies* (New York: 2003), 15–16.
3 Oates, *To Purge This Land with Blood*, 291–292.
4 Shepherdstown *Register*, October 29, 1859. See also Oates, *To Purge This Land with Blood*, 294.
5 Oates, *To Purge This Land with Blood*, 327.
6 Ibid., 335.
7 Shepherdstown *Register*, October 29, 1859.
8 Higginson, famously, would later command and write about a regiment of African American soldiers in the War. See R. D. Madison, ed., *Army Life in a Black Regiment and Other Writings* (London: 1997).
9 On South Carolina, see C. Vann Woodward, ed., *Mary Chesnut's Civil War* (New Haven, CT: 1981), and on Mississippi, Winthrop D. Jordan, *Tumult and Silence at Second Creek* (Baton Rouge, LA: 1993).
10 See, for instance, Steven A. Channing, *Crisis of Fear* (New York: 1974).
11 See Paul Christopher Anderson, *Blood Image: Turner Ashby in the Civil War and the Southern Mind* (Baton Rouge, LA: 2002), 60.
12 The phrase is borrowed from Kenneth Cmiel, *Democratic Eloquence: The Fight over Popular Speech in Nineteenth Century America* (Berkeley, CA: 1990).
13 The best place to begin on the vital language of republicanism is still Bernard Bailyn, *The Ideological Origins of the American Revolution* (Cambridge, MA: 2012). But see also Joyce Appleby, *Inheriting the Revolution* (Cambridge, MA: 2000) and Gordon S. Wood, *The*

Radicalism of the American Revolution (New York: 1991). For the ethic's translation into the Confederate experience, see George Rable, *The Confederate Republic* (Chapel Hill, NC: 1994).

14 On the Republicans, see Eric Foner, *Free Soil, Free Labor, Free Men* (New York: 1995) and William E. Gienapp, *The Origins of the Republican Party, 1852–1856* (New York: 1988). The Republicans emerged as the second major American party – there were other political possibilities – after the collapse of the American Whig party in the early 1850s. See Michael F. Holt's *The Rise and Fall of the American Whig Party* (New York: 1999).

15 See Potter, *The Impending Crisis*, 160. Douglas's motives cannot be divorced from the era's larger emphasis on progress and development. See Robert W. Johannsen, *Stephen A. Douglas* (Urbana, IL: 1997).

16 The conspiratorial and quasi-scriptural language of "true inwardness" would become especially important in Reconstruction. See Mark Wahlgren Summers, *A Dangerous Stir* (Chapel Hill, NC: 2009). On the relationship between European nationalist revolutions and the American experience, see Andre M. Fleche, *The Revolution of 1861* (Chapel Hill, NC: 2014).

17 See Garry Wills, *"Negro President": Jefferson and the Slave Power* (Boston: 2005). The ideological flux of nationalism and sectionalism is explored in Susan-Mary Grant, *North over South: Northern Nationalism and American Identity in the Antebellum Era* (Lawrence, KS: 2000).

18 Jean H. Baker, *James Buchanan* (New York: 2004) is the most recent biography.

19 The Southern reactions can be found in McPherson, *Battle Cry of Freedom*, 151. It is a longstanding but still useful exercise to pair the sectional conflict in biography, particularly in pairings of South Carolina and Massachusetts politicians who are taken to represent apposite ethics. The Brooks–Sumner episode, and much else of value besides, is handled expertly in David Donald, *Charles Sumner and the Coming of the Civil War* (New York: 1960) but see also his *Charles Sumner and the Rights of Man* (New York: 1970). Drew Gilpin Faust's *James Henry Hammond and the Old South* (Baton Rouge, LA: 1980) is still the best biography of an honor-driven planter, while Manisha Sinha, *The Counterrevolution of Slavery: Politics and Ideology in Antebellum South Carolina* (Chapel Hill, NC: 2000) takes the class as whole. A too-narrow focus on honor can obscure what was a vibrant intellectual culture in the antebellum

South. See Michael O'Brien's majestic *Conjectures of Order: Intellectual Life and the American South, 1810–1860* (Chapel Hill, NC: 2004).

20 Kansas is almost as much a bog for the student as for the settler, merely less (one hopes) bloody. The year of Lecompton, the Dred Scott case, and Buchanan is handled ably in Kenneth M. Stampp, *America in 1857* (New York: 1990). Douglas's retort to Buchanan is quoted on 293.

21 Yancey is quoted in McPherson, *Battle Cry of Freedom*, 215. On Yancey in particular, and secessionists and fire-eaters in general, see Eric H. Walther, *William Lowndes Yancey and the Coming of the Civil War* (Chapel Hill, NC: 2006), and William W. Freehling, *The Road to Disunion: Secessionists at Bay, 1776–1854* (New York: 1990) and his *The Road to Disunion: Secessionists Triumphant, 1854–1861* (New York: 2007).

22 Brady is quoted in Harold Holzer, *Lincoln at Cooper Union: The Speech that Made Abraham Lincoln President* (New York: 2004), 94. Lincolnia is its own genre in American history and so capacious as to be nearly biblical. Biographically, my views have been shaped by Richard Cawardine, *Lincoln: A Life of Purpose and Power* (New York: 2006); Douglas L. Wilson, *Honor's Voice: The Transformation of Abraham Lincoln* (New York: 1998); and David Herbert Donald, *Lincoln* (New York: 1995). I have also been profoundly impacted by William Lee Miller, *Lincoln's Virtues: An Ethical Biography* (New York: 2002).

23 Though Lincoln's collected works are now accessible online, David S. Reynolds's annotated compendium, *Lincoln's Selected Writings* (New York: 2015), which includes essays for context, is a valuable one-volume collection. It will be the main citation hereafter. The Cooper Union speech appears on 196–209, quote on 204.

CHAPTER 2

1 Tony Horwitz, *Confederates in the Attic: Dispatches from the Unfinished Civil War* (New York: 1998) is an engaging riff on some of these themes. See also David Goldfield, *Still Fighting the Civil War: The American South and Southern History* (Baton Rouge, LA: 2013).

2 See Varon, *Disunion!*, but also Wolfgang Schivelbusch, *The Culture of Defeat: On National Trauma, Mourning, and Recovery* (New York:

2001). See also Russell McClintock, *Lincoln and the Decision for War: The Northern Response to Secession* (Chapel Hill, NC: 2008).

3 For the quoted passages from the secession declarations, see *A Declaration of the Immediate Causes which Induce and Justify the Secession of South Carolina from the Federal Union* (Charleston, SC: 1860) and *A Declaration of the Immediate Causes which Induce and Justify the Secession of the State of Mississippi from the Federal Union* (Jackson, MS: 1861).

4 See Baptist, *The Half Has Never Been Told*; Sven Beckert, *Empire of Cotton: A Global History* (New York: 2014); and Walter Johnson, *River of Dark Dreams: Slavery and Empire in the Cotton Kingdom* (Cambridge, MA: 2013).

5 On Davis, see William J. Cooper, Jr., *Jefferson Davis, American* (New York: 2000). On the Confederate nationalists, see Emory M. Thomas, *The Confederate Nation, 1861–1865* (New York: 1979), and John McCardell, *The Idea of a Southern Nation: Southern Nationalists and Southern Nationalism, 1830–1860* (New York: 1979).

6 Baker, *James Buchanan*, 142. The exclamation point was used by Stampp – "Let him be remembered, then, for that!" – in *America in 1857*, 331.

7 Lincoln is quoted in Ayers, *In the Presence of Mine Enemies*, 109.

8 See McPherson, *Battle Cry of Freedom*, 262. The First Inaugural is in Reynolds, *Lincoln's Selected Writings*, 228–234, (quote on 234). See also Baker, *James Buchanan*, 140.

9 Davis is quoted in Cooper, *Jefferson Davis*, 342.

10 See Charles B. Dew, *Apostles of Disunion: Southern Secession Commissioners and the Causes of the Civil War* (Charlottesville, VA: 2001).

11 On honor culture in the antebellum South, see Bertram Wyatt-Brown, *Southern Honor: Ethics and Behavior in the Old South* (New York: 1982) and Kenneth S. Greenberg, *Honor and Slavery* (Princeton, NJ: 1997).

12 McPherson, *Battle Cry of Freedom*, 272. On the epic mode and the ladies of Charleston, see Julia A. Stern, *Mary Chesnut's Civil War Epic* (Chicago: 2010).

13 Charles Royster, *The Destructive War: William Tecumseh Sherman, Stonewall Jackson, and the Americans* (New York: 1991), xii.

14 W. Buck Yearns, ed., *The Confederate Governors* (Athens, GA: 2010), 46. See also Daniel W. Crofts, *Reluctant Confederates: Upper South Unionists in the Secession Crisis* (Chapel Hill, NC: 1989).

15 The Lincoln quotes are in McPherson, *Battle Cry of Freedom*, 286, 336. Almost every major Civil War engagement and personage has a study, and some their own literature. Most readers will still profit enormously by taking up Shelby Foote's three-volume *The Civil War: A Narrative* (New York: 1958–1974), which is monumental if tinged by the author's perspective as a Southern novelist. A more modern if equally comprehensive work is David J. Eicher, *The Longest Night: A Military History of the Civil War* (New York: 2002).

16 The full quote appears in Foote, *The Civil War*, 2: 119: "No general yet found can face the arithmetic, but the end of the war will be at hand when he shall be discovered."

17 This vital election fact is developed in Mark E. Neely, Jr., *The Union Divided: Party Conflict in the Civil War North* (Cambridge: 2002), 39.

18 Lincoln's use of "remorseless struggle" appears in his Annual Message to Congress, December 3, 1861, and his "people's contest" in his Message to Congress in Special Session, July 4, 1861, both of which appear in Reynolds, *Lincoln's Selected Writings*, 254–258 (quote on 255), 238–249 (quote on 247). Phillip Shaw Paludan, *A People's Contest: The Union and Civil War* (New York: 1988) remains the most accessible overview of the Northern home front.

CHAPTER 3

1 Lincoln's rumination on liberty is in his Address at Sanitary Fair, Baltimore, MD, April 18, 1864, in Reynolds, *Lincoln's Selected Writings*, 339–341 (quote on 340). Desmoulins is quoted in R. R. Palmer, *Twelve Who Ruled: The Year of Terror in the French Revolution* (Princeton, NJ: 2005), 260. Davis is quoted in Rable, *The Confederate Republic*, 122.

2 That general is George B. McClellan. He is quoted in Stephen W. Sears, *George B. McClellan: The Young Napoleon* (New York: 1988), 132.

3 Johnston is quoted in Charles P. Roland, *Albert Sidney Johnston: Soldier of Three Republics* (Lexington, KY: 2001), 252. Davis is quoted in Herman Hattaway and Archer Jones, *How the North Won: A Military History of the Civil War* (Urbana, IL: 1991), 58.

4 Lincoln is quoted in Ron Chernow, *Grant* (New York: 2017), 220.

5 Johnston is quoted in Steven E. Woodworth, *This Great Struggle: America's Civil War* (Plymouth: 2011), 96. Grant and Sherman are quoted in Chernow, *Grant*, 205.

6 That the War was won and lost in the west seems no longer a controversial point, though once it would have been. See most recently Earl J. Hess, *The Civil War in the West: Victory and Defeat from the Appalachians to the Mississippi* (Chapel Hill, NC: 2012). The War's border areas – Kentucky was one – have also attracted a great deal of attention. See for instance William W. Freehling, *The South vs. The South: How Anti-Confederate Southerners Shaped the Course of the Civil War* (New York: 2001).

7 Lincoln's support of Grant is quoted in Chernow, *Grant*, 211.

8 McClellan is quoted in Sears, *George B. McClellan*, 337. See also David Herbert Donald, *We Are All Lincoln Men: Abraham Lincoln and His Friends* (New York: 2003) and William C. Davis, *Lincoln's Men: How President Lincoln Became Father to an Army and a Nation* (New York: 1999).

9 Lincoln is quoted in Sears, *George B. McClellan*, 338.

10 Lincoln to Albert G. Hodges, April 4, 1864, in Reynolds, *Lincoln's Selected Writings*, 338–339 (quote on 339); see also Donald, *Lincoln*, 15. McClellan is quoted in McPherson, *Battle Cry of Freedom*, 360.

11 Douglas L. Wilson, *Lincoln's Sword: The Presidency and the Power of Words* (New York: 2007) and Garry Wills, *Lincoln at Gettysburg: The Words that Remade America* (New York: 1992) explore Lincoln as a writer. The quoted passages are the Appeal to Border-State Representatives for Compensated Emancipation, July 12, 1862, 267–268 (quote on 267); Annual Message to Congress, December 3, 1861, 254–258 (quote on 258); Annual Message to Congress, December 1, 1862, 286–296 (quotes on 296), all in Reynolds, *Lincoln's Speeches and Writings*.

12 The Natchez, Mississippi conspiracy, also mentioned in Chapter 2, is recounted in Jordan, *Tumult and Silence at Second Creek*. The debate over slave agency and emancipation is a fierce one. See, for one example, Kate Masur, *An Example for All the Land: Emancipation and the Struggle over Equality in Washington, D. C.* (Chapel Hill, NC: 2010). Movement – of people, of things, of words – is also a dynamic force to consider. See Yael A. Sternhill, *Routes of War: The World of Movement in the Confederate South* (Cambridge, MA: 2012).

13 Lincoln is quoted in Donald, *Lincoln*, 315. See also Lincoln to John C. Frémont, September 2, 1861 and September 11, 1861, 250–251, and Proclamation Revoking General Hunter's Emancipation Order, 265–266, both in Reynolds, *Lincoln's Speeches and Writings*.

14 The Union chaplain is quoted in Chernow, *Grant*, 222. On the confiscation acts, see Silvana R. Siddali, *From Property to Person: Slavery and the Confiscation Acts, 1861–1862* (Baton Rouge, LA: 2005).

15 The quotes from Lincoln's official communications are in his Message to Congress, March 6, 1862, 260, and Appeal to Border-State Representatives for Compensated Emancipation, July 12, 1862, 267–268, both in Reynolds, *Lincoln's Speeches and Writings*. Lincoln is quoted on embracing compensation in Willie Lee Rose, *Rehearsal for Reconstruction: The Port Royal Experiment* (Athens, GA: 1999), 151.

16 Lincoln to McClellan, July 2, 1862, in Roy P. Basler, ed., *Abraham Lincoln: Speeches and Writings* (Cleveland, OH: 1946), 645–646.

17 The phalanx of Lee biographers is nearly a match for Lincoln's. Douglas Southall Freeman's *R. E. Lee* (New York: 1934) is still grand – but because Freeman himself came to hulk nearly as heavily over the writing of Confederate history as Lee did the War itself, it should be paired with Keith D. Dickson, *Sustaining Southern Identity: Douglas Southall Freeman and Memory in the Modern South* (Baton Rouge, LA: 2011). Three other biographies have shaped my perspective: Emory M. Thomas, *Robert E. Lee* (New York: 1995); Richard B. McCaslin, *Lee in the Shadow of Washington* (Baton Rouge, LA: 2001); and Michael Fellman, *The Making of Robert E. Lee* (Baltimore: 2000).

18 See Thomas, *The Confederate Nation*, cited earlier, but also more recently Stephanie McCurry, *Confederate Reckoning: Power and Politics in the Civil War South* (Cambridge, MA: 2010).

19 See Gary W. Gallagher, *The Confederate War: How Popular Will, Nationalism, and Military Strategy Could Not Stave Off Defeat* (Cambridge, MA: 1997). But see also Richard E. Beringer, Herman Hattaway, Archer Jones, and William N. Still, Jr., *Why the South Lost the Civil War* (Athens, GA: 1986). On efforts to nationalize the Confederacy culturally and socially, see Anne Sarah Rubin, *A Shattered Nation: The Rise and Fall of the Confederacy, 1861–1868* (Chapel Hill, NC: 2005) and Michael T. Bernath, *Confederate Minds: The Struggle for Intellectual Independence in the Civil War South* (Chapel Hill, NC: 2010).

CHAPTER 4

1 On the shock of combat, see Earl J. Hess, *The Union Soldier in Battle: Enduring the Ordeal of Combat* (Lawrence, KS: 1997). The Confederate

officer-in-the-dark is quoted in Douglas Southall Freeman, *Lee's Lieutenants: A Study in Command* (New York: 1944), 1: 469. See also Joseph L. Harsh, *Taken at the Flood: Robert E. Lee and Confederate Strategy in the Maryland Campaign of 1862* (Kent, OH: 1999), 169–170. Here perhaps a further point is warranted. In recent years especially, as the narrative of Confederate heritage known as the Lost Cause (discussed later) has come under intense scrutiny, it has become something of a project among its defenders to establish that black soldiers fought for the Confederacy. (Hence: slavery could not have caused the War, hence, slavery could not have been the cause that even ordinary Confederates fought for.) Much in the way, say, that we can say slaves destroyed slavery from within during the War but did not emancipate themselves, we can say that a slave with the Confederate army might be considered a "black Confederate" only in the sense that he was a Confederate slave, held to or impounded for labor. He was not a soldier. The effort to make (up) black Confederate soldiers says less about the world of Confederates and much more about the desperate effort to curate a postwar myth and heritage. See Kevin M. Levin, *Searching for Black Confederates: The Civil War's Most Persistent Myth* (Chapel Hill, NC: 2019).

2 Johnston is quoted in Freeman, *Lee's Lieutenants*, 1: 264. See also James I. Robertson, Jr., *Stonewall Jackson: The Man, the Soldier, the Legend* (New York: 1997). The quartermaster is quoted on 362.

3 The "singular crawling effect" of Malvern Hill is quoted in Steven E. Woodworth, *Davis and Lee at War* (Lawrence, KS: 1995), 170. See also Peter S. Carmichael, ed., *Audacity Personified: The Generalship of Robert E. Lee* (Baton Rouge, LA: 2004). Harsh, *Taken at the Flood*, 57–65, is a careful evaluation of Lee's critical dispatch to Davis. Lee's famous assertion is quoted in McPherson, *Battle Cry of Freedom*, 471.

4 On Bragg, see Earl J. Hess, *Braxton Bragg: The Most Hated Man of the Confederacy* (Chapel Hill, NC: 2016). The previously disgusted biographer was Grady McWhiney, *Braxton Bragg and Confederate Defeat* (Tuscaloosa, AL: 1969), the second volume of which was indeed finished in 1991 by Judith Lee Hallock.

5 See Richard M. McMurry, *Two Great Rebel Armies: An Essay in Confederate Military History* (Chapel Hill, NC: 1996). See also W. J. Cash's classic *The Mind of the South* (New York: 1941), 44. That its democratic armies became the symbol of Confederate nationalism explains why the Confederate battle flag, not the national flag of the Confederacy, became the (still) visceral symbol of identification. See

John M. Coski, *The Confederate Battle Flag: America's Most Embattled Emblem* (Cambridge, MA: 2005) and Robert E. Bonner, *Colors and Blood: Flag Passions of the Confederate South* (Princeton, NJ: 2004). On Southern identity, see James C. Cobb, *Away Down South: A History of Southern Identity* (New York: 2005).

6 McClellan is quoted in Foote, *The Civil War*, 1: 465. The full text of the Harrison's Landing Letter accompanies McClellan's commentary on it as well as a revealing note, in George B. McClellan, *McClellan's Own Story* (New York: 1887), 487–490.

7 These two remarkable Lincoln letters, to Cuthbert Bullitt, on July 28, 1862, and to August Belmont on July 31, 1862, are two of his most widely cited. See for instance McPherson, *Battle Cry of Freedom*, 503. William Lee Miller, in *President Lincoln: The Duty of a Statesman* (New York: 2008), 226–227, rightly calls Lincoln's sentence on malicious dealing, in the letter to Bullitt, "one of Lincoln's great sentences."

8 See Eric Foner, *The Fiery Trial: Abraham Lincoln and American Slavery* (New York: 2010), quotes on 224–225.

9 Lincoln's quotes appear in Donald, *Lincoln*, 362, 366. The legal and policy aspects of hard war are developed in John Fabian Witt, *Lincoln's Code: The Laws of War in American History* (New York: 2012) and Mark Grimsley, *The Hard Hand of War: Union Military Policy Toward Southern Civilians, 1861–1865* (Cambridge: 1995).

10 Foner, *The Fiery Trial*, 225. See also James Oakes, *The Radical and The Republican: Frederick Douglass, Abraham Lincoln, and the Triumph of Antislavery Politics* (New York: 2007).

11 Lee's view of Pope, and his remark at Fredericksburg, are in Freeman, *R. E. Lee*, 2: 264, 462.

12 Lee's assessment was supposedly given to a family relative after the War, and it appears, as one instance, in James Havelock Campbell, *McClellan: A Vindication of the Military Career of George B. McClellan* (New York: 1916), 419. One cannot separate the question of its authenticity from the profound reemergence of conservatism after the War, and the reemergence of a virulent racism and white supremacy by the turn of the century, as a perusal of a source such as this one will readily reveal.

13 The quotes suggesting McClellan's glee and then caution at Antietam are in McPherson, *Battle Cry of Freedom*, 537, 543–544.

14 Annual Message to Congress, December 1, 1862, in Reynolds, *Lincoln's Selected Writings*, 286–296 (quote on 296). The Preliminary Emancipation Proclamation appears on 280–281. In it Lincoln notes

that efforts in colonization – with the consent of those freed – "will be continued." The formal Emancipation Proclamation, which does not contain colonization language but does authorize black troops, appears on 297–298.

15 McClellan on himself, Lincoln on McClellan, and Lincoln to Rosecrans all quoted in McPherson, *Battle Cry of Freedom*, 545, 569, 582–583.

CHAPTER 5

1 The theme was quintessential Faulkner: to tell about the South is from *Absalom, Absalom!* (1936); the past-not-past from *Requiem for a Nun* (1938); the quoted passage from *Intruder in the Dust* (1951). See Patrick Gerster and Nicholas Cords, eds., *Myth and Southern History* (Urbana, IL: 1989). On Pickett's Charge, see Carol Reardon, *Pickett's Charge in History and Memory* (Chapel Hill, NC: 1997).

2 The Gettysburg Address appears in Reynolds, *Lincoln's Selected Writings*, 328–329. See also Wills, *Lincoln at Gettysburg*, but also, importantly, Gabor S. Boritt, *The Gettysburg Gospel: The Lincoln Speech That Nobody Knows* (New York: 2006). The differences in the subtitles are telling.

3 Joyce is quoted in Richard Ellman, *James Joyce* (New York: 1982 edition), 397.

4 Ulysses S. Grant, *Personal Memoirs of U.S. Grant* (New York: 1885), 1: 53, 2: 489, 1: 250.

5 Lincoln on Halleck is quoted in Chernow, *Grant*, 220. The German officer is quoted in Ian Kershaw, *Hitler: Nemesis, 1936–1945* (New York: 2000), 450.

6 Grant, *Memoirs*, 1: 480. Lincoln to Grant, July 13, 1863, in Reynolds, *Lincoln's Selected Writings*, 313.

7 The Lost Cause has drawn a remarkable amount of attention in the last twenty years especially. Overviews are Gaines M. Foster, *Ghosts of the Confederacy: Defeat, the Lost Cause, and the Emergence of the New South, 1865–1913* (New York: 1987) and Charles Reagan Wilson, *Baptized in Blood: The Religion of the Lost Cause* (Athens, GA: 1982). See also W. Fitzhugh Brundage, *The Southern Past: A Clash of Race and Memory* (Cambridge, MA: 2005); two works by David W. Blight, *Race and Reunion: The Civil War in American Memory* (Cambridge,

MA: 2001) and *American Oracle: The Civil War in the Civil Rights Era* (Cambridge, MA: 2011).

8 See Mark E. Neely, Jr., *The Fate of Liberty: Abraham Lincoln and Civil Liberties* (New York: 1991); Iver Bernstein, *The New York City Draft Riots: Their Significance for American Society and Politics in the Age of the Civil War* (New York: 1990); and Foner, *The Fiery Trial*, 225–226.

9 The quote is from Lincoln's letter to Cuthbert Bullitt, July 28, 1862, in Miller, *President Lincoln*, 226.

10 Lincoln is quoted in Donald, *Lincoln*, 576. See also Nelson Lankford, *Richmond Burning: The Last Days of the Confederate Capital* (New York: 2002). By no means do the Lincoln myths mentioned above exhaust them. See Gerald J. Prokopowicz, *Did Lincoln Own Slaves?* (New York: 2008).

11 Lincoln to James C. Conkling, August 26, 1863, in Reynolds, *Lincoln's Selected Writings*, 318–321 (quote on 321).

12 The major points and counterpoints are narrated in Foote, *The Civil War*, 2: 430–433.

13 See James Longstreet, *From Manassas to Appomattox* (Philadelphia: 1896), 386–387, 358. On the army slaves with Lee, see Kent Masterson Brown, *Retreat from Gettysburg: Lee, Logistics, and the Pennsylvania Campaign* (Chapel Hill, NC: 2005).

14 Longstreet, *From Manassas to Appomattox*, 384; Grant, *Memoirs*, 2: 489.

15 Lee's quotes are in Thomas, *Robert E. Lee*, 300–301.

16 The Second Inaugural Address, delivered on March 4, 1865, mere weeks before Confederate surrender, appears in Reynolds, *Lincoln's Selected Writings*, 364–368 (quote on 367).

17 On Douglass, see his own, still-powerful narrative: John R. McKivigan, Peter P. Hinks, and Heather L Kaufman, eds., *Narrative of the Slave Life of Frederick Douglass* (New Haven, CT: 2016). It first appeared 1845, but Douglass revised almost continually for half a century until his death in 1895. On the black soldiery, see Joseph T. Glatthaar, *Forged in Battle: The Civil War Alliance of Black Soldiers and White Officers* (Baton Rouge, LA: 2000) and Steven V. Ash, *Firebrand of Liberty: The Story of Two Black Regiments that Changed the Course of the Civil War* (New York: 2008). On the empathy developed by British soldiers in the War of 1812, see Alan Taylor, *The Internal Enemy: Slavery and War in Virginia, 1772–1832* (New York: 2013), 339. Two other works, when paired, offer insight into soldiers' attitudes toward race and the

citizen-soldier ideal: Chandra Manning, *What This Cruel War was Over: Soldiers, Slavery, and the Civil War* (New York: 2007) and Gary W. Gallagher, *The Union War* (Cambridge, MA: 2011).

18 Lincoln is quoted in McPherson, *Battle Cry of Freedom*, 675. The observer is quoted in Foote, *The Civil War*, 3: 5.

19 Oakes, *The Radical and the Republican*, 226, 212, 232. In the nineteenth century "friend" connoted a political relationship – a close relation of interests – in ways its more affective meaning today has mostly shed. It does appear Lincoln used it here in both senses.

20 Lincoln "slow" and "scour" quotes appear in Donald, *Lincoln*, 456, 465. The Springfield Letter is Lincoln to James C. Conkling, August 26, 1863, in Reynolds, *Lincoln's Selected Writings*, 318–321.

CHAPTER 6

1 Lincoln to James C. Conkling, August 26, 1863, in Reynolds, *Lincoln's Selected Writings*, 319–321 (quotes on 321). The naval officer is quoted in McPherson, *Battle Cry of Freedom*, 381. See also Craig L. Symonds, *The Civil War at Sea* (New York: 2012).

2 The poet is John Greenleaf Whittier, quoted in Beckert, *Empire of Cotton*, 243.

3 Lee is quoted in Freeman, *R. E. Lee*, 3: 16.

4 Willard's Hotel is acidly rated in Chernow, *Grant*, 340. The description of Meade appears in Foote, *The Civil War*, 3: 297. See also Grant, *Memoirs*, 2: 143, and Donald, *Lincoln*, 520.

5 Grant is quoted in McPherson, *Battle Cry of Freedom*, 731. Lee is quoted in Freeman, *R. E. Lee,* 3: 398.

6 Lee's quote about death appears in Freeman, *R. E. Lee*, 4: 120, and Grant on Lee in Grant, *Memoirs*, 2: 489. A different view of Appomattox appears most recently in Jay Winik's excellent *April, 1865: The Month That Saved America* (New York: 2001).

7 Grant is quoted in McPherson, *Battle Cry of Freedom*, 726, and Lee's attempts to lead charges personally are described in Freeman, *R. E. Lee*, 3: 287–288, 317–319. The effects of Civil War combat on values is explored particularly in Gerald F. Linderman, *Embattled Courage: The Experience of Combat in the American Civil War* (New York: 1987), while Lincoln's famous quote is situated as a moral problem in Miller, *President Lincoln*, 217.

8 Only recently have war deaths been revised – for many years the standard of 620,000 dead, Union and Confederate, had been conventional. See J. David Hacker, "A Census Based Count of the Civil War Dead," *Civil War History* (December 2011): 307–348. In short: perhaps as many as 500,000 Union soldiers and as many as 350,000 Confederate soldiers perished in the War, though the destruction of many Confederate records makes even that reckoning an educated guess.

9 Bell Irvin Wiley's classic volumes on soldier life, *The Life of Johnny Reb* (Indianapolis: 1943) and *The Life of Billy Yank* (Indianapolis: 1951) are still deservedly in use. See also Noah Andre Trudeau, *Like Men of War: Black Troops in the Civil War, 1862–1865* (Boston: 1998); Reid Mitchell, *The Vacant Chair: The Northern Soldier Leaves Home* (New York: 1993); Kenneth W. Noe, *Reluctant Rebels: The Confederates Who Joined the Army after 1861* (Chapel Hill, NC: 2010); and James M. McPherson, *For Cause and Comrades: Why Men Fought in the Civil War* (New York: 1997).

10 See James Marten, *Sing Not War: The Lives of Union and Confederate Veterans in Gilded Age America* (Chapel Hill, NC: 2011), esp. 1–32, and Barbara A. Gannon, *The Won Cause: Black and White Comradeship in the Grand Army of the Republic* (Chapel Hill, NC: 2011).

11 The 50,000 figure is in McPherson, *Battle Cry of Freedom*, 619 n53. That it is given in a footnote suggests its tentativeness. Indeed for complex reasons – some of them matters of definition – civilian and slave deaths are elusive and probably will never be understood with even an approximate certainty. It suffices to say here that the failure to comprehend them is a failure deeper than computational calculus. Brian Steel Wills, *Inglorious Passages: Noncombatant Deaths in the American Civil War* (Lawrence, KS: 2017) offers something of a melancholy remedy. See also Drew Gilpin Faust, *This Republic of Suffering: Death and The American Civil War* (New York: 2008), esp. 137–142 (quote on 139).

12 See A. J. P. Taylor, *English History, 1914–1945* (New York: 1965), 492. Cleburne's proposal and the reaction are quoted in McCurry, *Confederate Reckoning*, 328, 340.

13 The quoted Sherman passage appears in Foote, *The Civil War*, 3: 357.

14 See Varon, *Disunion!*, 25. The particular warning is in Federalist #4.

15 On the guerrilla war, see Daniel Sutherland, *A Savage Conflict: The Decisive War of Guerrillas in the American Civil War* (Chapel Hill, NC: 2009) for an essential overview. See also Michael Fellman, *Inside War:*

The Guerrilla Conflict in Missouri During the American Civil War (New York: 1989) and T. J. Stiles, *Jesse James: Last Rebel of the Civil War* (New York: 2002). Mobberly is quoted in Scott Thompson, "The Irregular War in Loudoun County, Virginia," in Brian D. McKnight and Barton A. Myers, eds., *The Guerrilla Hunters: Irregular Conflicts during the Civil War* (Baton Rouge, LA: 2017), 123–124.

16 Lincoln's "tired spot" is in Foote, *The Civil War*, 3: 815. See also "Memorandum of Probable Failure of Re-election," August 23, 1864, in Reynolds, *Lincoln's Selected Writings*, 353.

17 Hood's attack on Johnston appears in his *Advance and Retreat: Personal Experiences in the United States and Confederate States Armies* (New Orleans: 1880), 130. Hood's quote on his courtship is in Woodward, *Mary Chesnut's Civil War*, 516. See also Stephen W. Berry, *All That Makes a Man: Love and Ambition in the Civil War South* (New York: 2003).

18 The lion-fox quote appears in McPherson, *Battle Cry of Freedom*, 753. Early's quote appears in Foote, *The Civil War*, 3: 460.

19 Hood reproduced his telegram of September 6, 1864, in *Advance and Retreat*, 247–248.

20 Grant is quoted in McPherson, *Battle Cry of Freedom*, 758, 778. But see also the author's important point on 719–720: had not these numbers of Union soldiers reenlisted and given Lincoln's armies an important veteran presence, the Confederacy "might well seize victory from the jaws of defeat."

21 Sherman quoted in Royster, *The Destructive War*, 340. The best traditional biographies of Sherman are John F. Marzalek, *Sherman: A Soldier's Passion for Order* (Carbondale, IL: 1993) and Michael Fellman, *Citizen Sherman: A Life of William Tecumseh Sherman* (New York: 1995).

22 Sherman is quoted in Royster, *The Destructive War*, 354. See also Anne Sarah Rubin, *Through the Heart of Dixie: Sherman's March and American Memory* (Chapel Hill, NC: 2014) and Joseph L. Glatthaar, *The March to the Sea and Beyond: Sherman's Troops in the Savannah and Carolinas Campaigns* (Baton Rouge, IL: 1985).

EPILOGUE

1 See J. Tracy Power, *Lee's Miserables: Life in the Army of Northern Virginia from the Wilderness to Appomattox* (Chapel Hill, NC: 1998),

esp. 302–315. On the diehards, see Jason Phillips, *Diehard Confederates: The Confederate Culture of Invincibility* (Athens, GA: 2007). See also Steven V. Ash, *A Year in the South: 1865* (New York: 2002).

2 The peace conference was the setting for some remarks by Lincoln from which some have conjured up a supposed, limited retreat on emancipation. More likely, the conjurers have confused the very points Lincoln tried to convey by them: as a practical matter the Confederacy was doomed, slavery doomed with it. See Donald, *Lincoln*, 556–561, and Foner, *The Fiery Trial*, 314–316.

3 Lee's farewell address is in Freeman, *R. E. Lee*, 4: 154–155. Lee is quoted in Phillips, *Diehard Confederates*, 169.

4 The Second Inaugural, March 4, 1865, appears in Reynolds, *Lincoln's Selected Writings*, 364–368. Lincoln is quoted on the Second Inaugural in Donald, *Lincoln*, 568.

5 Douglass is quoted in Donald, *Lincoln*, 568. Lincoln and Booth are quoted in Edward Steers Jr., *Blood on the Moon: The Assassination of Abraham Lincoln* (Lexington, KY: 2001), 91.

6 Booth is quoted in Steers Jr., *Blood on the Moon*, 204. Johnson remains a fascinating character study. See Eric McKitrick, *Andrew Johnson and Reconstruction* (New York: 1988).

7 Eric Foner's *Reconstruction: America's Unfinished Revolution, 1863–1877* (New York: 2014) is the best study of the period. Even earlier than W. E. B. DuBois, the great African American historian, a challenge to prevailing yet largely mythological "history" of the Reconstruction era appeared, but DuBois's *Black Reconstruction in America, 1860–1880* (New York: 1997) is still enlightening. See also Hahn, *A Nation Under our Feet*, and Leon F. Litwack, *Trouble in Mind: Black Southerners in the Age of Jim Crow* (New York: 1998).

8 Most general readers understand the violence of the Reconstruction era as synonymous with the Ku Klux Klan, but the resistance and its design began earlier than the Klan operation and outlasted it. See Richard Zuczek, *State of Rebellion: Reconstruction in South Carolina* (Columbia, SC: 1996) and two strong, general works on terror in the postwar: Stephen Budiansky, *The Bloody Shirt: Terror after the Civil War* (New York: 2008) and Douglas R. Edgerton, *The Wars of Reconstruction: The Brief, Violent History of America's Most Progressive Era* (New York: 2014).

9 In addition to the readings on memory and reconciliation suggested earlier, see Caroline E. Janney, *Remembering the Civil War: Reunion*

and the Limits of Reconciliation (Chapel Hill, NC: 2013) and Nina Silber, *The Romance of Reunion: Northerners and the South, 1865–1900* (Chapel Hill, NC: 1993).

10 Gabriel Garcia Marquez, *One Hundred Years of Solitude* (New York: 1970), 13.

Index